WITHDRAWN

MY
MASTER RECIPES

ALSO BY PATRICIA WELLS

The French Kitchen Cookbook

Simply Truffles

Salad as a Meal

We've Always Had Paris . . . and Provence
(with Walter Wells)

Vegetable Harvest

The Provence Cookbook

The Paris Cookbook

L'Atelier of Joël Robuchon

Patricia Wells at Home in Provence

Patricia Wells' Trattoria

Simply French

Bistro Cooking

The Food Lover's Guide to France

The Food Lover's Guide to Paris

My
Master Recipes

165 RECIPES TO INSPIRE CONFIDENCE IN THE KITCHEN
With Dozens of Variations

Patricia Wells

In collaboration with Emily Buchanan

wm

WILLIAM MORROW
An Imprint of HarperCollins*Publishers*

HarperCollins books may be purchased for educational, business, or sales promotional use. For information please e-mail the Special Markets Department at SPsales@harpercollins.com.

FIRST EDITION

Designed by Suet Yee Chong
Photographs by David Japy
Styled by Elodie Rambaud

Library of Congress Cataloging-in-Publication Data has been applied for.

ISBN 978-0-06-242482-2

17 18 19 20 21   QGT   10 9 8 7 6 5 4 3 2 1

As ever, for my husband,

Walter,

with gratitude for his love, dedication,

sharing, encouragement, and most of all,

for helping create such a perfect life!

And to Marc, Faye, and Marlow

for all their love and support, and for approaching all

recipe-tasting opportunities with never-ending gusto.

Contents

GRILL   173

ROAST   187

ROASTING VEGETABLES   188

ROASTING POULTRY AND MEAT   203

ROASTING FRUIT   214

INTRODUCTION

*A Formula for
Confidence in the Kitchen*

On the last day of each week of the cooking classes I hold, both in Paris and Provence, I regularly hear students remark: "Wow! I now have more confidence in the kitchen." Working toward that goal for all home cooks, *My Master Recipes* creates a framework for every cook to master fundamental techniques through various master recipes, securing a blueprint to expand and experiment with a whole new repertoire of recipes.

A friend who is a pianist told me that she perfected recipes the way she perfected pieces of music, repeating them over and over until she got it right. With this book, readers can perfect and experiment with particular techniques and recipes while they come to understand how they apply across a broader palette of recipes, expanding skills and increasing the joy of home cooking.

Simple but basic techniques—including blanching, steaming, simmering, poaching, infusing, emulsifying, grinding, searing, panfrying, deep-frying, grilling, roasting, braising, baking, folding, setting—are the foundation of this book. Once a home cook clearly understands and masters each simple technique, confidence soars and calmness in the kitchen reigns. With what seems like the flick of a switch, some recipes can be flipped from sweet to savory and back again. Once the cook truly understands the principles behind the recipes, conscious, intelligent creativity can follow.

Once a cook has prepared the Instant No-Knead Dough (page 280)—a foolproof recipe for homemade pizza, focaccia, and pinwheel breads—an entire repertoire of options becomes instantly available, opening up a new collection of specialties to bring to the table. No need to look elsewhere.

And there's an added advantage: Once proper equipment has been organized—ramekins for the *panna cotta*, a baking stone or metal plate for the pizza, the right pan for searing, the porcelain baking dish for the *frittata*, a rectangular loaf pan for the *nougat glacé* and *semifreddo*—kitchen items no longer have a single use, but can be relied upon endlessly.

Seasonality, the abundant use of fresh fruits, vegetables, zests, and herbs, substituting honey for sugar when possible, and olive oil for butter when it fits, are signatures of my very personal style of cooking and an integral part of *My Master Recipes*.

In this book, you will see an emphasis on a balance of flavors and textures—the importance of acidity and crunch in a dish. As a cook decides to prepare a recipe, it's best to imagine the finished version in one's mind: How will the flavors go together? Is there a balance of textures? Is it beautiful? Will a garnish of herbs add a sense of freshness and a welcome, essential burst of final color?

In some intriguing ways, this personal cookbook has influenced my cooking more than any of my other works. Thinking so systematically about the secrets to success and confidence in the kitchen has made me much more conscious of how I cook and why, and which techniques I use: why, how, and whether they really achieve the best results. I have also become acutely aware of the importance of keeping the kitchen as neat as humanly possible while cooking: One is calmer, there is less to clean up in the end, and there is a comforting reassurance that everything in life is almost "in its place."

INGREDIENTS AND THEIR IMPORTANCE: A CASE FOR ORGANIC

I don't know any cook who disagrees with this credo: Without fresh, high-quality ingredients, one might as well forget cooking. In all the ingredients lists in these recipes, I try to steer the cook toward the finest. And although I do not insist in the ingredients list that every single ingredient be organic, in my own kitchen I use organic products—fruits, vegetables, grains, flours, poultry, meat, herbs, honey, wine—about 95 percent of the time. We are fortunate enough to have been able to transform our land in Provence from a mildew-ridden vineyard and a property without wildlife into an organic haven, growing organic grapes, olives, honey, figs, herbs, vegetables, and flowers, all of which attract birds, bees, butterflies, and insects that help make our little world a true sanctuary.

I do know that eating organic all the time is not realistic for many cooks. Cost is a huge factor, and so is availability. I find it useful to have a go-to list of what is best to buy organic and what is fine to buy non-organic when organizing my shopping.

A few rules of thumb: Citrus fruit is often heavily sprayed with pesticides, so if you are zesting the peel to use in a recipe, go organic. If you are using just the juice or flesh, the thick skin barrier protects the interior, so non-organic is fine.

Most tropical fruits, especially those with thick, hardy skins, resist pesticides fairly well, so a non-organic choice is fine.

The Environmental Working Group (EWG) in Washington, D.C., has conducted extensive tests on pesticide residues on fruits and vegetables and publishes an annual list of the "Dirty Dozen" items to buy organic and a "Clean Fifteen" list of items that are safer to buy as conventional produce. I find these lists to be a very useful tool. (See www.ewg.org.)

The Dirty Dozen: Insist Upon Organic When Possible

Apples	Cucumbers	Strawberries
Celery	Grapes	Spinach
Cherries	Nectarines	Sweet Bell Peppers
Cherry Tomatoes	Peaches	Tomatoes

The Clean Fifteen: Non-Organic Is Okay

Asparagus	Eggplant	Onions
Avocados	Grapefruit	Papayas
Cabbage	Honeydew Melon	Pineapples
Cantaloupe	Kiwi	Sweet Corn
Cauliflower	Mangoes	Sweet Peas (frozen)

For ingredients other than produce, I do make an effort to make sustainable and ethical choices, choosing cage-free eggs, meat, and poultry fed a traditional diet for its species (grass-fed beef and grain-fed poultry).

Like most attentive cooks, I favor specific brands or varieties—mustard, nut oils, canned tomatoes, soy sauce, peppercorns—for I find that their top quality can make a difference in the final effort. I have included my preferred list at the back of this book (page 449).

MY GOAL FOR EVERY COOK

For some reason (perhaps the influence of my mother, who I always saw as a fearless cook) I have always been confident in the kitchen. Except for one weekend when Joël and Janine Robuchon spent several days with us in Provence after having worked together on the cookbook *Simply French*. They had visited us many times, but previously Joël and I had always cooked *his* food. Now that the book was completed we were just going to spend a friendly weekend together. But when I realized I was going to cook *my* food for him I felt a sudden panic, and for a moment I lost that confidence that had always come so naturally to me. But when he declared that my fish and fennel soup was an inspiration to him, I breathed a huge sigh of relief and all confidence returned.

I realized that all I had learned from spending years with him in his kitchen at Jamin was that there are essential formulas to be learned, and once they are learned, the cook becomes the master of the recipe, and not the other way around. Once a cook is confident and free to experiment, cooking becomes truly creative and rewarding, not just a rote effort.

It is my goal that this book will inspire every cook, inviting courage and confidence in the kitchen, pleasures at the table, and a whole new repertoire of culinary delights.

ORGANIZE

Organization, Neatness, Cleanliness,
and Essential Equipment

Keeping an organized, well-stocked kitchen does not mean that you have to have a million gadgets or spend a ton of money. It's really all about a state of mind. Also, being neat and clean in the kitchen costs nothing, save a bit of discipline and care.

One of the smallest kitchens I ever worked in was a square little box in an apartment in Madison, Wisconsin, when I was a graduate student. There was a huge window overlooking the university's stadium and the counter ran along three sides of the room. I could stand in the middle of the minuscule kitchen and reach absolutely everything. I had no choice but to keep it very neat and organized. I often look back on that kitchen and almost declare it a luxury.

On the first day of my cooking classes I rather tongue-in-cheek require all students to raise their hands and take The Pledge: "I do solemnly swear to keep my kitchen clean and spotless at all times. . . ." Some students tell me right out that it is not possible. (One student's wife later took photos of his spotless kitchen to document his advancement!) I often tell them to "keep things neat for your neighbor" as they cook, but it also means keeping everything neat for themselves. Here are some tips:

~ Keep pastry scrapers, damp sponges, and clean towels at the ready at all times. Pastry scrapers are invaluable tools: They are great for scraping minced or chopped ingredients into bowls from chopping boards and counters. And keeping your counters free of crumbs, chopped-off ends of vegetables, and peelings means when you turn around next time, you'll have a clean and ready-to-go counter.

~ Keep the sink totally empty of any dirty dishes or cooking utensils. There is nothing worse than turning around to drain something in the sink to find that the sink is barely accessible. In the end it takes less time to clean up and keep everything neat while actually cooking, rather than waiting until the bread is in the oven, the salad is made, and the main dish is simmering on top of the stove, and you still have a mess to clean up.

~ *Mise en place, mise en place, mise en place!!!* Okay, I am lecturing, but this is one subject that deserves extra emphasis. Even I need the advice every now and then. *Mise en place* simply means "everything in its place," and for me that means gathering all the ingredients, including any special equipment, set out on a tray. Weigh and measure all ingredients; if eggs need separating, do that now; if a lemon needs zesting, do that now; if confectioners' sugar needs sifting, do that now. Trust me. Nothing adds confidence in the kitchen like this kind of organization. Even I find that when I bend my rule (oh, yes, I'm in a hurry!), I invariably forget an ingredient! Being a stickler about *mise en place* can also help you keep your pantry organized; as you use up the last of the baking soda, whole peppercorns, or active dry yeast make a note on your shopping list to replace them.

~ Read the recipe all the way through first, not just the ingredients but the instructions, too. Having an idea of what is required of you from beginning to end will help avoid mistakes and surprises and ultimately help you be a better cook.

MY ESSENTIAL EQUIPMENT

Although I do consider myself a gadget girl, I find that about nine out of ten gadgets fail to deliver on their promise. I recently purchased a "floating thermometer" that I thought would be great for monitoring the temperature of water while simmering. The first time I used it, the face of the thermometer steamed up so seriously that I could not read the temperature! So it does well to choose wisely. Here's a list of the equipment that never fails me.

~ I use both gas and induction cooktops, and favor all of the Le Creuset cast-iron products for searing and braising. For sheer ease of cleaning, I find that All-Clad stainless steel pots are excellent for simple heating or reheating.

~ I am a fan of ceramic-coated nonstick frying pans, especially for cooking ingredients that will normally stick, such as scrambled eggs.

~ A pair of stainless steel pasta cooking pots (5 quart [5 l] and 10 quart [10 l]) fitted with colanders are my favorites. I use them not just for pasta but for all my stocks (just lift out the colander and all the stock has been filtered out!), as well as for blanching.

~ I love copper, and have a huge selection. I especially like to own equipment that will live longer than I do.

~ I adore the panini grill for all kinds of grilling tasks, from toast to vegetables, so much so that I no longer own a traditional toaster. I haven't had particular success with grilling meat, poultry, and fish on it, though, so I stick to my outdoor or stovetop grill for those.

~ A label maker! I label everything: my spices and salt infusions, my containers of soups and stocks; leftovers in the freezer. Even if it is quite clear that the liquid in that container is chicken stock, I date and label it anyway. One can never be too sure! Of course you don't need to buy a machine: a roll of labeling tape and a Sharpie will do in a pinch.

~ Date your oils, condiments, and so on. The day I open a flavored oil—such as walnut, hazelnut, sesame, you name it—I write the date on the label, so I know when it has been opened. When using, I always give the oils the sniff test. If they smell good, even if just a bit past the desirable use-by date, I use them.

~ Thermometers: Essentials include a good deep-fry thermometer, an instant-read thermometer for meats, and if, possible, an infrared thermometer that will instantly tell you the heat of your oven or the temperature of your freezer.

~ A digital scale. Measure, weigh, measure, weigh. Weighing ingredients, from flour to sugar, nuts to vegetables, is a much more accurate method than eyeballing or even using cup measures. All of the recipes in the book are written to accommodate this.

~ Multiple sets of measuring spoons: Have at least 4 or 5 sets and take them apart and recombine them, with the 1 tablespoon measures all hung together and so forth. You will always have a clean spoon at the ready. When, ever, did you need to use all of those spoons on the ring at the same time?

~ Timers: Timers are essential. Most cell phones today have excellent timers, but I also love to have a collection in my kitchen, especially when several items are being timed at once. Be sure to place the timer next to the pot or oven it relates to, so you know that it's time to intervene with that recipe!

~ An electric spice mill: This is a pure essential for grinding seeds, nuts, dried vanilla beans, and spices.

~ A small electric deep-fat fryer: Today one can find totally reliable miniature fryers that use no more than 1 quart (1 l) of oil for deep-frying. I find the machine indispensable, and much more accurate and less bothersome than frying on a burner and fumbling with deep-fry thermometers.

~ Knives, knives, knives: My husband, Walter, collects knives and instructs students on how to handle and sharpen them, so we do have an abundance at hand. I find knives to be very personal, and the one that may be my favorite may be rejected out of hand by another cook. One only really needs a few: a good small knife for everyday use, a larger chef's knife for larger tasks, and a serrated bread knife for even slicing.

~ Cold bowls for sorbets, hot plates for hot food: If space permits, keep a set of small bowls in the freezer, so any sorbets you make will stay well chilled at serving time. Likewise, I am a stickler for serving hot food on hot plates. I have warming ovens but I find that a five-minute or so warming in the microwave heats plates more efficiently and keeps them hotter for longer. Timing will vary according to the type of plates or bowls (pottery, clay, fine china, etc.) being heated, the quantity, and the wattage of the microwave. Five minutes is an average, and with trial and error cooks will learn what combination works best for their plates and their ovens.

BLANCH

Blanching is a super-simple technique of cooking foods briefly by plunging them into boiling water (for 2 to 8 minutes, depending on the food) and then immediately stopping the cooking process by submerging them in a bath of ice water. I use this technique most for lightly cooking vegetables for salads, which I find brings out their essential flavor. The process of blanching inactivates the vegetable's enzymes, limiting the loss of vitamins in the food and helping to retain its natural vibrant color. For this reason, it is also a useful way to treat vegetables before freezing them.

Tips

~ Use plenty of heavily salted water (1 tablespoon coarse sea salt per 1 quart [1 l] of water) to prevent a concentration of food acids in the water that can turn your food brown.

~ Do not blanch green vegetables for more than 7 minutes, in order to maintain their bright green color.

~ Do not cover the pot. Covering the pot can turn bright green vegetables a dull, drab color; leaving the pot uncovered allows volatile acids to escape and helps maintain bright colors.

~ You want the water to come to a boil as quickly as possible after the food is added to reduce the cooking time. This is essential for two reasons: to prevent the vegetables from getting soggy and to help retain the color of the vegetables. The pot of water should be kept on high heat, and you may need to blanch in batches.

~ Place blanched items on paper towels or a clean kitchen towel to dry them and prevent sogginess.

~ If making ahead of time, do not dress the vegetables with any kind of acidic vinaigrette or dressing, as this will cause the vegetables to become dull and turn brown. Wait until serving time to add the dressing.

Green Bean and Artichoke Salad
with Hazelnut Vinaigrette

On each visit to the popular Paris brasserie Lazare, I look forward to sampling this green bean salad, a dish I could easily enjoy on a regular basis. It's everything a salad should be: bright, light, colorful, and satisfying.

This recipe demonstrates two indispensable blanching techniques: refreshing blanched vegetables in an ice water bath to halt the cooking process and retain their natural vibrant color; and tossing warm, freshly blanched vegetables in vinaigrette so they soak up more of the delicious dressing. Both are quick and simple, can be applied to almost any vegetable, and are perfect for the make-ahead cook!

In my cooking classes, I find that most students have stayed away from using fresh artichokes because they are intimidated by the preparation. But once you have plunged into the world of fresh artichokes, you won't turn back. The process is simple, and I find the repetition of the preparation almost soothing and meditative.

4 SERVINGS

EQUIPMENT: *A grapefruit spoon or a melon baller; a 5-quart (5 l) pasta pot fitted with a colander.*

1/4 cup (50 g) hazelnuts
1/4 cup (60 ml) plus 1 teaspoon best-quality hazelnut oil
Fine sea salt
3 tablespoons (45 ml) freshly squeezed lemon juice
4 fresh, firm baby artichokes

(Ingredients continue)

6 tablespoons (75 g) coarse sea salt
1 pound (500 g) haricots verts, rinsed and trimmed at both ends
2 tablespoons finely minced shallot
Coarse, freshly ground black pepper

1. In a small skillet, combine the hazelnuts, 1 teaspoon of the hazelnut oil, and 1/8 teaspoon of fine sea salt and toss to blend. Cook over medium heat, shaking the pan regularly, until the nuts are fragrant, evenly toasted, and beginning to crackle and sizzle, 3 to 4 minutes. Watch carefully! They can burn quickly. Transfer the nuts to a large plate to cool. (If not using immediately, store in an airtight container at room temperature for up to 1 week.)

2. In a large bowl, whisk together the remaining 1/4 cup hazelnut oil, 1 tablespoon of the lemon juice, and 1/4 teaspoon of fine sea salt. Taste for seasoning.

3. Fill a large bowl with water and add the remaining 2 tablespoons lemon juice to the water. With a knife, trim off and discard most of the stem from the base of one of the artichokes, leaving about 1 inch (2.5 cm). Bend back the tough outer green leaves, one at a time, and snap them off at the base. Continue snapping off leaves until only the central cone of yellow leaves with pale green tips remains. Lightly trim the top cone of leaves to just below the green tips. Trim any dark green areas from the base. Halve the artichoke lengthwise. With the grapefruit spoon or melon baller, scrape out and discard the hairy choke (if present) from each half. Quarter each trimmed artichoke half lengthwise. Add the slices to the acidulated water. Repeat with the remaining artichokes. (The artichokes can be prepared several hours in advance and stored in the acidulated water in the refrigerator.)

4. Fill the pasta pot with 3 quarts (3 l) water and bring to a rolling boil over high heat. Add 3 tablespoons of the coarse sea salt. Using a slotted spoon,

lift the artichoke slices from the acidulated water and carefully drop them into the boiling water. Blanch the artichoke slices, uncovered, until soft, about 3 minutes, counting from when the water comes back to a boil. Drain well. Add the artichokes to the vinaigrette in the bowl and toss to coat. (Doing this while warm helps the artichokes better absorb the dressing.)

5. Prepare a large bowl of ice water.

6. Fill the same pasta pot with 3 quarts (3 l) water and bring to a rolling boil over high heat. Add the remaining 3 tablespoons coarse sea salt and the haricots verts and blanch, uncovered, until crisp-tender, about 5 minutes, counting from the time the water comes back to a boil. (Cooking time will vary according to the size and age of the beans.) Immediately remove the colander from the water, allow the water to drain from the beans, and plunge the colander with the beans into the ice water so they cool down as quickly as possible. (The beans will cool in 1 to 2 minutes. If you leave them in the ice water any longer, they will become soggy and begin to lose flavor.) Drain the beans and wrap them in a thick clean kitchen towel to dry. (The beans can be cooked up to 4 hours in advance. Keep them wrapped in the towel and refrigerate, if desired.)

7. Add the cooled beans to the artichokes and vinaigrette in the bowl and toss to evenly coat the beans. Garnish with the shallot and toasted hazelnuts and season with pepper. Serve.

Artichoke, Zucchini, Avocado, and Green Zebra Tomato Salad

This refreshing salad is a soothing landscape of green, yellow, and orange. The forward, vibrant flavors of grassy baby artichokes, raw zucchini, creamy avocado, and faintly acidic green tomatoes are all enlivened with the elegance of toasted pistachios and the citrusy tang of orange, lime, and lemon zests.

— 4 SERVINGS

EQUIPMENT: *A citrus zester; a small jar with a lid; a grapefruit spoon or a melon baller; a 5-quart (5 l) pasta pot fitted with a colander; a mandoline; 4 chilled salad plates.*

PISTACHIO AND CITRUS DRESSING

1 organic orange, zested, halved, and juiced, all elements reserved
1 organic lime, zested, halved, and juiced, all elements reserved
1 organic lemon, zested, halved, and juiced, all elements reserved
1/2 teaspoon fine sea salt
1/2 cup (125 ml) best-quality pistachio oil

TOASTED PISTACHIOS

1 cup (120 g) raw, unsalted shelled pistachio nuts
1 teaspoon best-quality pistachio oil
1/4 teaspoon fine sea salt

VEGETABLES

6 fresh, firm baby artichokes
3 tablespoons coarse sea salt
2 small zucchini
2 firm, ripe avocados
2 firm, green heirloom tomatoes (such as Green Zebra)

1. In the small jar, combine 2 tablespoons of the citrus juice (equal parts orange, lime, and lemon) and the salt. Cover the jar and shake to blend. Add the pistachio oil and shake to blend again. Taste for seasoning.

2. In a small skillet, combine the pistachios, oil, and salt and toss to coat evenly. Cook over medium heat, shaking the pan regularly, until the nuts are fragrant, evenly toasted, and beginning to crackle and sizzle, 3 to 4 minutes. Watch carefully! They can burn quickly. Transfer the nuts to a large plate to cool. (If not using immediately, store in an airtight container at room temperature for up to 1 week.)

3. Fill a large bowl of water and add the reserved citrus halves and 2 tablespoons of the citrus juice to the water. With a knife, trim off and discard the stem from the base of one of the artichokes, leaving about 1 inch (2.5 cm). Bend back the tough outer green leaves, one at a time, and snap them off at the base. Continue snapping off leaves until only the central cone of yellow leaves with pale green tips remains. Lightly trim the top cone of leaves to just below the green tips. Trim any dark green areas from the base. Halve the artichoke lengthwise. With the grapefruit spoon or melon baller, scrape out and discard the hairy choke (if present) from each half. Cut each trimmed artichoke half lengthwise into 6 thin slices. Add the slices to the acidulated water. Repeat with the remaining artichokes. (The artichokes can be prepared several hours in advance and stored in the acidulated water in the refrigerator.)

4. Fill the 5-quart (5 l) pasta pot with 3 quarts (3 l) water and bring to a rolling boil over high heat. Add the coarse sea salt. Use a slotted spoon to lift the artichoke slices from the acidulated water and carefully drop them into the boiling water. Blanch, uncovered, until soft, about 3 minutes, counting from when the water comes back to a boil. Drain well and transfer to a large salad bowl. Add the pistachio and citrus dressing and toss to generously coat the artichoke slices with the dressing. (Doing so while warm helps them better absorb the dressing.)

5. Trim the zucchini. On the mandoline, slice the zucchini into thin lengthwise strips, or, if desired, crosswise into thin rounds. Add to the artichokes in the bowl and toss to generously coat with the dressing.

6. Halve, pit, and peel the avocados. Cut each half crosswise into thin slices. Add to the artichokes and zucchini in the bowl and toss gently to coat with the dressing.

7. Core the tomatoes. With a very sharp knife, cut them in half and then cut each half into quarters. Add to the bowl with the vegetables and toss to coat with the dressing.

8. Divide the salad among the four chilled salad plates. Scatter with the toasted pistachios. Garnish with the orange, lime, and lemon zest. Serve.

VARIATION: *For a varied presentation, toss each of the ingredients in the dressing separately and arrange them artfully on a large dinner plate or salad plate, interlacing the ingredients with one another.*

Spring Pea Soup with
Goat Cheese, Radish, and Dill

This quick, easy, healthy pea soup is a welcome sign of the emergence of spring. The pea pods make a lovely, delicate stock, while the goat cheese, radish, and dill add final touches of color, crunch, and flavor.

4 APPETIZER SERVINGS

EQUIPMENT: *A 3-quart (3 l) and a 2-quart (2 l) saucepan; a blender, food processor, or immersion blender.*

1 pound (500 g) fresh peas in their pods, preferably organic
1 medium onion, peeled and halved
3 plump, fresh garlic cloves, peeled but left whole
1 tablespoon coarse sea salt
1/4 teaspoon fine sea salt
2 ounces (50 g) firm goat's milk cheese or feta
2 red radishes, trimmed and sliced paper-thin
Fresh dill, for garnish

1. Rinse the pea pods well. Shell the peas, reserving the pods. You should have about 2 cups (300 g) shelled peas.

2. In the 3-quart (3 l) saucepan, combine the pods, onion, and garlic with 1-1/2 quarts (1.5 l) water. Bring to a boil over high heat, then reduce the heat to medium and simmer until the stock is full flavored, about 30 minutes. Strain and set aside. Discard the pods, onion, and garlic.

3. Prepare a large bowl of ice water.

4. In the 2-quart (2 l) saucepan, bring 1 quart (1 l) water to a boil over high heat. Add the coarse sea salt and the shelled peas and blanch, uncovered,

for 2 minutes, counting from the time the water comes back to the boil. Taste for doneness: The peas should still be a bit firm. Drain well. Plunge the peas into the bowl of ice water to halt cooking and help them maintain their bright green color. Drain the peas, reserving a handful for garnish.

5. In the blender or food processor or in a large bowl using the immersion blender, combine the peas, fine sea salt, and 1-1/3 cups (330 ml) of the pea stock and blend until smooth and velvety. Serve chilled or at room temperature, garnished with the reserved whole peas, crumbled goat's milk cheese, radish slices, and dill.

Spring Pea and Mint Salad

There is no more welcome sign of spring than the sight of a market stall overflowing with mounds of fresh peas in their pods.

4 SERVINGS

EQUIPMENT: *A 2-quart (2 l) saucepan.*

1 pound (500 g) fresh peas in their pods
1 tablespoon coarse sea salt
1 shallot, peeled and minced
1 leek, white part only, halved lengthwise, rinsed, and thinly sliced
1/2 teaspoon fine sea salt
Zest and juice of 1 organic lemon
1/4 cup (60 ml) extra-virgin olive oil
1/4 cup (60 ml) fresh mint leaves, cut into a chiffonade, for garnish

1. Shell the peas. You should have about 2 cups (300 g).

2. Prepare a bowl of ice water.

3. In a 2-quart (2 l) saucepan, bring 1 quart (1 l) water to a boil over high heat. Add the coarse sea salt and the peas and blanch, uncovered, for 2 minutes, counting from the time that the water comes back to a boil. Taste for desired doneness. The peas should still have a touch of crunch. Drain well. Plunge into the bowl of ice water to halt cooking and help keep their bright green color. Drain the peas and pat dry with a clean kitchen towel. Transfer to a salad bowl. Add the shallot and leek and toss to combine.

4. In a small bowl, combine the fine sea salt, lemon zest, lemon juice, and olive oil and whisk to blend. Add to the bowl with the vegetables and toss to coat. Garnish with the mint leaves and serve.

STEAM

Steaming sometimes gets a bad rap as a boring way to prepare vegetables, destined for unsophisticated children or those on a diet or suffering from some kind of illness. But used in the proper way, steaming is one of the best ways to achieve clean, bright flavors, and can be anything but boring. There's nothing to get in the way of the pure flavor of the food, and it's a very gentle way of cooking delicate foods such as fish and seafood, which, under the spell of the evaporating water, become creamy and tender.

Tips

~ If possible, use a bamboo steamer: The bamboo collects condensation in the lid, keeping it from dripping on the food as it cooks.

~ Make sure you have abundant water in the pan below the steamer, so the pan does not boil dry during the cooking process.

~ If possible, wrap meat and poultry in a lettuce or cabbage leaf, banana leaf, a bed of fresh herbs, or baking parchment to protect them. This also helps keep the bamboo from absorbing strong odors, and in the case of fresh herbs will add flavor at the same time.

~ For vegetables, bring the water to a rolling boil with the lid on the steamer before adding the vegetables, so that the steamer is full of vapor when you place the vegetables inside.

~ Pay attention to the cooking times. While it's true that you can't burn food when steaming, overcooking can leave vegetables, in particular, limp and lifeless.

Steamed Fish and Shellfish

Steamed Turbot with Lemongrass, Peas, and Baby Spinach

This recent favorite recipe has become a standby—and a hit—in my cooking classes. Sweating and steaming are two techniques I love to teach, and I find that so many students are amazed at how easy and healthful it is to steam fish. Many tell me that they have a bamboo steamer, but never quite knew what to do with it! So here's a masterful way to put the steamer to use, in a warming, colorful dish that combines the steamed fish and a fragrant, full-flavored blend of lemongrass, peas, and spinach.

— 6 SERVINGS —

EQUIPMENT: *A 2-quart (2 l) saucepan; a 9-inch (22 cm) bamboo steamer; a large, fine-mesh sieve; 6 warmed, shallow bowls.*

1 tablespoon coarse sea salt
2 cups (300 g) fresh or frozen shelled peas
2 tablespoons unsalted butter
2 shallots, peeled and finely chopped
Fine sea salt
1/4 cup (60 ml) chopped fresh lemongrass (from 4 to 8 stalks), tender pale parts only, or 1/4 cup (60 ml) Kaffir Lime Powder (page 443)

(Ingredients continue)

3 cups (750 ml) Fish Stock (page 404) or Shellfish Stock (page 406) or clam broth
1 cup (250 ml) heavy cream
Six 4-ounce (125 g) boneless, skinless turbot fillets (see Note)
4 cups (6 ounces; 170 g) fresh baby spinach leaves
Grated lime zest or fresh mint leaves, for garnish (optional)
Kaffir Lime Powder (page 443), for garnish (optional)

1. Prepare a bowl of ice water.

2. In the 2-quart (2 l) saucepan, bring 1 quart (1 l) water to a boil over high heat. Add the coarse sea salt and the peas and blanch, uncovered, for 2 minutes, counting from when the water comes back to a boil. Taste for the desired doneness; the peas should still have a touch of crunch. Drain well. Plunge into the bowl of ice water to halt the cooking and help preserve their bright green color.

3. In a medium saucepan, combine the butter, shallots, 1/8 teaspoon fine sea salt, and the lemongrass and sweat—cook, covered, over low heat—until softened, about 5 minutes. Add the stock and cook until it has reduced to 1/2 cup (125 ml), 10 to 12 minutes. Add the cream and cook until slightly thickened, 2 to 3 minutes more. Strain the sauce through the fine-mesh sieve into another medium saucepan, pressing hard on the solids to extract maximum flavor. Discard the solids. Taste for seasoning. (The sauce can be made up to 1 day in advance. Refrigerate in a covered container.)

4. Bring 1 quart (1 l) water to a simmer in the bottom of a medium saucepan. Arrange the fish fillets in the bamboo steamer. Place the steamer over the simmering water, cover, and steam just until the fish is cooked to the desired doneness and flakes easily with a fork, 2 to 3 minutes.

5. Place the spinach leaves and several tablespoons water in a large skillet. Cover and wilt the spinach over medium-high heat. Once wilted, add the blanched peas to warm them. Transfer the spinach and peas to the fine-mesh sieve to drain.

6. To serve, gently reheat the sauce if necessary. Divide the vegetables among the six warmed, shallow bowls and set a fish fillet on top of each. Spoon the sauce over all. Garnish with the lime zest or mint leaves and/or kaffir lime powder. Serve immediately.

NOTE: *Any firm, white-fleshed fish fillets—such as halibut, flounder, trout, or perch—can be used here.*

WINE MATCH: *A current favorite white wine is the northern Rhône Condrieu from the vineyards of François Villard, particularly his cuvée De Poncins. To my palate, it is the richest and most flattering expression of the Viognier grape: mineral-rich, pure, and full-bodied but not overly fruity.*

Steamed Shrimp in Saffron Sauce

Inspired by a saffron-rich sauce served with mussels at our neighborhood Provençal restaurant Bistro du'O, this quick and easy dish offers a lot of bang for its buck. The technique of warming the saffron for 30 minutes in just a tablespoon of warm broth extracts the rich color and flavor of the rare saffron threads.

4 SERVINGS

EQUIPMENT: *A 9-inch (22 cm) bamboo steamer; a blender or immersion blender; 4 warmed, shallow soup bowls.*

3 cups (750 ml) Fish Stock (page 404) or Shellfish Stock (page 406)
1 teaspoon saffron threads
1 cup (250 ml) heavy cream
8 large, fresh shrimp, peeled and deveined, or 8 ounces (250 g) fish fillets (see Note)
Aïoli Piquant (page 94; optional)
Toasted Pain au Levain (page 293) or Socca (page 437), for serving (optional)

1. In a large saucepan, warm the stock over low heat. In a small bowl, combine 1 tablespoon of the warm stock with the saffron. Stir gently to color the liquid and set aside to infuse until the liquid is a bright saffron color, at least 30 minutes. Pour the saffron liquid into the cream and stir until the cream turns a bright saffron yellow.

2. Just before steaming the shrimp or fish, add the saffron-infused cream to the pan with the stock and bring the sauce to a gentle simmer over low heat.

3. If you are using fish, cut the fillets into 8 even pieces. Bring 1 quart (1 l) water to a simmer in the bottom of a medium saucepan. Arrange the

shrimp or fish fillets in the steamer. Place the steamer over the simmering water, cover, and steam just until the shrimp are evenly pink or the fish flakes easily with a fork, 3 minutes, or until both are cooked to the desired doneness.

4. In the blender, or directly in the saucepan using the immersion blender, blend the sauce until frothy. Divide the sauce among the four warmed, shallow soup bowls. Top with several pieces of shrimp or the steamed fish. If desired, pass a bowl of *aïoli* to stir into the soup. Serve with slices of toasted Pain au Levain or *socca* (chickpea crêpes).

NOTE: *Any firm, white-fleshed fish fillets—such as monkfish, halibut, flounder, trout, or perch—can be used here.*

WINE MATCH: *Our winemaker Yves Gras's daily drinking white Sablet is ideal here: A blend of Viognier, Bourboulenc, Grenache Blanc, and Clairette Blanc, the wine is fresh, juicy, and peppy—all qualities to love in a young white wine.*

Steamed Cod with Rosemary
and Seaweed Butter

On Sunday mornings in Paris I always make a tour of the neighborhood organic market on Boulevard Raspail. There our fishmonger always offers the brightest, freshest cod fillets, which I bring home for a quick and satisfying lunch. To me, steamed fish is a miracle of flavor and healthfulness. I grow a hedge of fresh rosemary outside my back door, so I use the herb liberally in my cuisine. I like to steam on a bed of herbs, as this prevents the fish from sticking to the steamer basket and flavors the fish at the same time. Here the fish is simply anointed with a blend of sliced scallions and seaweed butter, a perfect match for the mild-flavored fish.

— 4 SERVINGS —————————————————————

EQUIPMENT: *A 9-inch (22 cm) bamboo steamer; 4 warmed, shallow soup bowls.*

6 scallions, trimmed and thinly sliced on the diagonal
4 tablespoons (60 g) Seaweed Butter (page 79)
Several fresh rosemary branches
1 pound (500 g) skinless cod fillets, cut into 8 equal pieces
Fine sea salt
Minced fresh chives, for garnish

1. In a small saucepan, combine the scallions and butter and warm, over low heat, until the butter is melted and bubbling. Remove from the heat, cover, and keep warm while steaming the cod.

2. Bring 1 quart (1 l) water to a simmer in the bottom of a medium saucepan. Arrange the rosemary in the steamer. Carefully place the fish

on top of the rosemary. Place the steamer over the simmering water, cover, and steam just until the fish flakes easily with a fork, and is opaque throughout and cooked to the desired doneness, 4 to 5 minutes. Season the fish lightly with fine sea salt.

3. Place two pieces of the fish in the center of each warmed, shallow soup bowl. Pour the seaweed butter sauce all over. Garnish with chives and serve.

Steamed Vegetables

Steamed Corn on the Cob
with Piment d'Espelette Butter

I am not sure how long ago I began steaming corn on the cob, but today that is my only method for cooking this warming, reliable vegetable. Fresh corn needs only a few moments of steaming, and the result is a vegetable that is firm, flavorful, and honest. No more soggy boiled corn! And with a variety of compound butters in the freezer, there are always inventive ways to season the corn: My favorite is piment d'Espelette butter. During the summer months, we have steamed corn for lunch once or twice a week, often served with a simple salad and maybe a touch of cheese and toast. Sometimes I fully shuck the corn, as is traditional; other times I leave some husk on for a more rustic, casual look.

— 4 SERVINGS

EQUIPMENT: *A 9-inch (22 cm) bamboo steamer.*

4 ears fresh corn, shucked or left partially shucked
Piment d'Espelette Butter (page 79) or other compound butter (pages 77–80), for
  serving
Fine sea salt

Bring 1 quart (1 l) water to a simmer in the bottom of a medium saucepan. Arrange the corn in the steamer and place it over the simmering water. Cover and steam just until the corn is cooked through but still slightly firm, about 8 minutes. Remove and serve with the compound butter and a sprinkling of salt.

*Fregola—the golden toasted Sardinian pasta—
is a favorite ingredient to slip into bouillon-based
long-simmered soups to add body and texture.*

SIMMER

Simmering is a method of cooking using water or a flavored liquid heated to around 180° to 185°F (82° to 85°C), just under boiling (212°F/100°C); you should see a few bubbles rising to the top here and there. Using a lower simmering temperature can sometimes involve long cooking times, allowing for an exchange of flavors between the ingredient and the flavored liquid, which is often included as part of the final dish. Simmering is an excellent technique for tenderizing tough cuts of meat or cooking vegetables for a long time to draw out more flavor, such as with soups.

Cooking fish, poultry, or meat at a temperature any higher than a simmer is not advisable, as it will toughen and dry out the flesh and can damage the food as it is pushed around the pot by the bubbles.

Tips

~ To achieve an even simmer, use a heavy-duty pot that will distribute the heat evenly.

~ Place the pan of liquid over high heat, and when the liquid comes to a boil, reduce the heat to its lowest setting, so that the liquid calms down to a gentle simmer, with just a few bubbles rising to the top.

~ If your lowest gas or electric cooktop settings are too hot to achieve a gentle simmer, you can invest in a heat diffuser, a relatively compact kitchen tool that diffuses the heat coming from the heating element to lower the temperature under the pan if the heat source is too hot. These are often sold as "flame tamers" or under the brand name SimmerMat—both do the same thing. Look for diffusers made from quality material such as steel or cast iron, which will distribute heat evenly.

~ For dishes that you plan to simmer for a long time, use a large pot that will hold enough water to keep the food submerged for the duration of the cooking time as water evaporates. For dishes that have a short cooking time or require less water, a small pot will do.

~ A skillet or shallow pan works best with delicate foods that may crumble easily. Fish and chicken can be plunged into boiling water (blanched) for 30 seconds to 1 minute, to freshen the ingredients and remove any unwanted strong odors.

~ A baking parchment lid (see opposite) sits on top of the water and has several useful functions: to keep the food submerged for even cooking; to prevent delicate food from being tossed about by the bubbles; and to help increase the cooking time and concentrate flavors.

Baking Parchment Lids

Wooden Japanese drop lids, which come in several sizes and are designed to snugly but very delicately float on the liquid surface inside a pot, are ideal for using with simmered dishes. They are expensive and hard to come by, however, so making a baking parchment lid is a useful alternative.

Measure a length of baking parchment slightly larger than the diameter of the pot you are going to simmer in. Fold the piece of parchment in half on the diagonal to make a triangle. Fold the triangle in half again along the closed edge. Continue to fold the paper in half three more times, always using the closed folded corner as the pivot for the fold. Holding the pointed end of the folded paper measure at the center of the pot with the wide end toward the outer edge, use a pair of scissors to cut the wide end in a softly rounded arc following the curve of the pot. Snip off about 1 inch (2.5 cm) from the pointed end to create a steam vent. Unfold the paper and you should have a circular paper lid perfectly sized to the surface area of your pot.

Fregola, White Bean, and Pumpkin Minestrone

This welcoming winter soup—almost a winter *pistou*—was inspired by a version I sampled at the hands of chef Akihiro Horikoshi at his minuscule yet spectacular restaurant La Table d'Akihiro in Paris's 7th *arrondissement*. This soup contains many of my favorite colorful and healthy winter vegetables, including carrots, celery, and pumpkin. During the summer months, when the fresh white beans known in France as *cocos blanc* are in season, I shell the beans and freeze them uncooked to have on hand come winter. For the pumpkin, I prefer the smaller, firm-fleshed vegetable (such as delicata, kabocha, or butternut*)*, in place of larger, fibrous varieties that can be watery and lack flavor. As the pasta component, I like to add the golden *fregola*, a Sardinian specialty somewhat similar in shape to large Israeli couscous, made from semolina dough and toasted in the oven. Let this simmer away on top of the stove on a cold winter's day and you will be duly rewarded!

— 8 TO 12 SERVINGS ———————————————————————

EQUIPMENT: *A 6-quart (6 l) cast-iron pot with a lid; 8 to 12 warmed, shallow soup bowls.*

2 medium onions, peeled, halved lengthwise, and cut into thin half-moons
1 garlic head, cloves peeled and halved, green germ removed if present
1 leek, white and tender green parts only, quartered lengthwise, rinsed, and thinly sliced
1/4 cup (60 ml) extra-virgin olive oil
Fine sea salt

(Ingredients continue)

3 carrots, unpeeled, halved lengthwise and cut into thin half-moons

4 celery ribs, cut into thin slices

4 cups (1 kg) peeled and cubed delicata, kabocha, or butternut squash

1 pound (500 g) fresh white beans (or dried; see Note)

Two 14-ounce (400 g) cans diced Italian tomatoes in juice

1 cup (170 g) fregola

Freshly grated Parmigiano-Reggiano cheese, for garnish

1. In the cast-iron pot, combine the onions, garlic, leek, oil, and salt to taste. Stir to coat the vegetables with the oil. Sweat—cook, covered, over low heat—until softened, about 5 minutes.

2. Add the carrots, celery, squash, beans, tomatoes, 2 teaspoons salt, and 2 quarts (2 l) cold water. Bring just to a simmer over medium heat. Simmer, covered (so as not to reduce the liquid), until the vegetables are soft and the beans are cooked through, 45 minutes to 1 hour.

3. Add the *fregola* and simmer until the pasta is cooked through, about 15 minutes more. Taste for seasoning. Serve in the warmed soup bowls, garnished with cheese.

NOTE: *If using dried beans, rinse them, place them in a large heatproof bowl, cover with boiling water, and set aside for 1 hour. Drain the beans and use as directed in the recipe.*

VARIATIONS

~ I sometimes add bits of cooked ham or a swirl of a quick, non-garlic pesto (basil leaves with a touch of olive oil and salt pureed in a blender).

~ Add a Parmigiano-Reggiano rind in step 2 to further flavor the broth. Remove the rind before serving.

MAKE-AHEAD NOTE: *The soup can be prepared and stored in airtight containers in the refrigerator for up to 3 days or frozen for up to 1 month.*

Stracciatella (Roman "Egg Drop" Soup) with Spinach

This soup is light, flavorful, and so very quick to prepare! It's a favorite weeknight supper when I want something that's truly satisfying but I'm not in the mood for a complicated preparation. Removing the pot from the heat before adding the eggs allows them to cook slowly, achieving a delicately silken texture.

6 SERVINGS

EQUIPMENT: *A 3-quart (3 l) saucepan; 6 warmed, shallow soup bowls.*

2 large eggs, free-range and organic
6 tablespoons (45 g) grated Parmigiano-Reggiano cheese, plus more for serving
Coarse, freshly ground black pepper
1 quart (1 l) Chicken Stock (page 402) or Vegetable Stock (page 408)
4 cups (60 g) loosely packed spinach leaves, cut into a chiffonade
Fine sea salt

1. Crack the eggs into a medium bowl. With a fork, very gently break up the egg yolks. Do not whisk. Gently stir in the cheese and season lightly with pepper.

2. In the saucepan, bring the stock to a boil over high heat, then reduce the heat to its lowest setting to achieve a gentle simmer. Add the spinach and cook until wilted, about 1 minute. Remove the pan from the heat. (The heat allows the eggs to cook gently to achieve a delicately silken texture.)

3. Very slowly pour the egg mixture in a thin stream from about 8 inches (20 cm) above the pot into the stock, at the same time stirring carefully with a wooden spoon in one direction, until the eggs turn into elegant ribbons. This is a very delicate operation, so move slowly but deliberately. If the stock is too hot or the eggs are overbeaten or whisked, the eggs could turn into rubbery clumps. Taste for seasoning and add additional pepper and salt as needed.

4. Transfer the soup to the warmed soup bowls and garnish with more cheese. Serve immediately.

Ginger and Enoki Mushroom "Egg Drop" Soup

This Japanese-inspired version of the "egg drop" soup master shows how versatile this simmering technique is. This soup has a warming, ginger kick that works wonders for a cold, or when you're in need of a deeply nourishing broth. Many other flavors can be added or substituted here: lemongrass, a few drops of lime for acidity, bird's-eye chile for heat, or a carrot cut into julienne and lightly simmered so it retains a slight crunch.

— 6 SERVINGS ————————————————————————————

EQUIPMENT: *A 3-quart (3 l) saucepan; 6 warmed, shallow soup bowls.*

2 large eggs, free-range and organic
1 quart (1 l) Chicken Stock (page 402) or Vegetable Stock (page 408)
1 teaspoon finely grated fresh ginger
1-1/2 teaspoons soy sauce
4 cups (60 g) loosely packed baby spinach leaves
1/2 cup (40 g) enoki mushrooms, well rinsed
Fine sea salt (optional)

1. Crack the eggs into a medium bowl. With a fork, very gently break up the egg yolks. Do not whisk.

2. In the saucepan, combine the stock, ginger, and soy sauce and bring to a boil over high heat, then reduce the heat to its lowest setting to achieve a gentle simmer. Add the spinach and mushrooms and cook until tender, about 30 seconds.

3. When the spinach is wilted, remove the pot from the heat. (This allows the eggs to cook gently and reach the desired silky texture.) Very slowly pour

the egg mixture in a thin stream from about 8 inches (20 cm) above the pot into the stock, at the same time stirring carefully with a wooden spoon in one direction, until the eggs turn into elegant ribbons. This is a very delicate operation, so move slowly but deliberately. If the stock is too hot or the eggs are overbeaten or whisked, the eggs could turn into rubbery clumps. Taste for seasoning and add salt if necessary. Transfer to the warmed, shallow soup bowls and serve immediately.

William's Thai Vegetable Bouillon

This zillion-ingredient vegetable bouillon is adapted from a version offered by one of my favorite Parisian chefs, William Ledeuil of Ze Kitchen Galerie in the 6th *arrondissement*. The richly perfumed liquid is an ideal example of how a long, gentle simmer can draw out dense, intense flavors from vegetables, herbs, and spices. Unlike most vegetable bouillons, in which most of the ingredients are cooked whole or in chunks, here the aromatics are minced and sweated, resulting in a deeper, more complex-flavored liquid. As with all of William's food, this one is aromatically enriched with Asian ingredients, including lemongrass, ginger, Thai basil, kaffir lime leaves, and fresh cilantro. The bouillon can stand alone as a soothing soup, or can be used as a vegetable stock when an Asian flavor would be welcome.

MAKES 3 QUARTS (3 L) BOUILLON

EQUIPMENT: *A 10-quart (10 l) stockpot; a large colander lined with a double layer of dampened cheesecloth.*

1 cup (250 g) white button mushrooms, rinsed, trimmed, halved lengthwise
4 medium carrots, scrubbed
1 medium onion, peeled and minced
8 large shallots, peeled and minced
1 leek, white part only, halved lengthwise, rinsed, and minced
2 celery ribs, minced
1 small fennel bulb, trimmed and minced
6 fresh lemongrass stalks, halved lengthwise
1/2 bird's-eye chile or other small hot chile, seeded

(Ingredients continue)

A 1-1/2-inch (3 cm) knob of fresh ginger, peeled and minced

4 plump, fresh garlic cloves, peeled, halved lengthwise, and green germ removed if
*   present*

1 tablespoon black peppercorns, crushed

2 tablespoons extra-virgin olive oil

2 fresh Thai basil sprigs

2 fresh cilantro sprigs

6 fresh, frozen, or dried kaffir lime leaves (optional)

2 whole star anise

1 tablespoon coarse sea salt

1. In the stockpot, combine all the ingredients and toss to coat with the oil. Sweat—cook, covered, over low heat—until softened, about 5 minutes. Add 2 quarts (2 l) cold water and bring to a boil over high heat. Lower the heat to achieve a gentle simmer and cook, uncovered, for 1-1/2 hours. Remove from the heat, cover the pot with plastic wrap, and let the bouillon rest for 30 minutes to let any impurities settle to the bottom.

2. Place the large colander lined with cheesecloth over a large bowl. Ladle— do not pour, to avoid stirring up the impurities on the bottom of the pot— the liquid through the sieve to strain.

3. Transfer the bouillon to airtight containers and let cool slightly, then cover and refrigerate.

MAKE-AHEAD NOTE: *Store in airtight containers in the refrigerator for up to 3 days, or in the freezer for up to 3 months.*

POACH

Poaching is a moist-heat cooking method in which food is cooked gently, submerged in water or a flavored liquid, at 160° to 180°F (70° to 80°C), as opposed to boiling or simmering, which cooks food at higher temperatures.

This is a great method to use with very delicate foods such as eggs, fish, poultry, or fruit, which can easily dry out, break up, or overcook with more forceful kinds of cooking. It's my preferred method for cooking chicken breasts, as it gives such tender and flavorful results.

Because there is no fat added in the cooking process, it's not only a healthy option, but also an ideal method when you want to achieve bright, clean, pure flavors.

The trick is keeping the temperature constant, never reaching a boil, which can be tricky. A heat diffuser (see page 27) can be used if your heat source is too forceful to keep the liquid's temperature on the verge of simmering (almost bubbling, but not quite).

Traditionally, poaching liquid is a flavored stock enhanced with aromatic herbs (known as a *court bouillon*, an acidulated cooking liquid flavored with vegetables, herbs, vinegar or lemon juice, and seasoning) that will flavor the food as it cooks. Stock can also be used, as can milk, water, and syrup. Eggs are one of the only foods that should be poached in just water.

Tips

~ Poaching can be done starting with hot or cold liquid. If the liquid is at room temperature and the liquid and food are heated to a gentle simmer at the same time, there is more exchange of flavors between the two, and in my experience, for delicate ingredients such as chicken breasts, the result is much more tender poultry.

~ Any impurities that rise to the surface of the water ("scum") should be removed with a skimmer and discarded. This can be done as often as necessary during poaching.

~ Tender ingredients (such as chicken breasts) should be poached until just cooked through, or they will become tough.

~ Fruit is usually poached in a sugar syrup, which can be flavored with spices such as cinnamon, vanilla, star anise, cardamom, or allspice and laced with some fiery ginger. Traditionally, a sugar syrup is made with regular refined white sugar, but all sorts of sweeteners, such as Demerara sugar, honey, or maple syrup, can be substituted to achieve more depth of flavor. This is a great technique for cooking underripe fruit, as the sugar syrup helps sweeten and soften the fruit.

Poaching Eggs

You can scramble them, fry them, bake them, boil them. But my preferred way to enjoy this rich, nutrient-dense, and endlessly versatile food is to poach them in barely simmering water until the whites are just cooked and the golden yolk, when pierced with a knife, flows out to create a luscious sauce. Almost anyone can cook an egg, but to cook one to elevate it to the elegant heights it deserves, one must follow a few simple but important rules:

~ The number one rule: Make sure you have the freshest eggs possible. As eggs age, the tight protein structure of the whites begins to break down, causing them to become more watery, spreading quickly into wispy trails when dropped into simmering water. Fresher eggs will have plump whites that hold together better during cooking.

~ If possible, seek out cage-free eggs, preferably from organic chickens who are fed a natural diet.

~ Storing eggs at room temperature quickens the aging process, so it's best to keep them refrigerated.

~ Cracking eggs into a fine-mesh sieve is a great trick for separating any watery exterior from the bouncy firm inner egg white. If you crack an egg into the sieve and find that the whole white is very watery and weak, rather than firm as it should be, cut your losses and save that egg for another use, as it will never plump up when poached.

~ Water temperature is also extremely important when poaching eggs. Eggs are incredibly delicate and can overcook in just a matter of seconds. The cooking water must be at the most gentle of simmers when the eggs are slipped into the water, not a rolling boil, which would toss the egg around, cooking it too fast and tearing apart the white.

Poached Eggs

Many, many eggs were sacrificed in our test kitchen trying to determine the very best way to poach the perfect egg. We tried vinegar in the water, but found that although it helped give shape to the egg whites, they became rubbery and were laced with a faint unappealing acidic flavor. We tried simmering on the heat; taking off the heat and covering; swirling the water in a whirlpool, leaving the egg untouched after it hit the water—you name it, we tried it. The number one principle is to use the freshest eggs possible; if you start with less than that, all the other steps are more or less in vain (see page 41 for more tips).

— 4 SERVINGS

EQUIPMENT: *A 3-quart (3 l) saucepan about 9 inches (23 cm) in diameter; a mini fine-mesh sieve or tea strainer; 4 small bowls or ramekins; a slotted spoon; paper towels, folded in quarters.*

1/2 teaspoon fine sea salt
4 large, ultra-fresh eggs, free-range and
   organic, at room temperature

1. In the saucepan, bring 1-1/2 quarts (1.5 l) water to a gentle simmer. Add the salt.

2. Place the sieve over a ramekin and crack the egg into the sieve, allowing any thin watery egg white to drain away. Discard the drained egg white.

Very gently, so as not to dislodge the white from the yolk, slide the egg from the sieve into the ramekin. Repeat with the remaining eggs and ramekins.

3. Gently dip the edge of each ramekin into the simmering water, so that the egg slides smoothly into the water. Turn off the heat and cover the pot until the eggs are cooked through, about 3 minutes for room-temperature eggs. The white should be firm, with no translucent areas remaining, and the yolk should have a thin opaque film over the top, but still be soft and liquid inside.

4. With the slotted spoon, carefully remove the eggs one at a time, holding the folded paper towels underneath to absorb any water. Serve immediately.

NOTE: *If poaching one egg at a time, and if your egg white is plump and not watery, try swirling the water in a whirlpool before adding your egg to the water. The motion will help the egg white wrap around itself, creating a very neat and round cooked white. If the white is watery, however, the motion will simply tear the white apart, leaving streaks through the water. Using this technique for multiple eggs can get tricky, as the motion of the water can cause them to bump into one another.*

Teapot Onsen Eggs

Onsen tamago is a Japanese tradition of cooking eggs in their shells at low temperatures in hot springs. This home version simply uses a teapot and a kitchen towel to create a warm bath for the eggs. The result: a luxurious, silken texture throughout the whole egg, transforming the humble poached egg into a delicacy to be enjoyed on its own, or to sit atop a side dish of mushrooms or grilled asparagus, or to accompany a salad as a luscious, rich sauce.

— 2 SERVINGS ————————————————————————————

EQUIPMENT: *A ceramic or porcelain teapot or small, heat-retaining vessel with a lid.*

2 large, ultra-fresh eggs, free-range and organic, at room temperature

1. Preheat the teapot: Fill it with boiling water and let it sit for several minutes.

2. Empty the teapot. With a spoon, gently lower the eggs, intact in their shells, into the teapot, being careful not to crack the shells.

3. In a saucepan or kettle, bring 1 quart (1 l) water to a boil. Remove from the heat, wait for 2 minutes, then pour the water over the eggs in the teapot. Cover with the lid and wrap with a thick kitchen towel to help retain the heat.

4. Leave the eggs in the hot water for 16 to 17 minutes. (Note that this time may vary depending on how well the teapot is able to retain heat.)

5. Remove the eggs from the teapot. Rinse them briefly under cold water, then crack the shells, separating each side with your thumbs as you would an uncooked egg. The eggs will emerge in the form of a poached egg, but both the whites and yolks will have an almost creamy, silken texture.

Seared Garlic Mushrooms, Chile Ricotta, and Poached Egg on Comté and Paprika Brioche

Seared mushrooms are my ultimate pairing with poached egg, at once creamy and earthy, balanced by the lactic tang of ricotta and just that little kick of chile to brighten your senses. This recipe is a reason to keep slices of Comté and paprika brioche in your freezer for when you're in the mood for a decadent weekend brunch.

— **2 SERVINGS** —

EQUIPMENT: *A colander lined with cheesecloth (optional); a 3-quart (3 l) saucepan about 9 inches (23 cm) in diameter; a mini fine-mesh sieve or tea strainer; 2 small ramekins or bowls; a slotted spoon; paper towels, folded in quarters; 2 warmed plates.*

1/4 cup (80 g) best-quality fresh ricotta
1/8 teaspoon dried chile flakes
1/4 teaspoon dried oregano
Fine sea salt
3 tablespoons unsalted butter or Ghee (page 411)
7 ounces (200 g) mixed fresh mushrooms, such as button, shiitake, and chanterelle, trimmed, wiped clean with a damp cloth (see Note), and thinly sliced
2 plump, fresh garlic cloves, halved, green germ removed if present, and minced
3 tablespoons finely chopped fresh parsley leaves, plus more for garnish
2 slices Comté and Paprika Brioche (page 272)
2 large, ultra-fresh eggs, free-range and organic, at room temperature
Coarse, freshly ground black pepper

1. If time permits, place the ricotta in a colander lined with cheesecloth. Set the colander over a bowl and refrigerate for 1 to 2 hours to drain excess liquid from the ricotta.

2. In a small bowl, mix together the ricotta, chile flakes, oregano, and 1/8 teaspoon salt until well combined. Set aside.

3. Melt 2 tablespoons of the butter in a large skillet over medium-high heat. When the butter begins to fizz, add the mushrooms in a single layer. Do not overcrowd the pan or the mushrooms will steam rather than sear. You may have to sear in batches. Leave the mushrooms untouched until they are seared to a deep golden brown, about 2 minutes. Toss the mushrooms to cook evenly on all sides, about 2 minutes more.

4. Reduce the heat to medium and add the remaining 1 tablespoon butter, the garlic, and the parsley. Toss to cover evenly and cook for 1 minute more. Be careful not to burn the garlic. Transfer the mushrooms to a bowl.

5. In the fat remaining in the pan, toast the sliced brioche for about 30 seconds on each side.

6. In the saucepan, bring 1-1/2 quarts (1.5 l) water to a gentle simmer. Add 1/2 teaspoon of salt.

7. Place the sieve over a ramekin. Crack one egg into the sieve, allowing any thin watery egg white to drain away. Discard the drained egg white. Gently slide the egg from the sieve into the ramekin. Repeat with the remaining egg and ramekin.

8. Gently dip the edge of each ramekin into the simmering water, so that each egg slides smoothly into the water. Turn off the heat and cover the pot until the eggs are cooked through, about 3 minutes for room-temperature eggs. The white should be firm, with no translucent areas remaining, and the yolk should have a thin opaque film over the top, but still be soft and liquid inside.

9. With the slotted spoon, carefully remove the eggs one at a time, holding the folded paper towels underneath to absorb any water.

10. To assemble the dish, place a slice of toasted brioche on a warmed plate, spread generously with the chile ricotta, heap with the seared mushrooms, and top each slice with a poached egg. Season with salt and black pepper and garnish with parsley.

NOTE: *Wipe the mushrooms clean with a damp cloth, removing any dirt with the tip of a sharp knife. Do not soak the mushrooms in water: They are very porous and will easily absorb excess water. If the mushrooms are damp from rinsing, they will not sear properly.*

Artichokes with Poached Egg in Cèpe Cream with Truffles

This quartet of artichokes, poached egg, powerfully flavored *cèpe* (*porcini*) mushrooms, and dreamy, fresh winter truffles could not be more satisfying. This is a great teaching recipe and one we use during my truffle classes, where cooks get to master preparing artichokes, sweating leeks, poaching eggs, and working with truffles. Don't worry if fresh truffles are not at hand: The remaining trio of ingredients will hold their own just fine.

My good friend and great cook Jeffrey Bergman generously shared this recipe with me.

--- 4 SERVINGS ---

EQUIPMENT: *A grapefruit spoon or melon baller; a small saucepan with a lid; a large skillet with a lid; a 3-quart (3 l) saucepan about 9 inches (23 cm) in diameter; a mini fine-mesh sieve or tea strainer; 4 small bowls or ramekins; a slotted spoon; paper towels, folded in quarters; 4 warmed, shallow soup bowls.*

3 tablespoons freshly squeezed lemon juice

8 firm, fresh baby artichokes

1 cup (250 ml) heavy cream

1 tablespoon Cèpe Mushroom Powder (page 432)

Fine sea salt

Coarse, freshly ground black pepper

1 tablespoon extra-virgin olive oil

2 tablespoons unsalted butter, at room temperature

1 large leek, white and tender green parts only, quartered, rinsed, and thinly sliced

4 large, ultra-fresh eggs, free-range and organic, at room temperature

1 ounce (15 g) fresh black truffle, peeled and cut into matchsticks (optional)

2 tablespoons minced fresh chives

1. Fill a large bowl with water and add the lemon juice. With a knife, trim off and discard the stem from the base of one of the artichokes, leaving about 1 inch (2.5 cm). Bend back the tough outer green leaves, one at a time, and snap them off at the base. Continue snapping off leaves until only the central cone of yellow leaves with pale green tips remains. Lightly trim the top cone of leaves to just below the green tips. Trim any dark green areas from the base. Halve the artichoke lengthwise. With a grapefruit spoon or melon baller, scrape out and discard the hairy choke (if present) from each half. Quarter each trimmed artichoke half lengthwise. Add the slices to the acidulated water. Repeat with the remaining artichokes. (The artichokes can be prepared several hours in advance and stored in the acidulated water in the refrigerator.)

2. In the small saucepan, warm the cream over medium heat. Whisk in the mushroom powder until the mixture is smooth. Season with salt and pepper. Cover and set aside to keep warm.

3. In the skillet, combine the oil and butter and melt the butter over low heat. Add the leeks and sweat—cook, covered, over low heat—until softened, about 5 minutes. Drain the artichokes, add them to the skillet, and cook, covered, until soft, about 5 minutes more. Taste for seasoning. Cover and set aside to keep warm.

4. In the 3-quart (3 l) saucepan, bring 1-1/2 quarts (1.5 liters) water to a gentle simmer.

5. Place the mesh sieve over a ramekin. Crack an egg into the sieve, allowing any thin watery egg white to drain away. Discard the drained egg white. Gently slide the egg from the sieve into the ramekin. Repeat with the remaining eggs and ramekins.

6. Gently dip the edge of each ramekin into the simmering water, so that each egg slides smoothly into the water. Turn off the heat and cover the pot until the eggs are cooked through, about 3 minutes for room-

temperature eggs. The white should be firm, with no translucent areas remaining, and the yolk should have a thin opaque film over the top, but still be soft and liquid inside.

7. With the slotted spoon, carefully remove the eggs one at a time, holding the folded paper towels underneath to absorb any water.

8. Evenly divide the artichoke mixture among the centers of the warmed bowls, creating a little platform for the poached egg. Place a poached egg in the center of each artichoke bed. Evenly spoon the mushroom cream around the base of the artichokes. Garnish with the truffle matchsticks (if using) and the chives.

WINE MATCH: *I love this dish with a white Châteauneuf-du-Pape Domaine Saint Préfert from the talented winemaker Isabel Ferrando: Her outstandingly appealing wine is a blend of Clairette Blanc and Roussanne, my favorite Rhône white grape.*

Poaching Poultry and Fish

Poached Chicken Breasts with Morels, Peas, and Tarragon

In my cooking classes, no matter the season, poached chicken breasts and morel mushrooms are a favorite. During the January truffle week, we toss in thick slices of fresh black truffles, and in the spring Paris classes, fresh peas add a touch of greenery, crunch, and a healthful lift. Fresh button mushrooms can be substituted for the morels and cooked in the mixture of cream and stock for a few minutes.

As to poaching chicken breasts, should we use cold water or hot? I have done side-by-side tests with breasts from the same chicken, using the same aromatics. Without a doubt, the poultry that is put into a room-temperature liquid, then brought to a very gentle simmer comes out more tender, less rigid than its counterpart put into simmering liquid. Chicken breasts can be poached in just water or just stock, and with or without added aromatics. I prefer to use both stock and aromatics, which gives the poultry more flavor, and also creates a rich and flavorful stock. Note that I do not peel the onion, as the skin is a natural dye and helps add color to the stock. Reserve the resulting stock for soups and sauces.

EQUIPMENT: *A 2-quart (2 l) saucepan; dampened cheesecloth; a colander; a 6-quart (6 l) cast-iron pot with a lid; an instant-read thermometer (optional); 8 warmed dinner plates.*

PEAS

1 tablespoon coarse sea salt

2 cups (300 g) fresh or frozen shelled peas

MOREL SAUCE

1-1/2 ounces (40 g) dried morel mushrooms (about 12 large)

3/4 cup (185 ml) heavy cream

3/4 cup (185 ml) Chicken Stock (page 402)

2 teaspoons freshly squeezed lemon juice, or to taste

Fine sea salt

Coarse, freshly ground black pepper

CHICKEN AND POACHING LIQUID

4 boneless, skinless free-range chicken breasts (about 8 ounces/250 g each)

1-1/2 quarts (1.5 l) Chicken Stock (page 402) or water

1 onion, unpeeled and quartered

Several fresh thyme sprigs

6 fresh parsley sprigs

2 bay leaves

6 black peppercorns

1 teaspoon fine sea salt

TO SERVE

Cooked petit épeautre (farro) or rice

Fresh tarragon leaves

Coarse, freshly ground black pepper

1. Prepare a large bowl of ice water.

2. In the same saucepan, bring 1 quart (1 l) water to a boil over high heat. Add the coarse sea salt and the peas and blanch, uncovered, for 2 minutes, counting from when the water comes back to a boil. Taste for the desired doneness. The peas should still have a bit of crunch. Drain well. Plunge into the ice water until cool to halt the cooking and help the peas retain their bright green color, 1 to 2 minutes. Drain well and set aside.

3. Rinse the morels in a colander under cold running water to rid them of any grit. Transfer them to a heatproof cup or bowl and pour in 2 cups (500 ml) hottest possible tap water. Set aside for 15 minutes to plump them up. With the slotted spoon, carefully remove the mushrooms from the liquid, leaving behind any grit that has fallen to the bottom, and set aside, reserving the liquid.

4. Place the dampened cheesecloth in the colander set over a large bowl. Carefully spoon the mushroom soaking liquid into the colander, leaving behind any grit at the bottom of the measuring cup. You should have 1-1/2 cups (375 ml) liquid. (If there is too much liquid, discard it or save it for another use. If there is not enough liquid, top it off with water to make 1-1/2 cups/375 ml.)

5. In a large saucepan, combine the strained soaking liquid, cream, and stock and cook over high heat, uncovered, until reduced by half, 15 to 20 minutes. Season with the lemon juice, and salt and pepper. Add the plumped morels and heat until warmed through, 2 to 3 minutes.

6. In the cast-iron pot, combine the chicken and all the poaching liquid ingredients, partially cover, and bring to a very gentle simmer over medium heat, until bubbles begin forming around the edge of the pot, about 5 minutes. Reduce the heat to medium-low and simmer, still partially covered, until a knife inserted into the thickest part of the breast shows that the chicken is white and is cooked through, not pink, or an instant-

read thermometer inserted into the chicken registers 165°F (74°C), about 5 minutes more, for a total of 10 minutes. Do not overcook the poultry or it may turn rigid and tough. Remove the pot from the heat, cover, and let rest for 15 minutes. The resting will help keep the poached poultry moist, tender, and buttery.

7. Remove the chicken from the poaching liquid and slice the breasts diagonally into strips. Add the warm sliced chicken to the morel sauce and toss to coat (warm chicken will more readily absorb the sauce). Keep the sauce warm and let rest for at least 5 minutes and up to 15 minutes, to allow the chicken to absorb the sauce. Add the peas and warm through. Taste for seasoning. With a slotted spoon, lift the chicken, mushrooms, and peas from the sauce and arrange them on the warmed dinner plates. With a large spoon, drizzle the sauce over all. Serve, if desired, with *petit épeautre* or rice. Garnish with tarragon and pass the pepper mill alongside.

Poached Chicken Breast Salad
with Lemon and Mint

If I had to make a list of my favorite lunchtime foods, chicken salad would be near the top. Poached chicken breasts are a standby in my kitchen—I love the way lean protein satisfies hunger—and this version, flavored with lemon and mint, works in any season.

4 SERVINGS

EQUIPMENT: *A 3-quart (3 l) saucepan with a lid; an instant-read thermometer (optional).*

CHICKEN AND POACHING LIQUID

2 boneless, skinless free-range chicken breasts (about 8 ounces/250 grams each)

1 quart (1 l) Chicken Stock (page 402) or water, at room temperature

1 onion, unpeeled and quartered

Several fresh tarragon leaves

Several fresh thyme sprigs

6 fresh parsley sprigs

1 celery stalk or several celery leaves, chopped

2 bay leaves

6 black peppercorns

1 teaspoon fine sea salt

DRESSING

1/4 cup (60 ml) extra-virgin olive oil

2 tablespoons freshly squeezed lemon juice

1 tablespoon French mustard

1/4 cup (60 ml) capers in vinegar, drained

6 scallions, white and green parts, trimmed and thinly sliced

1/4 teaspoon fine sea salt

1/4 cup fresh mint leaves, cut into a chiffonade, for garnish
Coarse, freshly ground black pepper

1. In the saucepan, combine the chicken and all the poaching liquid ingredients, partially cover, and bring to a very gentle simmer over medium heat, until bubbles begin forming around the edge of the pan, about 5 minutes. Reduce the heat to medium-low and simmer, partially covered, until a knife inserted into the thickest part of the breast shows that the chicken meat is white and cooked through, not pink, or until an instant-read thermometer inserted into the chicken registers 165°F/74°C, about 10 minutes total. Do not overcook the poultry or it may turn rigid and tough. Remove the pan from the heat, cover, and let rest for 15 minutes to help keep the poached poultry moist, tender, and buttery (see Note).

2. PREPARE THE DRESSING: In a large bowl, combine the oil, lemon juice, mustard, capers, scallions, and salt.

3. Remove the chicken from the poaching liquid and, with a fork, hold the chicken firmly on a cutting board. With a second fork, carefully shred the chicken. While still warm, place the chicken in the dressing and toss to coat. (Warm chicken will more readily absorb the dressing.) Taste for seasoning.

4. Serve the chicken salad in mounds on a salad plate, garnished with the mint chiffonade. Pass the pepper mill alongside.

NOTE: *The chicken may be used immediately or refrigerated, covered in the stock. The stock may be strained and used to prepare chicken soup or reduced to use for a sauce. Store the chicken in the stock in the refrigerator for up to 3 days.*

Salt Cod Brandade

Salt cod *brandade* is a classic French Provençal specialty, a creamy, garlic-rich puree of salt cod, milk, and oil, enhanced with a touch of nutmeg, a squeeze of lemon juice, and a hit of freshly ground black pepper. It's an ideal appetizer, made for a dip with fresh vegetables or for spreading on toasted sourdough bread. It's the poaching in a broth of garlic and bay leaves that gives it a dense, forward flavor.

NOTE: *You will need to begin this recipe the day before in order to desalt the cod.*

— 8 APPETIZER SERVINGS

EQUIPMENT: *A food processor.*

1 pound (500 g) boneless, skinless salt cod
5 plump, fresh garlic cloves, peeled, halved, green germ removed if present
4 bay leaves, crushed and halved, to release flavor
3/4 cup (185 ml) whole milk
3/4 cup (185 ml) extra-virgin olive oil
1/2 teaspoon freshly grated nutmeg
2 teaspoons freshly squeezed lemon juice
Coarse, freshly ground black pepper
About 12 best-quality brine-cured black olives (no need to pit), for garnish
Toasted sourdough bread, for serving

1. Place the cod in a large, shallow container and pour in cold water to cover. Cover securely and refrigerate for 24 hours, changing the water several times to desalt the fish.

2. Drain the cod and cut it into 4 pieces. Place the cod, garlic, and bay leaves in a large saucepan. Add cold water to cover. Bring just to a simmer over

medium heat and gently poach the cod until softened, about 10 minutes. Drain the cod and the garlic, discarding the bay leaves. When cool enough to handle, break the cod into flakes with a fork.

3. In a medium saucepan, heat the milk over medium-low heat just until small bubbles form around the edge of the pan. In a separate medium saucepan, heat the oil just until warmed.

4. Place the cod and garlic in the food processor. While pulsing on and off, add the warm oil in a steady stream; do not overmix the cod. When the oil is incorporated and the mixture is quite smooth, slowly add the milk in a steady stream, again pulsing on and off to avoid overmixing, which could turn the *brandade* into a gummy mass. The *brandade* should be light, white, and fluffy, not thin and runny; you may not need to add all the milk. Add the nutmeg and lemon juice to the mixture and pulse once or twice just to incorporate. Season with pepper and taste for seasoning. (If you do make the *brandade* too thin, pour the mixture into a fine-mesh sieve set over a bowl to drain out excess liquid. Discard the liquid.)

5. Transfer the *brandade* to a shallow serving bowl, mounding it in the center, and garnish with the black olives. Serve with plenty of crusty, toasted sourdough bread.

Poaching Fruits

Poached Pears in Beaumes-de-Venise Wine with Ginger and Honey

Pears are a favorite fruit year-round and my preferred fruit for poaching. Here I call upon the sweet muscat-based Provençal wine Beaumes-de-Venise (from the town of the same name), matching it up with vanilla, cloves, rosemary, allspice, cinnamon, and, of course, honey from our property. When cooking with wine, be sure to leave the pot uncovered, letting most of the alcohol evaporate and allowing for rounder, fruitier, firmer flavors. I like to serve this with fresh rosemary sorbet.

— 6 SERVINGS

EQUIPMENT: *6 chilled dessert plates.*

1 plump, fresh vanilla bean
6 small firm pears, peeled, with stems intact
1/4 cup (60 ml) mild honey, such as clover
1-1/2 bottles Beaumes-de-Venise or other sweet muscat-based wine (750 ml each)
2 tablespoons freshly squeezed lemon juice
3 fresh ginger slices
4 fresh rosemary sprigs
4 whole cloves
8 black peppercorns

8 whole allspice berries

2 cinnamon sticks

Fresh Rosemary Sorbet (page 91), for serving (optional)

1. Halve the vanilla bean lengthwise and use the tip of a small spoon to scrape out the seeds.

2. In a large saucepan that will hold the pears upright and snug, combine all the ingredients, including the vanilla bean and seeds. Bring to a gentle simmer over medium heat and cook, uncovered, just until the pears are cooked through—tender but not mushy—15 to 20 minutes. Using a slotted spoon, very gently turn the pears from time to time so they are evenly coated in the poaching liquid.

3. Remove from the heat and, using a slotted spoon, transfer the pears to a large, shallow bowl. Strain the liquid, reserving the vanilla pod for making Vanilla Sugar (page 441) and discarding the other solids. Return the liquid to the saucepan and cook over high heat until it has reduced by half, about 10 minutes. The liquid should be light and syrupy. Allow the liquid to cool slightly, then pour it over the cooled pears. Cover and refrigerate for up to 24 hours before serving.

4. To serve, cut each pear in half lengthwise and place cut side down on a small chilled dessert plate, spooning the liquid over the pears.

Cherries, Peaches, and Blackberries Poached in Elderflower-Vanilla Syrup

The heady floral fragrance of elderflower marries beautifully with summer fruits, poached ever so gently in a light syrup and served with a refreshing lemon verbena sorbet. Perfect for balmy summer nights.

── 4 SERVINGS ────────────────────────────

1/4 cup (60 ml) elderflower syrup or elderflower liqueur

3 tablespoons fragrant honey, such as lavender

1 plump, fresh vanilla bean

1 cup (250 g) dark, sweet cherries, such as Bing, halved and pitted

2 firm yellow or white peaches, halved and pitted, each half cut into quarters

12 blackberries

Lemon verbena sorbet (page 92), for serving

1. In a large saucepan that will hold the fruit in a single layer, combine the elderflower syrup, honey, vanilla pod, and 3 cups (750 ml) water and heat over medium heat, stirring to dissolve the honey. Reduce the heat to low, set the cherries and peach slices in the poaching liquid, and cook at a gentle simmer just until the fruit is cooked through—tender but not mushy, with the skins intact—about 5 minutes. Add the blackberries and poach for 1 minute more, until just warmed through.

2. Remove from the heat and, using a slotted spoon, transfer the fruit to a large, shallow bowl. Set aside to cool.

3. Return the saucepan with the poaching liquid to the stove and cook the poaching liquid over high heat until it has reduced by a third, 25 to 30 minutes. The liquid should be light and syrupy. Set aside to cool, then pour over the poached fruit and refrigerate until chilled, about 1 hour.

4. Divide the fruit evenly among four dessert plates. Spoon over the reduced poaching liquid. Serve with lemon verbena sorbet.

VARIATION: *If you do not have an ice cream maker, substitute Whipped Yogurt Cream (page 416) for the lemon verbena sorbet.*

Lemon Verbena and Rosemary Poached Apricots with Almond Crumble

Gently poached apricots are a real treat in summer, especially when enlivened by the bright flavor of lemon verbena, piney notes of rosemary, and a scattering of *sbrisolona* (an Italian almond cookie) crumbled on top for that essential crunch.

— 4 TO 6 SERVINGS

EQUIPMENT: *A food processor; a baking sheet lined with baking parchment; a heavy-duty mixer fitted with the whisk attachment or a handheld electric mixer; 4 to 6 dessert plates.*

LEMON VERBENA CREAM
1/3 cup (80 ml) heavy cream
1 tablespoon packed fresh or dried lemon verbena leaves

ALMOND CRUMBLE (SBRISOLONA)
8 ounces (250 g) whole unblanched almonds
2-1/4 cups (320 g) unbleached, all-purpose flour
7/8 cup (105 g) instant polenta
1 cup (8 ounces/250 g) unsalted butter, melted
3/4 cup (150 g) Vanilla Sugar (see page 441)
1 large egg, free-range and organic
1/2 teaspoon pure almond extract
3/4 teaspoon fine sea salt

APRICOTS
1/4 cup (60 ml) fragrant honey, such as lavender
1 tablespoon packed fresh or dried lemon verbena leaves

3 fresh rosemary sprigs

1-1/2 pounds (750 g) firm apricots (about 20 small), halved lengthwise and pitted

1. PREPARE THE LEMON VERBENA CREAM: Several hours before serving, combine the heavy cream and lemon verbena leaves in a small saucepan and bring barely to a simmer over medium heat, until small bubbles appear around the edge of the pan. Remove from the heat, cover, and set aside to infuse. When the cream mixture has cooled, transfer to a container, cover, and refrigerate for at least 4 hours, or until well chilled.

2. PREPARE THE ALMOND CRUMBLE: Center a rack in the oven. Line the baking sheet with baking parchment. Preheat the oven to 350°F (170°C).

3. In the food processor, coarsely chop the almonds.

4. In a medium bowl, combine the almonds, flour, and polenta. Toss to blend.

5. In a large bowl, combine the melted butter, sugar, egg, almond extract, and salt and stir to blend. Add the flour mixture and stir until the dough is well combined. The texture should resemble a rough cookie dough.

6. Rub the dough between your hands and let it drop onto the parchment-lined baking sheet in clumps, pressing it lightly together so that it covers the sheet without any spaces in between. Bake until deep golden and crisp, 20 to 30 minutes. Set aside to cool.

7. POACH THE APRICOTS: In a large saucepan that will hold the apricot halves in a single layer, combine the honey, lemon verbena leaves, rosemary, and 1 quart (1 l) water and heat over medium heat, stirring to dissolve the honey. Reduce the heat to low, place the apricot halves in the poaching liquid in a single layer, and cook at a gentle simmer just

until the apricots are cooked through—tender but not mushy, with the skins intact—about 5 minutes.

8. Remove from the heat and, using a slotted spoon, transfer the apricots to a large, shallow bowl. Return the saucepan to the heat and cook the liquid over high heat until it has reduced by a third, about 15 minutes. The liquid should be light and syrupy. Strain the liquid, discarding the rosemary and lemon verbena. Let the liquid cool slightly, then pour it over the apricots.

9. Strain the chilled cream and discard the lemon verbena leaves. In the bowl of the mixer or in a bowl using the handheld electric mixer, whip the cream to soft peaks.

10. To serve, divide the apricot halves among the dessert plates. Spoon over the warm reduced poaching liquid. Break up a handful of the almond crumble into bite-size pieces. Scatter the crumble sparingly over the apricots and dot with small spoonfuls of the lemon verbena cream.

NOTE: *This* sbrisolona *recipe makes much more than is required for this recipe, but keeps beautifully for at least a week if stored at room temperature in an airtight container. Serve with coffee or sweet wine, or crumbled over Greek yogurt with fresh fruit.*

INFUSE

Having an army of homemade pantry items can really take your cooking to another level with minimal effort. Infused oils take little time to make, will easily last up to a month or more, and can add uplifting fragrance and flavor notes to a meal just before serving.

Fat is an excellent carrier of flavor. When herbs and spices are soaked or heated in oil or cream or combined with butter, their essential oils combine with the fats, making for heady aromatic condiments to add nuance and complexity to just about any dish. Infused (compound) butters keep amazingly well in the freezer, and add a dramatic touch to any dish from steamed vegetables to all manner of seafood to seared beef. A sprinkle of truffle salt—which also keeps for many months in the freezer, so the aroma of truffles can be enjoyed all year round—can elevate Sunday brunch eggs from ordinary to spectacular.

Magic Cèpe Mushroom Soup

I call this crowd-pleasing soup my magic recipe. It is so amazing that so few ingredients—and a soup made in a matter of minutes—can have so much depth of flavor. It really is a fine example of the miracles of infusion. The dried *cèpe* (*porcini*) mushroom powder packs a maximum of fragrance and flavor and takes well to many variations: pair it with paper-thin slices of raw domestic mushrooms or seared domestic or wild mushrooms showered in the bowl at serving time; prepare with dried morel powder in place of *cèpes*; top with thin slices of raw black truffles; or add a dollop of mushroom-powder-infused whipped cream.

— 8 SERVINGS

EQUIPMENT: *A large jar with a lid; a 3-quart (3 l) heavy-duty saucepan with a lid; 8 warmed, shallow soup bowls.*

2 cups (500 ml) heavy cream
2 tablespoons Cèpe Mushroom Powder
    (page 432)
1/2 teaspoon fine sea salt
3 cups (750 ml) Chicken Stock (page 402)
    or Vegetable Stock (page 408)
Chopped fresh chives, for garnish
Extra-virgin olive oil or Chive Oil
    (page 83), for garnish

1. If time permits, combine the cream and mushroom powder in a jar, seal,

and refrigerate for 24 hours to infuse the cream with the mushroom flavor and aroma. (Alternatively, combine the cream and mushroom powder in the heavy-duty saucepan, bring just to a simmer, cover, remove from the heat, and set aside for 30 minutes to infuse the cream.)

2. At serving time, in heavy-duty saucepan, combine the infused cream, salt, and stock and bring to a gentle simmer over medium heat. Remove from the heat and taste for seasoning

3. Serve in the warmed soup bowls, garnished with chives and a drizzle of oil.

VARIATIONS: *Add sliced raw domestic or wild mushrooms to the soup and cook for several minutes; add grilled, sliced fresh cèpes or domestic mushrooms; add truffle matchsticks at serving time.*

MAKE-AHEAD NOTE: *The soup can be prepared up to 3 days in advance and stored in airtight containers in the refrigerator.*

Spaghetti Nests with Cèpe Mushroom Cream Sauce

Dried wild mushrooms and their accompanying powder have become huge players in my infusion game. This forward-flavored sauce tastes remarkably rich yet is not the least bit heavy, since infusing the cream with *cèpe* powder and making a *cèpe* reduction imparts such intense flavors and bold results.

— 4 SERVINGS

EQUIPMENT: *A small jar with a lid; a 1-quart (1 l) heatproof bowl; dampened cheesecloth; a fine-mesh sieve; a 10-quart (10 l) pasta pot fitted with a colander; 4 warmed pasta bowls.*

4 tablespoons heavy cream

1 teaspoon Cèpe Mushroom Powder (page 432)

2 cups (40 g) dried cèpe mushrooms

2 tablespoons salted butter

3 tablespoons coarse sea salt

13 ounces (400 g) best-quality dried spaghetti or fresh spaghetti (see Note)

1/2 teaspoon fresh thyme leaves

1 cup (100 g) freshly grated Parmigiano-Reggiano cheese

3 tablespoons minced fresh chives

1. If time permits, combine the cream and mushroom powder in a jar, seal, and refrigerate for 24 hours to infuse the cream with the mushroom flavor and aroma. (Alternatively, combine the cream and mushroom powder in a small, heavy-duty pot, bring just to a simmer, cover, remove from the heat, and set aside for 30 minutes to infuse the cream.)

2. Place the mushrooms in a colander and rinse well under cold running water to rid them of any grit. Transfer them to the heatproof bowl. Pour 2 cups

(500 ml) hottest possible tap water over the mushrooms. Set aside for 20 minutes to plump them up. With a slotted spoon, carefully remove the mushrooms from the liquid, leaving behind any grit that might have fallen to the bottom; reserve the soaking liquid. Place the cheesecloth in the sieve and set over a large bowl. Carefully pour the mushroom soaking liquid through the cheesecloth, leaving behind any grit at the bottom of the bowl.

3. Transfer the mushroom soaking liquid to a large saucepan (big enough to hold the pasta) and cook over high heat until it has reduced to 1/2 cup (125 ml), about 10 minutes. Add the mushrooms, butter, and infused cream.

4. Fill the pasta pot with 8 quarts (8 l) water and bring to a rolling boil over high heat. Add the salt and stir to dissolve. Add the pasta and cook until *al dente* or slightly resistant to the bite. Drain, reserving 2 tablespoons of the pasta cooking liquid. Immediately add the pasta to the pan with the mushroom sauce. Add the reserved pasta cooking liquid and the thyme. Toss to blend and cook over low heat until the pasta is well coated in the sauce. Remove the pan from the heat, add the cheese and chives, and toss once more. Taste for seasoning.

5. To create spaghetti nests, scoop a generous portion of spaghetti onto a large fork or meat prong. Place the fork into a ladle and rotate the fork in a continuous motion to wind the spaghetti around on itself. Gently place the spaghetti nest in a warmed pasta bowl. Serve immediately.

NOTE: *When buying dried spaghetti, choose a brand made in Italy and pay attention to the cooking time, as a longer cooking time usually indicates a higher-quality pasta. When following the instructions on the package, take the pasta out 1 to 2 minutes before the indicated time, as the pasta will continue to cook in the pan with the sauce.*

Scallop Carpaccio with Lime-Vanilla Sauce

I love plump, alabaster scallops in any form: as heavenly petals in a carpaccio, seared to a crisp in a skillet, or grilled in the shell with lots of butter, herbs, and sometimes fresh black truffles. This lime-vanilla-infused sauce was inspired by chef Fréderic Anton of Le Pré Catelan, the three-Michelin-star Parisian restaurant. Here, lime, vanilla, and mint form a powerful trio, infusing the thin, raw petals of scallop with their heady aroma.

—— 4 SERVINGS ————————————————————————

EQUIPMENT: *A small jar with a lid; a sharp, flexible knife; 4 chilled salad plates.*

LIME-VANILLA SAUCE
1 plump, fresh vanilla bean, halved lengthwise
1/4 cup (60 ml) extra-virgin olive oil
1/2 teaspoon fine sea salt
Grated zest of 2 organic limes
2 tablespoons freshly squeezed lime juice

1 pound (500 g) well-chilled, ultra-fresh sea scallops (see Note)
Fine sea salt
Vanilla Powder (page 442), for garnish
Fresh mint leaves, cut into a chiffonade, for garnish
Toasted sourdough bread, for serving

1. Using the tip of a small spoon, scrape out the vanilla bean seeds and place them in a small jar. (Reserve the pods for another use; see page 441.) Add the oil and salt, cover with the lid, and shake to blend. Let the mixture infuse for several hours before using. Add the lime zest and juice and shake to blend.

2. Gently rinse the scallops and pat dry with paper towels. Remove and discard the little muscle on the side of each scallop. With a very sharp knife (a flexible fish boning knife is ideal here), cut each scallop crosswise into 4 thin, even slices. Toss with the sauce, evenly coating the scallop slices. Season lightly with fine sea salt.

3. Arrange the seasoned scallop slices, overlapping them slightly, on the chilled plates. Garnish with salt, vanilla powder, and mint chiffonade and serve with plenty of toasted sourdough bread.

NOTE: *If scallops are not available, use any skinless, firm white-fleshed fish fillets, such as monkfish, sea bass, or halibut, cut into medallions the size of a sea scallop.*

Compound Butters

A refrigerator or freezer stocked with just a few infused butters can change a cook's life, adding new dimensions to just about any dish or slice of naked toast waiting to be dressed with flavors of the sea, the earth, the garden. Let your imagination go wild! Here are some suggestions.

Tips

~ Use the best-quality butter you can afford, preferably from grass-fed cows.

~ Store compound butter in the refrigerator for up to a week, or in the freezer for up to 2 months. Make sure you wrap it well in baking parchment and protective plastic wrap to avoid freezer burn. To use, remove from the freezer, let soften at room temperature (about 15 minutes), slice off as much as you need, and return the rest to the freezer.

Clockwise from bottom left: Lemon, Mustard, Garlic, and Chile Butter; Honey and Orange Butter; Tarragon and Lime Butter; Candied Lemon and Ginger Butter; Caper, Cornichon, Mustard, and Parsley Butter; Parsley and Garlic Butter

Lemon, Mustard, Garlic, and Chile Butter

This favored compound butter offers a wide range of flavors, as the gentle acidity of the citrus pairs beautifully with the tang of mustard, garlic, and hot pepper flakes. I spread it on toast, melt it over steamed or roasted vegetables (such as Roasted Broccoli, page 194), toss it with rice or pasta, or use it as a quick and vibrant garnish for warm fish, shellfish, meat, or poultry.

--- MAKES 8 TABLESPOONS (4 OUNCES/125 G) ---

1/2 cup (4 ounces/125 g) unsalted butter, at room temperature

1/4 teaspoon fine sea salt

1 teaspoon French whole-grain mustard

1/4 teaspoon hot red pepper flakes

1 plump, fresh garlic clove, peeled, halved, green germ removed if present, and minced

1 teaspoon grated organic lemon zest

1. Place all the ingredients on a large plate and mash with a fork until well blended.

2. Transfer to a serving container and refrigerate until firm, 30 minutes to 1 hour. (Alternatively, transfer the butter to a 7 × 12-inch (17.5 × 30 cm) sheet of baking parchment and use the paper to roll the butter into a log.) Wrap securely with plastic wrap and freeze for later use, up to 2 months. Thaw in the refrigerator before using.

VARIATIONS

Each of these variations uses 1/2 cup (4 ounces/125 g) unsalted butter, at room temperature.

TARRAGON AND LIME BUTTER

A great match for scallops or any fish or shellfish dish. Equally good served with steamed or roasted vegetables such as Whole Roasted Cauliflower (page 200).

1/4 teaspoon fine sea salt
Grated zest of 1 organic lime
2 tablespoons finely minced fresh tarragon leaves

PARSLEY AND GARLIC BUTTER

This is much like the classic beurre maître d'hôtel *that is used on almost anything from steak to vegetables. I like to use it on any fish or shellfish, such as Monkfish with Polenta-Parmesan Crust and Capers (page 141).*

1/4 teaspoon fine sea salt
3 tablespoons finely minced fresh flat-leaf parsley leaves
1 plump, fresh garlic clove, peeled, halved, green germ removed if present, and
   minced

CAPER, CORNICHON, MUSTARD, AND PARSLEY BUTTER

Use on Grilled Scallops in Their Shells (page 175) or any grilled or steamed fish.

1 tablespoon minced capers
1 tablespoon minced cornichons (about 4)
1 teaspoon French whole-grain mustard
1 tablespoon finely minced fresh flat-leaf parsley leaves

SEAWEED BUTTER

Use on Steamed Cod with Rosemary (page 22) or spread on Seaweed Quick Bread (page 259).

1 tablespoon finely chopped dried wakame seaweed flakes

PIMENT D'ESPELETTE BUTTER

Use this anywhere a little butter and mild spice is called for. It is a favorite condiment on Steamed Corn on the Cob (page 24).

1/4 teaspoon fine sea salt
1 teaspoon ground Espelette pepper or other mild ground chile

DRIED CÈPE BUTTER

Use this to spread on toast or on Mushroom Brioche Rolls (page 175) for an extra mushroom hit.

1/4 teaspoon fine sea salt
 2 teaspoons Cèpe Mushroom Powder (page 432)

TRUFFLE BUTTER

Because this butter freezes so well, I have it on hand all year long, to spread on toast or to season fish, poultry, or shellfish.

1/4 teaspoon fine sea salt
2 tablespoons minced fresh black truffle peelings

VANILLA BUTTER

Use as a replacement for regular butter in baking when the heady aroma of vanilla is required.

2 teaspoons Vanilla Powder (page 442)

CANDIED LEMON AND GINGER BUTTER

Use on toasted fruit bread, such as the Candied Lemon Quick Bread (page 253) or Cranberry, Pistachio, and Almond Sourdough Loaf (page 296).

2 tablespoons finely minced fresh ginger
2 tablespoons finely minced Candied Lemon (page 414)
1/8 teaspoon fine sea salt

HONEY AND ORANGE BUTTER

Use on Blueberry and Orange Blossom French Toast (page 268).

2 tablespoons intensely flavored honey, such as chestnut, buckwheat, or mountain
    honey, or pure maple syrup
1/8 teaspoon fine sea salt
Grated zest of 1/2 organic orange

HONEY BUTTER

Freshly prepared honey butter is astonishingly good spread on sourdough bread, especially one flavored with dried cranberries, pistachios, and almonds (page 296). The honey butter should be used within a day or so and can be stored at room temperature.

1/2 cup room-temperature unsalted butter
1 teaspoon honey of choice

Herb-Infused Oils

I generally reach for olive oil when cooking, a natural choice for me in Provence, but its often strong fruity and peppery notes can compete with other flavors, so a mild-flavored vegetable oil (such as sunflower) is often preferable to use for infusing.

Tips

~ Always use fresh herbs, not dried ones.

~ Clean and dry any herbs you are using to infuse the oil.

~ Blanching and refreshing herbs before infusing will help retain their bright color.

~ Never use flavored oils for deep-frying—any herb particles will burn at high frying temperatures.

~ Oils should be stored in the refrigerator. Fat crystals appear when the oil is stored at a cool temperature, giving it a cloudy appearance that will disappear when the oil comes back to room temperature. Be sure to remove your oils from the refrigerator 15 to 20 minutes before using and return them to the refrigerator promptly once used.

Basil Oil

I delight in having a fridge full of herb-infused oils. Basil is a longtime favorite that I use often to bring fragrance, color, and a final touch of drama to dishes like Thin Crust Pizza with Mozzarella and Capers (page 283), Chickpea Crêpe with Fresh Goat Cheese, Zucchini Ribbons, and Toasted Pine Nuts (page 144), or a 40-Minute Cheese Pinwheel Loaf (page 285); to simply drizzle over grilled eggplant or a tomato salad; or to garnish soups. I blanch and refresh the basil so it keeps its brilliant green color. I use olive oil here, for I feel the basil would feel betrayed if I did not. For all other herbs, I prefer sunflower oil. All of the recipes can easily be halved. I also find that a blender—as opposed to a food processor or immersion blender—does a superior job of completely and thoroughly integrating the herbs with the oil.

— Makes about 1 cup (250 ml)

EQUIPMENT: *A 5-quart (5 l) pasta pot fitted with a colander; a fine-mesh sieve; a blender; a small jar with a lid or a plastic squeeze bottle.*

3 tablespoons coarse sea salt
4 cups loosely packed fresh basil leaves
1 cup (250 ml) extra-virgin olive oil

1. Prepare a large bowl of ice water.

2. In the pasta pot, bring 3 quarts (3 l) water to a rolling boil over high heat. Add the salt and the basil leaves and blanch for 25 seconds. Drain the basil and transfer the leaves to a fine-mesh sieve. Dip the sieve into the ice water to refresh the basil and help retain its bright green color. Transfer the basil

leaves to a thick, clean kitchen towel. Roll the towel and squeeze to dry the leaves.

3. In the blender, combine the basil leaves and oil and blend for a full minute. Transfer to the jar or squeeze bottle. Store the infused oil in the refrigerator for up to 1 week or freeze for up to 1 month. Remove from the refrigerator at least 10 minutes before using if the oil has congealed.

VARIATIONS

Follow the recipe above, with these adjustments:

CHIVE OIL
Use on fish and shellfish, especially raw oysters on the half shell; as a garnish on Blanched and Grilled Asparagus with Chives (page 181); or drizzled on soups such as Magic Cèpe Mushroom Soup (page 69).

No need to blanch; place 1 cup packed chopped fresh chives in a fine-mesh sieve and run hot water over them for several minutes to soften and remove the chlorophyll flavor. Blend with 1 cup (250 ml) sunflower oil.

ROSEMARY OIL
Use on steamed or blanched vegetables, on sliced summer tomatoes, or roasted lamb, beef, or chicken.

Blanch 1 cup fresh rosemary leaves for 30 seconds as directed. Blend with 1 cup (250 ml) sunflower oil.

MINT OIL
Drizzle on grilled lamb.

Blanch 4 cups fresh mint leaves for 15 seconds as directed. Blend with 1 cup (250 ml) sunflower oil.

Infused Salts

Salt absorbs the aromas and flavors of whatever you infuse it with, and infused salts will become the stars of your pantry. My favorites include piment d'Espelette salt (used almost daily, sprinkled on pizzas, pastas, cottage cheese—anything that loves a touch of heat and hint of salt) and wild mushroom salts (*cèpe* and morel), used on simple fare such as pastas and mushroom soups. And of course during truffle season in Provence—from November to March—I always keep truffle salt on hand, though this salt needs to be kept in the freezer and taken out about 10 minutes before using. I find that 1:1 proportions are ideal, usually combining 1 tablespoon Maldon sea salt flakes (I prefer flaky salt here, perfect for the table and for the tactile enjoyment of rubbing the salt mixture between your fingers as you season) with 1 tablespoon ground powder or spice.

PIMENT D'ESPELETTE SALT: *1 tablespoon salt flakes, 1 tablespoon ground Espelette pepper*

DRIED CÈPE OR MOREL SALT: *1 tablespoon salt flakes, 1 tablespoon Cèpe (Porcini) Mushroom Powder (page 432) or morel powder (page 432)*

TRUFFLE SALT: *1 tablespoon salt flakes, 1 tablespoon minced fresh black truffle. (Store in the freezer for up to 6 months. Remove from the freezer at least 10 minutes before using to soften.)*

TOASTED CUMIN SALT: *Toast cumin seeds in a small saucepan over medium heat until fragrant, about 2 minutes. Transfer to a dish to cool, then grind to a fine powder in an electric spice grinder. For the salt, combine 1 tablespoon salt flakes and 1 tablespoon ground toasted cumin.*

Clockwise from center top: Red Chile Salt; Dried Morel Salt; Piment d'Espelette Salt;
Toasted Cumin Salt; Maldon Sea Salt Flakes; Saffron Salt; Dried Cèpe Salt

RED CHILE SALT: *1 tablespoon salt flakes, 1 tablespoon hot red pepper flakes*

LEMON SALT: *1 tablespoon salt flakes, 1 tablespoon finely grated organic lemon zest.*
Combine in a spice grinder and pulse 5 times to blend. Store in the refrigerator.

SAFFRON SALT: *1 tablespoon salt flakes, 1 teaspoon ground saffron threads*

Infused Cheeses

Many cheeses—from Coulommiers to Saint-Félicien to Saint-Marcellin—are welcome theaters for absorbing the flavors of such ingredients as fresh mushrooms, mushroom powder, and fresh truffles. It's an area ripe for experimentation and discovery.

Rosemary-Infused Goat's Milk Cheese

Fresh, young, soft goat's milk cheese infused with the vibrant herbal flavors of fresh rosemary is the perfect example of infusing less assertive flavors with stronger ones. Two plus two equals ten! Use to stuff zucchini blossoms or as a topping on toast rounds with a dollop of Spicy Tomato Marmalade (page 422).

MAKES 8 OUNCES (250 G)

EQUIPMENT: *A mini food processor or a standard food processor fitted with a small bowl.*

2 disks fresh, soft goat's milk cheese (about 8 ounces/250 g total)
1/4 cup (60 ml) heavy cream
2 tablespoons finely minced fresh rosemary leaves

In the food processor, combine the cheese, cream, and rosemary. Process until smooth. Store in an airtight container in the refrigerator for up to 3 days.

Cèpe-Infused Coulommiers

Each season I experiment with different cheeses to pair with black truffles, and one Christmas I purchased a fragrant Coulommiers cheese from Marie Quatrehomme in Paris. She had sliced the soft-ripened cow's milk cheese in half and topped each half with mascarpone and a showering of dried *cèpe* powder. The Coulommiers itself was so ripe, we savored it by simply scooping up servings with a spoon. Coulommiers comes from the Île-de-France village of the same name and is a lesser-known cousin of Brie. It is smaller and thicker than Brie, with a pronounced aroma and flavor of toasted nuts and mushrooms, making it a perfect match for wild mushrooms. The cheese is made with either raw or pasteurized milk, can be either *fermier, artisanal,* or *industriel,* weighs about 1 pound (500 g), measures about 6 inches (15 cm) in diameter, and is about 1-1/2 inches (3 cm) high. It can be aged from 3 to 8 weeks. Slice it in half and slather it with fragrant truffle *crème fraîche* or thick cream flavored with minced dried morels.

— 12 SERVINGS

EQUIPMENT: *Unflavored dental floss or a very sharp knife.*

1 Coulommiers cow's milk cheese (a little more than 1 pound/650 g), well chilled
  (or substitute Camembert)
1 tablespoon mascarpone cheese
2 tablespoons dried Cèpe Mushroom Powder (page 432)

1. With the dental floss or very sharp knife, carefully slice the cheese horizontally into two even disks, like a layer cake. Spread a thin layer of mascarpone cheese on the cut side of each half. Shower with the mushroom powder. Reconstruct the cheese by putting the two halves together again.

Wrap it securely in plastic wrap. Refrigerate for 24 to 48 hours to infuse the cheese with the mushroom powder.

2. To serve, let the cheese come to room temperature. Unwrap and place it on a cheese tray. Cut into thin wedges.

MAKE-AHEAD NOTE: *Store, securely wrapped, in the refrigerator for up to 2 days. Remove from the refrigerator 30 minutes before serving.*

Infused Sorbets

Fresh Rosemary Sorbet

My bountiful herb garden serves as a welcome canvas for all manner of sorbets, and when I entertain, an infused herb variation invariably turns up at dessert time, paired with Chestnut Honey Madeleines (page 311), one of my favorite Almond Bars (page 300), or with fresh, poached, or roasted fruit. While this is neither a classic sorbet (which normally does not contain dairy) nor an ice cream (which normally contains whole eggs), it's what I personally call a sorbet: light, flavorful, refreshing. The addition of homemade invert sugar syrup helps give a smooth mouthfeel to the sorbet and also prevents it from crystallizing.

12 SERVINGS

EQUIPMENT: *A fine-mesh sieve; an ice cream maker; 12 ice cream bowls, chilled in the freezer.*

1/2 cup (100 g) sugar
2 cups (500 ml) whole milk
1 cup (250 ml) heavy cream
2 tablespoons Invert Sugar Syrup (page 438) or light corn syrup
About 1 cup fresh rosemary leaves, plus more for garnish

1. In a large saucepan, combine the sugar, milk, cream, sugar syrup, and rosemary. Stir to dissolve the sugar. Heat over medium heat, stirring from time to time, just until tiny bubbles form around the edges of the pan.

2. Remove from the heat, cover, and let infuse for at least 1 hour at room temperature. Refrigerate until thoroughly chilled or overnight.

3. Strain the chilled sorbet base, discarding the rosemary leaves. Transfer to an ice cream maker and freeze according to the manufacturer's instructions. Serve the sorbet in the chilled ice cream bowls, garnished with leaves of fresh rosemary.

VARIATIONS

LEMON VERBENA SORBET
Substitute 1 cup fresh or dried lemon verbena leaves for the rosemary leaves.

FRESH THYME SORBET
Substitute 1 cup fresh or dried thyme leaves for the rosemary leaves.

FRESH BASIL SORBET
Substitute 1 cup fresh basil leaves for the rosemary leaves.

KAFFIR LIME SORBET
Substitute 20 fresh or dried ground kaffir lime leaves for the rosemary leaves.

EMULSIFY

This chapter calls for a little bit of scientific background. An emulsion is the mixture of two liquid ingredients that normally don't mix, held together by a third ingredient that stabilizes the mixture and prevents it from separating. Two liquids can form an emulsion by being vigorously shaken together—like oil and vinegar in a jar—but the emulsion will not hold, and the two will eventually separate. That is something we call a temporary emulsion, not to be scorned! But adding an emulsifying agent like egg yolk, egg white, flour, lemon juice, or mustard will create a thick and velvety sauce that holds together permanently, such as mayonnaise, *aïoli*, vinaigrettes, and roux-based sauces. Understanding how emulsions hold and stay together can help us make better sauces every time and help prevent the emulsion from breaking—or allow us to fix it easily when it does. Emulsions can be delicate, but a split emulsion is both avoidable and repairable. See the tips under each sauce or condiment recipe for how to avoid or fix a broken emulsion.

Emulsified Sauces

Aïoli Piquant (Spicy Garlic Mayonnaise)

Thick, golden, unctuous *aïoli* is a theme song I live to sing. We make it regularly in the summertime, using it as a little dip for raw vegetables, slathering it on toasted homemade sourdough bread, teaming it up with grilled, steamed, fried fish, shellfish, even oysters, such as Steamed Shrimp in Saffron Sauce (page 20), Crispy Golden Squid (page 149), and Oysters with Parmesan-Polenta Crust (page 157). Go wild here—it's a holiday food!

While this is a fairly simple process, it is easy for the emulsion to break if a few basic rules aren't followed.

Tips

~ Because mayonnaise and *aïoli* contain raw eggs, use the freshest possible eggs to avoid any food contamination.

~ The ingredients must be at room temperature. If the oil has been stored in a cool place, bring it to room temperature by pouring it into a glass and standing it in a bath of warm water. If this step is not followed and the emulsion splits, a few drops of warm water added to the mixture can bring it back together.

~ In the beginning, the oil must be added in a very, very slow trickle or it will not emulsify with the egg yolk.

~ If the egg yolk appears on the small side, you may need to double the amount of yolk or reduce the amount of oil in the recipe.

~ If the emulsion begins to separate after refrigeration, bring it up to room temperature, then beat vigorously until the emulsion comes back together.

~ If the *aïoli* is too thick, you can add a little water.

~ To fix a broken emulsion: Place an additional large egg yolk in a separate bowl, whisk vigorously, and then slowly add the separated aïoli or mayonnaise to the egg yolk, whisking continuously until the mixture comes together.

— MAKES 1/2 CUP (125 ML) ——————————————————————————

EQUIPMENT: *A mortar and pestle, a mini food processor, or a standard food processor fitted with a small bowl.*

1/2 cup (125 ml) mild-flavored extra-virgin olive oil, at room temperature (see Note)
3 plump, fresh garlic cloves, peeled, halved, green germ removed if present, and minced
1/4 teaspoon fine sea salt
1 large egg yolk, free-range and organic, at room temperature (see Note)

IF MIXING BY HAND

1. Pour boiling water into a large mortar to warm it (see Note); discard the water and dry the mortar. Place the oil in a measuring cup or in a bottle with a pouring spout. Place the garlic and salt in the mortar and mash together evenly with the pestle to form as smooth a paste as possible. (The fresher the garlic, the easier it will be to crush.)

2. Add the egg yolk. Stir, pressing slowly and evenly with the pestle, always in the same direction, to thoroughly blend the garlic paste and yolk. Continue stirring, gradually adding just a few drops of the oil, mixing

until thoroughly incorporated. Do not add too much oil in the beginning or the mixture will not emulsify. As soon as the mixture begins to thicken, add the remaining oil in a slow, steady stream, mixing continuously until thickened. Taste for seasoning. Transfer to a bowl. Cover and refrigerate for at least 1 hour to allow the flavors to infuse. Store in an airtight container in the refrigerator for up to 3 days.

IF USING A FOOD PROCESSOR

1. In the food processor, combine the garlic, egg yolk, and salt and process until well blended.

2. With the motor running, very slowly add several tablespoons of the oil, processing until the mixture begins to thicken and scraping down the sides of the bowl as necessary. With the motor running, slowly add the remaining oil in a slow, steady stream, stopping to scrape down the bowl as necessary. Taste for seasoning. Transfer to a small bowl. Cover and refrigerate for at least 1 hour to allow the flavors to blend. Store in an airtight container in the refrigerator for up to 3 days.

NOTE: *This will help encourage a stable emulsion, since oil and egg yolk bind together more successfully at room temperature.*

VARIATION

CHILE-LIME MAYONNAISE
Add 1 teaspoon fresh lime juice and 1 teaspoon ground Espelette pepper or other ground chile.

Lime Mayonnaise

This bright and zesty mayonnaise gives many opportunities for indulgence, as an alternative dipping sauce to *aïoli* for Oysters with Parmesan-Polenta Crust (page 157) and Crispy Golden Squid (page 149), with Roasted Autumn Rainbow Vegetables (page 189), or to be enjoyed with Four-Hour Aromatic Braised Pork leftovers (page 223).

If making mayonnaise by hand, there are two things you need: patience and stamina. If you add too much oil too early in a race to the finish line, your emulsion won't take and you will have a sad, liquid mess. The key is to thicken the egg yolk first as the basis of a stable emulsion and then add the oil in the thinnest stream possible. A metal pouring spout fitted to the olive oil bottle will do the trick nicely.

For tips on creating a stable emulsion, see the master recipe on page 94.

— MAKES 1/2 CUP (125 ML) ————————————————————————

EQUIPMENT: *A measuring cup with a pouring spout; a mini food processor or a standard food processor fitted with a small bowl.*

1/2 cup (125 ml) mild-flavored vegetable oil, such as sunflower oil
1 large egg yolk, free-range and organic, at room temperature
1/4 teaspoon fine sea salt, or to taste
1 teaspoon freshly squeezed lime juice
1/2 teaspoon brown rice vinegar or white wine vinegar
2 tablespoons thick Greek-style yogurt or sour cream (optional)

IF MIXING BY HAND

1. Place the oil in the measuring cup. In a medium bowl, whisk the egg yolk and salt for several minutes, until light and thick and beginning to pale in color. While whisking, gradually add just a few drops of the oil and whisk

until thoroughly incorporated. Do not add too much oil at the beginning or the mixture will not emulsify.

2. Continue adding the oil a few drops at a time until the mixture begins to thicken. Once you are confident you have a thick, stable emulsion, add the remaining oil in a slow, steady stream, whisking constantly. (The mixture may begin to look oily, even a little gelatinous. Don't worry: As soon as you add the acid—the lime and the vinegar—the mayonnaise will instantly become smooth and velvety.) Whisk in the lime juice and vinegar. Taste for seasoning. Transfer to a bowl. Fold in the yogurt, if using.

IF USING A FOOD PROCESSOR

1. Place the oil in the measuring cup. In the food processor, combine the egg yolk and salt and pulse until well blended.

2. With the motor running, very slowly add several teaspoons of the oil, processing until the mixture thickens. Keep the motor running and slowly add the remaining oil in a slow, steady stream. Add the lime juice and vinegar and pulse to incorporate. Taste for seasoning. Transfer to a bowl. Fold in the yogurt, if using.

MAKE-AHEAD NOTE: *Store the mayonnaise in an airtight container in the refrigerator for up to 3 days.*

Anchoïade
(Anchovy Sauce)

This classic Provençal sauce finds its way onto my table on many occasions. It's ideal to use as a dip for a platter of raw vegetables and is particularly delicious served with Whole Roasted Cauliflower (page 200). Much like a vinaigrette, this is a temporary emulsion, where the oil separates from the other ingredients rather quickly because there is no egg to bind them, a totally normal reaction.

— MAKES 1 CUP (250 ML) —————————————————

EQUIPMENT: *A mini food processor or a standard food processor fitted with a small bowl.*

4 plump, fresh garlic cloves, peeled, halved, green germ removed if present, and minced
About 16 oil-cured anchovy halves, drained
2 teaspoons best-quality red wine or sherry vinegar
1 cup (250 ml) mild-flavored extra-virgin olive oil
Coarse, freshly ground black pepper

In the food processor, combine the garlic, anchovies, and vinegar and process to blend. With the machine running, slowly add the oil, processing until you have a smooth sauce. Taste for seasoning, but add pepper only at serving time.

MAKE-AHEAD NOTE: *Store in an airtight container in the refrigerator for up to 3 days. Shake the jar vigorously at serving time to bring the emulsion back together.*

Beurre Blanc
(Butter Sauce)

One summer a student made a special advance request to make *beurre blanc* in class. She had been frustrated for years by not succeeding at this classic French sauce. I happily incorporated it into my class menu, serving it with some steamed turbot fresh from Brittany (see Steamed Turbot with Lemongrass, Peas, and Baby Spinach for the steaming fish method, page 17). It was a huge success and is now a staple sauce I teach in all my classes.

Tips

~ The flavor of butter is very pronounced in this sauce. Don't skimp on a cheap brand; use the best-quality butter you can afford, and the final results will reward you.

~ Make sure the butter is properly chilled. This will help keep the emulsion cool as it is added to the sauce. If your butter is at room temperature, cut it into cubes, wrap it in its original packaging or in baking parchment, and freeze it for 5 minutes to chill.

~ *Beurre blanc* splits when the sauce gets too hot, causing the emulsion to break, so use a small heavy-duty saucepan that will heat evenly. A large saucepan will heat the butter too quickly, making a stable emulsion harder to achieve.

~ If your stovetop does not have a reliably low setting, you may want to use a heat diffuser (see page 27) to keep the heat low, or remove the pan from the heat occasionally to cool the sauce.

EQUIPMENT: *A fine-mesh sieve.*

1/4 cup (60 ml) dry white wine, such as a young Chardonnay
2 tablespoons best-quality white wine vinegar or cider vinegar
2 tablespoons finely minced shallot
1/3 cup (80 ml) heavy cream
1/4 teaspoon fine sea salt
1 cup (8 ounces/250 g) unsalted butter, cut into cubes and chilled

1. In a small heavy-duty saucepan, combine the wine, vinegar, and shallot. Bring to a boil over medium heat and cook until the liquid has reduced to 2 to 3 tablespoons, about 5 minutes. Add the cream and salt and boil for 1 minute. Reduce the heat to medium-low and add a few tablespoons of the butter, whisking as it melts and emulsifies into the cream sauce. Add the remaining butter a few pieces at a time, whisking constantly, making sure that the previous cubes of butter have been fully emulsified into the sauce before adding more. Lift the pan from the heat occasionally to cool the sauce, if necessary.

2. When all the butter has been whisked in, remove the pan from the heat. Taste for seasoning. Pour the sauce through the sieve into a bowl, pressing on the shallot to extract maximum flavor. Discard the shallot and transfer the sauce to a jug or sauceboat. Serve immediately.

VARIATIONS: *In place of the plain unsalted butter, use any of the compound butters (pages 77–80), such as Tarragon and Lime, or Lemon, Mustard, Garlic, and Chile.*

Emulsified Soups

Emulsified soups are a dream: Thick and creamy, they make you insist that they are filled with cream, when in reality the vegetables and oil come together to form a voluptuous and elegantly textured soup with no added dairy. I prefer preparing soups in a blender versus a food processor, since the force of the blender helps give a smoother, thicker, more velvety finish to the final product. If prepared in advance, be sure to reblend at serving time.

Artichoke Soup

This recipe—inspired by the remarkable artichoke soup that Parisian Michelin three-star chef Guy Savoy has served for decades (with fresh black truffles!)—perfectly exemplies the magic of emulsified soups. The mixture of artichoke hearts simmered in a rich chicken stock, when blended into a thick emulsion, is a rich, intensely satisfying creation, one in which you would swear there is added cream. This is my go-to soup when I really don't have the time to cook but want to put a delicious soup on the table. Despite its simplicity, I have worked endlessly to perfect this recipe and have found that frozen artichoke bottoms are the key; canned or jarred artichokes tend to taste either too acidic or too oily and don't offer the pure artichoke flavor. Chef Savoy's addition of the Parmigiano-Reggiano garnish is brilliant, and adds a touch of elegance and drama to this simple soup.

Note that using a good-quality blender here is essential to achieving a thick and creamy emulsion. A food processor or immersion blender will not accomplish the same results.

— 6 SERVINGS

EQUIPMENT: *A 6-quart (6 l) cast-iron pot with a lid; a blender; 6 warmed, shallow soup bowls.*

7 frozen artichoke bottoms (about 10 ounces/300 g total)
2 quarts (2 l) Chicken Stock (page 402)
Fine sea salt (optional)
Slivers of Parmigiano-Reggiano cheese, for garnish
Fresh thyme leaves, for garnish
Coarse, freshly ground black pepper, for garnish (optional)

1. In the 6-quart (6 l) pot, combine the artichoke bottoms and the stock. Cover, bring to a simmer over medium heat, and simmer for 1 hour.

2. Transfer the mixture, in batches, to the blender and blend until thick and creamy. Taste for seasoning. (I don't always find that salt is necessary, as the soup has so much flavor on its own.) Serve in the warmed bowls, garnished with the cheese, thyme, and pepper. I find that this soup is best served as it is made, with no storage or freezing; the emulsion tends to fade away if prepared in advance.

Red Tomato Gazpacho

A cool summer gazpacho soup is a wonderful example of a quick and easy emulsion, as the blender and golden olive oil work their magic to transform a handful of ingredients into a velvety chilled delight.

— 8 SERVINGS

EQUIPMENT: *A blender; 8 chilled, shallow soup bowls or glasses.*

2 pounds (1 kg) ripe red tomatoes, rinsed, cored, and cut into chunks
1 small, cucumber (about 6 ounces / 180 g), peeled and cut into chunks
1 small, mildly hot pepper, such as Anaheim, stemmed and cut into chunks
1 small red onion, peeled and cut into chunks
2 plump, fresh garlic cloves, peeled, halved, and green germ removed if present
2 teaspoons best-quality red wine or sherry wine vinegar
1 teaspoon fine sea salt
1/2 cup (125 ml) mild extra-virgin olive oil

1. In the blender, combine the tomatoes, cucumber, pepper, onion, and garlic. Blend at the highest speed until well emulsified and very smooth, a full 2 minutes. With the motor running, add the vinegar and salt. Slowly drizzle in the olive oil until the mixture is smooth, thick, and emulsified.

2. Cover and refrigerate until well chilled. Pour into the chilled bowls or glasses and serve.

MAKE-AHEAD NOTE: *The soup can be prepared up to 3 days in advance and stored in an airtight container in the refrigerator. Reblend at serving time.*

Tigerella Gazpacho

Striped Tigerella heirloom beauties, with their sweet, tangy flavor, create a wonderful variation on the classic gazpacho when teamed up with grassy and lightly bitter green peppers.

— 6 SERVINGS

EQUIPMENT: *A blender; 6 chilled, shallow soup bowls.*

1 pound (500 g) Tigerella heirloom tomatoes or other fresh red tomatoes

1 small cucumber (about 6 ounces/180 g), peeled and cut into chunks

1 small green bell pepper, seeded and cut into chunks

1/3 cup (80 ml) mild extra-virgin olive oil

2 tablespoons best-quality sherry wine vinegar

1 teaspoon fine sea salt

Combine all the ingredients and 1 cup (250 ml) water in the blender. Blend thoroughly to create a thick emulsion. Chill until very cold before serving in the chilled soup bowls.

MAKE-AHEAD NOTE: *The soup can be prepared up to 1 day in advance and stored in an airtight container in the refrigerator. Reblend at serving time.*

Roasted Cherry Tomato Soup
with a Touch of Spice

Here, fresh tomatoes swap their fruity acidic flavors for sweeter caramelized ones when roasted, giving this soup distinctive warming notes that are richly satisfying, even when the soup is served chilled. Roasting the tomatoes slowly at a low temperature reduces their moisture and condenses the rich tomato flavor. This is also a great trick for boosting the flavor of winter hothouse tomatoes. Serve this warm on a chilly night when dreaming of warmer weather.

— 8 SERVINGS

EQUIPMENT: *2 baking sheets; a blender; 8 chilled, shallow soup bowls.*

2 pounds (1 kg) variously colored heirloom cherry tomatoes
Fine sea salt
1/3 cup plus 2 tablespoons (110 ml) mild extra-virgin olive oil, plus more for serving
1/8 teaspoon ground Espelette pepper or other mild ground chile, or to taste
Fresh basil leaves, for garnish

1. Center a rack in the oven. Preheat the oven to 275°F (135°C).

2. Arrange the tomatoes side by side on the baking sheets. Sprinkle lightly with salt. Drizzle with 2 tablespoons of the olive oil. Bake until the tomatoes have shrunk by about one-third, 1 to 1-1/2 hours. (The tomatoes can be baked up to 1 day in advance and stored in an airtight container in the refrigerator.)

3. Place the roasted tomatoes in the blender. Add 1 cup (250 ml) water, the remaining 1/3 cup (80 ml) olive oil, 1/2 teaspoon salt, and the Espelette

pepper and blend well to create a thick emulsion. Since tomatoes vary in the amount of water they may retain, you may want to add more water to reach the desired consistency. Taste for seasoning. Chill until very cold before serving in the chilled bowls. Serve garnished with fresh basil leaves and a drizzle of olive oil.

MAKE-AHEAD NOTE: *The soup can be prepared up to 1 day in advance and stored in an airtight container in the refrigerator. Reblend at serving time.*

Yellow Tomato and Toasted Cumin Soup

While I grow many types of red, yellow, and green heirloom tomatoes in my garden, a favorite is the yellow *Ananas* (pineapple) variety, an organic tomato that is a pale yellow beefsteak with a red blush on the bottom end and subtle red streaking through the flesh. It is sweet, mildly acidic, and delicious. Other yellow varieties one might find at the farmers' market or grow in the garden include Amber, Aunt Gertie's Gold, and Amana Orange.

— 6 SERVINGS —

EQUIPMENT: *An electric spice mill; a blender; 6 chilled, shallow soup bowls.*

1 teaspoon cumin seeds, plus more for garnish.
1-1/2 pounds (750 g) yellow Ananas heirloom tomatoes, cored and quartered
1/3 cup (80 ml) mild extra-virgin olive oil
1 teaspoon fine sea salt
Garlic-Yogurt Sauce (page 425), for garnish

1. In a small skillet, toast the cumin seeds over medium heat until they are fragrant, shaking the skillet to keep the seeds from burning, about 1 minute. Transfer to a plate to cool.

2. In the spice mill, grind the seeds to a fine powder and transfer to a small bowl.

3. Combine the tomatoes, olive oil, toasted cumin (reserving a little for the garnish), salt, and 1/3 cup (80 ml) water in the blender. Blend for a full 3 minutes to create a thick emulsion. Chill until very cold before serving in the chilled bowls. Garnish with the reserved toasted cumin and swirls of garlic-yogurt sauce.

MAKE-AHEAD NOTE: *The soup can be prepared up to 1 day in advance and stored in an airtight container in the refrigerator. Reblend at serving time.*

GRIND

Why grind your own meat or poultry? Because it means you have total control over the ingredients, the type of cuts, and the meat's provenance. It also means that you can avoid any unwanted fillers or bacterial contamination that may make its way into industrially prepared ground meat. The ingredients will taste much fresher when ground right before you want to cook them.

Tips

~ Cut the meat or poultry into small, uniform cubes for even grinding.

~ Chill the meat or poultry and the food processor blade in the freezer for at least 15 minutes, or long enough to firm up the ingredient, as the meat is prone to smearing if too warm.

~ Pulsing will provide a more even grind. Always grind in batches to control the texture.

~ For the appliance-free cook, meat can be ground with a knife. A cleaver is useful for this. Meat and poultry must be cold and the knife very sharp, but you will get very little smearing, resulting in a good structure and juice retention during cooking.

Pork and Fennel Sausage

Pork and fennel sausage always reminds me of my childhood days in Milwaukee, Wisconsin, when my Italian mother made incredible thick-crust pizzas topped with homemade tomato sauce and fennel-rich pork sausage. This is my go-to pork sausage, based on a recipe from chef Nancy Silverton. I like to make a big batch, storing the leftovers in small packages in the freezer to keep on hand for pizza (page 279; 8 ounces/250 g sausage is enough for one 13-inch/33 cm pizza), pasta, and pinwheel bread (page 285).

MAKES 2-1/4 POUNDS (1.25 KG) BULK SAUSAGE

EQUIPMENT: *A baking sheet lined with baking parchment; a food processor.*

3 tablespoons fennel seeds
3 plump, fresh garlic cloves, peeled, halved, green germ removed if present, and
   minced
1 tablespoon fine sea salt
1 tablespoon plus 1 teaspoon sugar
1 tablespoon plus 1 teaspoon coarse, freshly ground black pepper
1 tablespoon plus 1 teaspoon hot Spanish paprika (not smoked)
2 pounds (1 kg) boneless pork shoulder
8 ounces (250 g) pork fatback

1. In a small skillet, toast the fennel seeds over medium heat until they are fragrant, shaking the skillet to keep the seeds from burning, about 1 minute. Transfer to a plate to cool.

2. In a large bowl, combine the garlic, salt, sugar, pepper, paprika, and toasted fennel seeds and toss to blend. Cut the pork and the fatback into 1-inch

(2.5 cm) cubes and add to the bowl. Toss to evenly coat the meat with the spice mixture. Cover the bowl and refrigerate for at least 24 hours and up to 2 days.

3. Spread the seasoned meat and fat in a single layer on the baking sheet and freeze for 30 minutes. The edges should be stiff but the middles still pliable. (Freezing will help the food processor blade cut the meat cleanly rather than tearing or smearing it.)

4. Working in about five batches and keeping the meat and fatback proportional in each, place the cubes in the food processor and grind in thirty to forty 1-second pulses until coarsely ground. (As the meat and fatback warm up, it may take less time to achieve a coarse grind.) Transfer to a platter and repeat with the remaining meat and fatback.

5. To cook the sausage (either the entire recipe or in small batches), panfry the sausage in a skillet over medium heat, using a spatula to break up the pieces, and cook until lightly browned, 5 to 10 minutes. The cooking time will depend upon the quantity of sausage used. Taste for seasoning.

6. Use the sausage immediately or cover and refrigerate for up to 3 days, or freeze, carefully wrapped, for up to 3 months.

Merguez Lamb Sausage with Harissa

Spicy lamb sausage, inspired by North African cuisine, is my go-to recipe in Provence for festive summertime parties beneath our verdant pergola. I love to serve it with an herb-laden couscous salad and generous servings of my spicy *harissa* and *harissa* yogurt sauce.

--- MAKES 18 HAND-ROLLED CIGARS OR PATTIES ---

EQUIPMENT: *An electric spice mill; a baking sheet lined with baking parchment; a food processor.*

1 tablespoon fennel seeds
2 teaspoons coriander seeds
2 teaspoons cumin seeds
3 plump, fresh garlic cloves, peeled, halved, green germ removed, and minced
2 teaspoons fine sea salt
1 teaspoon Spanish smoked hot paprika
1 teaspoon cayenne pepper
1 teaspoon Harissa (page 417), plus more for serving
2 pounds (1 kg) lamb shoulder meat
Sunflower oil, for cooking
Harissa Yogurt Sauce (page 425), for serving
Herbed Couscous Salad (page 436), for serving

1. In a small skillet, toast the fennel, coriander, and cumin seeds over medium heat until they are fragrant, shaking the skillet to keep the seeds from burning, about 1 minute. Transfer to a plate to cool.

2. In the spice mill, grind the seeds to a fine powder and transfer to a large bowl. Add the garlic, salt, paprika, cayenne pepper, and *harissa* and toss to blend.

3. Cut the lamb into 1-inch (2.5 cm) cubes and place them in the bowl with the seasoning. Toss to evenly coat the meat.

4. Spread the seasoned lamb in a single layer on the baking sheet. Cover with plastic wrap and freeze for at least 30 minutes, or until the edges of the meat are stiff but the centers are still pliable. (Freezing will help the food processor blade cut the meat cleanly rather than tearing or smearing it.)

5. Place about a quarter of the lamb cubes in the food processor and process until the meat is coarsely ground, about 12 seconds. Transfer to a platter. Repeat with the remaining lamb.

6. Wet your hands with cold water to prevent the meat from sticking. Roll about 1/4 cup (45 g) of the lamb mixture into a cylinder or cigar about 1 inch (2.5 cm) thick by 4 inches (10 cm) long, or form it into a small patty. Brush this sample sausage with oil. In a large, heavy-duty frying pan, cook the sample sausage over low heat, turning regularly, until the sausage is browned and cooked through, 3 to 4 minutes. Taste for seasoning and adjust in the remaining ground lamb as desired.

7. Form the remaining lamb into cigars or patties as desired and cook as above. You should be able to make about 17 more cigars or patties. Serve with additional *harissa and harissa* yogurt sauce as a garnish, with the couscous salad alongside.

MAKE-AHEAD NOTE: *The uncooked sausages can be stored in the refrigerator for up to 1 day before cooking, or frozen, uncooked, for up to 1 month. Thaw in the refrigerator before cooking.*

Duck Breast Burgers

Years ago, this became a favorite in my Paris cooking classes, inspired by a dish chef Eric Trochon served me at Semilla, our local hangout around the corner from my cooking studio. As always, grinding your own poultry and meat improves flavor and texture dramatically.

─── MAKES 8 BURGERS ─────────────────────────────────────

EQUIPMENT: *A sharp knife; a baking sheet lined with baking parchment; a food processor; a kitchen scale; a 3-1/4-inch (8 cm) hamburger press (optional).*

4 magret duck breasts, each about 1 pound (500 g)
5 ounces (150 g) smoked bacon, diced
1/4 cup (60 ml) toasted sesame oil
1/4 cup (60 ml) soy sauce
2 teaspoons fine sea salt
Coarse, freshly ground black pepper
8 slices Comté and Paprika Brioche (page 272), cut into 4-inch (10 cm) rounds and toasted, for serving
Spicy Tomato Marmalade (page 422), for serving

1. Using the tip of a sharp knife, carefully separate the duck fat from the breast meat. Cut the meat into 1/2-inch (1 cm) cubes and the fat of 1 duck breast into 1/4-inch (0.5 cm) cubes. (The remaining fat can be rendered—melted over low heat until liquid—then strained to remove any solids, and used for cooking in place of oil or butter. Store it in the refrigerator for up to 6 months.) Spread the cubed meat and fat (keeping the two separate) in a single layer on the baking sheet, and freeze for 30 minutes. The edges of the meat and fat should be stiff but the middles still pliable. (Freezing will help the food processor blade cut the meat

cleanly rather than tearing or smearing it, and keep the fat firm when mixed with the meat.)

2. While the meat is chilling, in a small, dry skillet, brown the bacon over medium heat until crisp and golden, about 5 minutes. With a slotted spoon, transfer the bacon to several layers of paper towels to drain. Blot the top of the bacon with several layers of paper towels to absorb any additional fat.

3. Working in two batches, place the chilled meat in the food processor and grind it in fifteen to twenty 1-second pulses, until it looks coarsely ground. Transfer the mixture to a large platter and repeat with the remaining meat. Inspect the meat for any large pieces, regrind as needed, and discard any tough gristle.

4. Add the sesame oil, soy sauce, salt, cooked bacon, cubed fat, and pepper to the ground duck meat. With your hands, work the ingredients into the meat, until evenly seasoned and well combined.

5. Portion the mixture and weigh it on the scale. I find 4 ounces (125 g) per patty is just right. You can go to 6 ounces (180 g) for larger appetites. I like the look of a perfectly round patty, so I use a hamburger press or a round metal form with a "pusher" or metal topper to very gently press the meat and fat mixture into the form. But hand-molded patties are also perfectly acceptable.

6. Heat a dry nonstick skillet over medium-high heat. When the skillet is hot but not smoking, carefully transfer the patties to the pan with a wide spatula. Reduce the heat to medium and cook for about 2 minutes per side, turning only once, until the burger is well browned on the outside and still rare on the inside, or until cooked as desired.

7. Remove the burgers from the pan and season both sides lightly with sea salt and generously with pepper. Carefully place each burger on top of a toasted brioche. Serve with Spicy Tomato Marmalade.

Asian Chicken and Cilantro Meatballs

My love for Asian food is never-ending, and this easy, quick chicken meatball creation is a favorite. The secret here is to steam the meatballs so they remain tender and succulent. Searing briefly afterward adds a wonderfully caramelized crust without overcooking.

— MAKES 25 TO 30 MEATBALLS —————————————————

EQUIPMENT: *A baking sheet lined with baking parchment; a food processor; a bamboo steamer.*

1 pound (500 g) boneless, skinless free-range chicken breast meat

2 tablespoons toasted sesame oil

1 tablespoon soy sauce

1 tablespoon Vietnamese fish sauce

3 tablespoons minced fresh ginger, or 1 tablespoon ground ginger

1 teaspoon fine sea salt

1/2 cup (40 g) plain dry bread crumbs

1/2 cup (125 ml) minced scallions, white and green parts

1 large egg, free-range and organic

1/4 cup minced fresh chives

1 cup loosely packed fresh cilantro leaves, plus more for garnish

1 tablespoon Kaffir Lime Powder (page 443; optional)

Chicken Stock (page 402) or William's Thai Vegetable Bouillon (page 37), warmed, for serving

1. Cut the chicken into 1-inch (2.5 cm) cubes. Spread the meat in a single layer on the baking sheet, cover with plastic wrap, and freeze for 1 hour. The chicken should be stiff. (Freezing will help the food processor blade cut the meat cleanly rather than tearing or smearing it.)

2. Place the cubes in the food processor and process for about 15 seconds, until the chicken is coarsely ground. Transfer the chicken to a large bowl, add 1 tablespoon of the sesame oil and the remaining ingredients (except the stock), and use your hands to blend the mixture.

3. To prevent the mixture from sticking, wet your hands with cold water, then shape the mixture into 1-1/2-inch (3 cm) balls, about the size of golf balls.

4. In a medium saucepan, bring 1 quart (1 l) water to a boil over high heat.

5. Arrange the meatballs side by side in the steamer, cover, and place on top of the saucepan. Steam until cooked through, about 5 minutes (see page 15 for best tips on steaming techniques and equipment). In a skillet, heat the remaining 1 tablespoon sesame oil over medium-high heat and sear the meatballs for a few minutes to create a crunchy, colorful exterior. Serve in the chicken stock or vegetable stock, and garnish with fresh cilantro leaves.

VARIATIONS: *Serve with Asian dipping sauces—Quick Asian Dipping Sauce (page 428), Sweet and Spicy Dipping Sauce (page 430), and Vietnamese Dipping Sauce (page 431)—or deep-fry for 2 minutes and garnish with a mixture of fresh cilantro, basil, and mint.*

SEAR

What do the crusty coating of fried potatoes, dark beer, chocolate, coffee, the mahogany surface of well-browned meat, and the burnished surface of brioche, cakes, breads, and a slice of toast all have in common? They get much of their color and flavor as a result of the Maillard reaction, also known as the "browning reaction." The cooking "miracle" gets its name from the French scientist Louis-Camille Maillard, who studied the browning of foods in the early 1900s. As the surface of foods warms in dry heat, amino acids (proteins) and sugars react together and the surface becomes brown, crunchy, and fragrant, with a rich, deep flavor.

This, more than anything else, is what distinguishes the depth of flavor of meat cooked at a high heat (baked, fried, roasted, grilled, and pan-fried) from that of food that is poached, simmered, steamed, or cooked at a low temperature. Dryness and temperature are the two main factors that create the Maillard reaction. Searing, therefore, is an essential technique to maximize flavors when braising, stewing, and roasting. See the Roast (page 203), Grill (page 173), and Braise (page 219) chapters for more searing tips using those techniques.

Tips

~ The drier the meat, the faster the Maillard reaction occurs. Patting food dry with a paper towel will speed up the browning process, which is particularly useful if you are searing the outside of a cut of meat before cooking it using another technique such as braising or slow cooking, making sure the meat does not overcook while the browning occurs.

~ The sizzle is the telltale sound that a nice, caramelized crust is forming on whatever it is you are searing. If the temperature of the pan is too low, or too much liquid is escaping from the food and pooling in the pan, you won't get a good sizzle, meaning there is not enough moisture evaporation happening and the temperature will not rise to sufficient levels to create the Maillard reaction. So a hot pan is essential, as is not overcrowding the pan, which will also force down the temperature of the pan.

Seared Beef Rib-Eye Steak

The French have an expression: *"Il n'y a pas trente-six solutions,"* or, "There are not thirty-six solutions," by which they mean there's only one true and effective answer to any question. That's surely not the case when asking the best way to cook a beef rib steak. Disagreement on every step of the cooking is rampant. Most butchers and chefs insist that the meat be cooked at room temperature (meaning not straight from a very cold refrigerator), but agreement stops there. Some prefer roasting or broiling; some season well in advance; some turn the steak every few minutes; some insist on extremely high heat, others turn to moderate. After many, many tests of recommendations from many, many butchers, this is my preferred method. Simple, easy, and a sure way for your searing confidence to soar.

4 SERVINGS

EQUIPMENT: *A large seasoned cast-iron skillet; an instant-read thermometer (optional).*

1 bone-in beef rib-eye steak, about 2 pounds (1 kg) and 1-1/2 inches (3 cm) thick
Fine sea salt
Coarse, freshly ground black pepper
Lemon wedges, Mint Chimichurri (page 423), and/or compound butter (pages 77–80) such as Lemon, Mustard, Garlic, and Chile; Parsley and Garlic; or Caper, Cornichon, Mustard, and Parsley, for serving

1. Remove the meat from the refrigerator at least 4 hours before cooking. This will help prevent the meat from steaming as it sears, and help it cook more evenly.

2. When you are ready to cook the beef, dry the meat well to maximize the browning effect. Preheat the skillet over high heat for 2 minutes. Season the meat well on both sides with salt and pepper. Reduce the heat to medium, then add the meat and sear for at least 8 minutes. (Resist the temptation to turn the meat too early since the meat will stick until the Maillard reaction kicks in, caramelizing the sugars and proteins on the surface of the meat, resulting in more intense flavors and an attractive crust.) Turn the meat and cook for 8 minutes more for rare meat, or cook to the desired doneness. Use an instant-read thermometer to test for temperatures ranging from 125°F (52°C) for rare to 155°F (68°C) for well-done.

3. Remove the steak from the pan and season both sides once again with salt and pepper. To keep the meat from sitting in any juices that are released as it rests, arrange the meat against an inverted shallow bowl on a cutting board and tent very loosely with foil to prevent the surface from cooling off too quickly. As the muscle fibers relax, they reabsorb the juices expelled during the cooking process, resulting in a much juicier and more flavorful steak. The angle of the steak helps to retain the juices while protecting the seared crust from becoming soggy. Let the meat rest for 10 minutes.

4. To serve, carefully cut away the bone. Carve the steak into thick slices. Pour any reserved juices over the meat. Serve with lemon wedges, *chimichurri*, and/or a selection of compound butters.

WINE MATCH: *If the budget allows, go for a sturdy red Châteauneuf-du-Pape here; a new favorite comes from the sandy-soil vineyards of Château de Vaudieu, black raspberry and cherry rich.*

Seared Chicken Hearts and Livers
with Fresh Thyme

Antoine Westerman of Le Coq Rico in Paris's 18th *arrondissement* taught me to value and appreciate the power of poultry innards, especially the livers and hearts, which he cooks in various magical ways. A favorite Provençal country restaurant—Le Dagobert in the Drôme—then taught me the magic of gently sweating, then forcefully searing tender lamb livers and richly flavored hearts with celery and shallots and showering them with fresh thyme leaves.

— 4 SERVINGS

4 celery ribs, rinsed and cut into thin half-moons
4 shallots, peeled and cut crosswise into thin slices
2 tablespoons extra-virgin olive oil
About 1/2 teaspoon fine sea salt
4 chicken livers, trimmed of any fat and gristle and cut into bite-size pieces
4 chicken hearts, trimmed of any fat and gristle and cut into bite-size pieces
2 teaspoons fresh thyme leaves, for garnish

1. In a medium skillet, combine the celery, shallots, oil, and salt and sweat—cook, covered, over low heat—until softened, about 5 minutes. Set aside in a bowl.

2. In the same skillet, sear the livers and hearts over high heat, tossing regularly, until browned around the edges and cooked through, about 5 minutes. Transfer the innards to the bowl with the celery-shallot mixture and toss to blend. Shower with the thyme leaves. Serve warm.

VARIATIONS: *The livers and hearts can also be garnished with mint or tarragon, or teamed up with a few capers.*

Seared Eggplant Caponata

Eggplant is the star player in this popular Sicilian vegetable dish, so the goal here is to extract as much of its dense, smoky, earthy flavor as possible. To achieve this, I cook the eggplant separately, searing it to intensify and concentrate its flavors. I don't agree with the common belief that eggplant should be cooked with huge amounts of oil: I find that if you sear cubed eggplant in a moderate amount of oil over fairly high heat and toss it regularly until soft, you don't have to exaggerate with the fat. Likewise, I find the advice to salt eggplant slices to draw out bitter liquid an antiquated custom. Bitterness has been bred out of today's eggplant, and in my experience, when eggplant is firm and fresh, it is never bitter.

— MAKES 1 QUART (1 L), TO SERVE 4 TO 6 —

1 pound (500 g) firm eggplant, washed but not peeled, cut into 3-inch (7.5 cm) chunks

6 to 8 tablespoons extra-virgin olive oil

1-1/2 teaspoons fine sea salt

2 teaspoons fresh or dried oregano

2 medium onions, peeled, halved lengthwise, and cut into thin half-moons

4 celery ribs, with leaves, chopped

1 cup (250 ml) tomato sauce or one 8-ounce can diced tomatoes

1/4 cup (50 g) organic unrefined raw sugar

1/4 cup (60 ml) best-quality red wine vinegar

2 tablespoons capers in vinegar, drained

Minced fresh oregano leaves, for garnish

1. In a large saucepan, combine the eggplant, 4 tablespoons of the oil, 1 teaspoon of the salt, and the oregano and toss to coat well. Sear the eggplant over high heat, tossing regularly to keep the eggplant from

sticking, until the flesh is soft and charred on the edges, about 8 minutes. If the eggplant becomes too dry, add 1 to 2 tablespoons additional oil and continue to sear until soft, about 2 minutes more.

2. In another saucepan, combine 2 tablespoons of the oil, the onions, celery, and remaining 1/2 teaspoon salt and toss to coat the vegetables with the oil. Sweat—cook, covered, over low heat—until the vegetables are soft, 5 to 7 minutes. Do not let the onions brown. Add the seared eggplant, tomato sauce, sugar, vinegar, and capers and simmer, covered, over low heat until very tender, about 10 minutes. Taste for seasoning.

3. At serving time, taste for seasoning again and garnish with minced fresh oregano leaves. Serve at room temperature as part of an antipasto assortment or as a side vegetable dish.

MAKE-AHEAD NOTE: *Store in an airtight container in the refrigerator for up to 3 days.*

Chickpea Crêpe with Fresh Goat Cheese, Zucchini Ribbons, and Toasted Pine Nuts (page 144)

PANFRY

Panfrying—shallow frying in a small amount of fat at medium-high in a frying pan or skillet—is one of the most common cooking techniques, yet it's often poorly executed. It's worth taking the time to hone your pan-frying skills, and you'll really see the results with better crusts, more even and precise cooking, and less food stuck to the bottom of the pan!

Tips

~ Use a heavy-duty pan made from good-quality materials that heat up at a moderate speed and distribute and maintain heat evenly, such as stainless steel, cast iron, or stainless steel lined copper. Cheap frying pans heat up too quickly and unevenly.

~ When I require a nonstick surface, I go for a well-seasoned cast-iron or ceramic-coated pan.

~ I prefer to panfry using extra-virgin olive oil, sunflower oil, clarified butter, or *ghee*, depending on which foods I am frying. There has been a lot of press demonizing cooking with olive oil at high temperatures, but the research is contradictory at best, and when in doubt, I look to history for guidance. The traditional Mediterranean diet, known as one of the healthiest diets in the world, has long fried vegetables in olive oil, with seemingly no long-term negative health effects. Olive oil can have a pungent flavor, however, so I use sunflower oil when I don't want to distract too much from the flavor of the food I am frying. Clarified butter and *ghee* have very high smoke points and so make an ideal fat to panfry in, but *ghee* in particular has a very rich, nutty flavor that isn't suitable for every dish.

~ Ideally, food should be at room temperature and patted dry before panfrying (where appropriate), as it speeds up the Maillard reaction, the caramelizing of the sugars and proteins on the surface of the food (see page 123 for more on the Maillard reaction).

~ Knowing when to add your food to a hot pan is key to successful panfrying. The fat should be hot but not smoking; in the case of olive oil, look for the surface of the oil to be shimmering to know that the oil temperature is right to begin frying. Food should sizzle vigorously as it makes contact with the oil. If it doesn't, the oil is not yet hot enough.

~ Don't be tempted to move or turn the food until one side is properly cooked and has developed a golden-brown crust. Flipping too early, before the Maillard reaction has kicked in, can result in your food sticking to the pan, and turning too much can cause more delicate foods to fall apart and will result in less caramelization.

~ It's important not to overcrowd the pan, as this will cause the oil temperature to drop and the food will steam rather than caramelize.

Swiss Potato Galette

A winter weekend trip to Switzerland, where I sampled a perfectly crisp and golden *galette* known as *rösti*, inspired a frenzy in the kitchen to perfect a version of this deceptively simple jewel. While the ingredients list is simple, the instructions must be followed to the letter. This rule holds true for all panfrying, a technique that we think we all know well, but we don't always pay careful attention to the pan being used, the intensity of the heat, and the timing. In this *galette*, the grated potatoes should form an intricate lattice, with a crunchy, golden exterior and light, fluffy interior. To achieve this, the potatoes are parboiled to avoid any raw flavors in the finished dish, then chilled for a few hours so they are easier to grate. I find there is no need to peel them first, making full use of all the nutrition the potato offers. Try cooking these in clarified butter or *ghee* for sweeter, more intense flavors.

---

4 SERVINGS

EQUIPMENT: *A 4-quart (4 l) saucepan; a four-sided grater or a coarse-holed grater; a 10-inch (24 cm) nonstick frying pan; a flat splatter guard, plate, or flat lid.*

1 tablespoon coarse sea salt
1 pound (500 g) russet potatoes, scrubbed but not peeled
1 fresh rosemary sprig
About 4 tablespoons (60 g) extra-virgin olive oil, clarified butter, or Ghee (page 411)
Fine sea salt
Coarse, freshly ground black pepper
Crème fraîche or sour cream, for serving
Fresh salad greens, for serving

1. Begin at least 5 hours before you want to panfry the *galette*. In the saucepan, combine 2 quarts (2 l) cold water, the coarse sea salt, potatoes, and rosemary sprig. Cover partially and bring to a boil over medium-high heat. Cook until the tip of a knife inserted into the potato meets slight resistance, about 15 minutes total. Err on the side of undercooking, as overcooked potatoes will turn to mush as you grate them. Drain the potatoes and refrigerate until well chilled, at least 4 hours and up to 1 day in advance (doing so will make them easier to grate). The potatoes can be grated up to 6 hours in advance and stored, covered, at room temperature.

2. At serving time, grate the potatoes on the coarse holes of the grater. In the skillet, heat the olive oil over medium heat until shimmering. Add the grated potatoes, pressing them down with a large, flat spatula so they form a solid cake. Panfry, without turning, until the first side is a deep golden brown, about 6 minutes. Keep the heat moderate so the potatoes brown but do not burn. At all times, the potato cake should glide easily in the pan as you shake it; add additional fat as needed.

3. Invert the potato cake out onto the splatter guard (or a flat plate or flat lid). Slide the *galette* back into the skillet (cooked side up) and panfry until the second side is a deep golden, about 6 minutes more. Transfer the *galette* to a flat serving plate. Season with salt and pepper, cut into 4 wedges, and serve immediately with *crème fraîche* and fresh salad greens.

MAKE-AHEAD NOTE: *The potatoes can be parboiled 1 day in advance and refrigerated. The potatoes can be grated up to 6 hours in advance and stored, covered, at room temperature.*
WINE MATCH: *A chilled, light, refreshing Swiss white is called for here: Try a dry white from the Vaud region of Switzerland, from the Chasselas grape.*

Charred Green Bean and Almond Salad with Smoky Baba Ghanoush

This dish is inspired by Chinese-style wok-fried green beans, blanched until tender to leave just a little crunch, then panfried over high heat so their exteriors are slightly charred and smoky. Drizzled with a fragrant almond oil, tossed with crunchy toasted almonds, parsley, and chives, and served on a layer of smoky *baba ghanoush*, this dish is a meal all in itself. In place of the *baba ghanoush* you can easily use classic or herbed *hummus* (page 419) or simply cooked chickpeas pureed with a little stock or water and seasoned with sea salt and toasted cumin seeds. This also makes for a wonderful side dish to my Four-Hour Aromatic Braised Pork (page 223), Poached Chicken Breast Salad with Lemon and Mint (page 56), or Roasted Beef Rib-Eye Steak (page 212).

—— 2 MAIN-COURSE SERVINGS OR 4 SIDE-DISH SERVINGS ——

EQUIPMENT: *A 5-quart (5 l) pasta pot, fitted with a colander; a large, heavy-duty skillet.*

3 tablespoons coarse sea salt
8 ounces (250 g) haricots verts, rinsed and trimmed at both ends
1 tablespoon extra-virgin olive oil
2 tablespoons sliced almonds
1 tablespoon best-quality almond oil
1/4 cup tightly packed fresh parsley leaves
1/4 cup chopped fresh chives
Fine sea salt
1 cup (about 8 ounces/250 g) Baba Ghanoush (page 420)
Grated zest of 1 organic orange

1. Prepare a large bowl of ice water.

2. Fill the pasta pot with 3 quarts (3 l) water and bring to a rolling boil over high heat. Add the coarse sea salt and the haricots verts and blanch, uncovered, until crisp-tender, about 2 minutes, counting from when the water comes back to a boil. (Cooking time will vary according to the size and age of the beans.) Immediately remove the colander from the water, let the water drain from the beans, and plunge the colander with the beans into the ice water so they cool down as quickly as possible. (The beans will cool in 1 to 2 minutes. If you leave them in the ice water any longer, they will become soggy and begin to lose flavor.) Drain the beans and wrap them in a thick kitchen towel to dry. (The beans can be cooked up to 4 hours in advance. Keep them wrapped in the towel and refrigerate, if desired.)

3. In the skillet, heat the olive oil over high heat until shimmering. Add the green beans and panfry, moving the beans around with a wooden spoon, until blistered and beginning to char and blacken, about 3 minutes. Remove from the heat.

4. In a small skillet, toast the sliced almonds over medium heat, shaking the pan regularly, until the nuts are fragrant and evenly toasted, 2 to 3 minutes. Watch carefully! They can burn quickly. Transfer the nuts to a large plate to cool. (If not using immediately, store in an airtight container at room temperature for up to 1 week.)

5. At serving time, toss the beans with the almond oil, parsley, and chives. Season with fine sea salt. On a serving platter, spread the *baba ghanoush* in a generous layer. Top with the beans and herbs. Scatter with the sliced almonds and the orange zest. Serve at room temperature.

Monkfish with Polenta-Parmesan Crust and Capers

Inspired by a presentation at Freddy's—a favorite Parisian wine bar around the corner from my cooking *atelier*—I created this polenta and Parmesan crust to encase delicate fresh fish fillet strips. I garnish them with a handful of capers warmed in a compound butter and a shower of salad greens. I have used firm white fish in this recipe, but it could work equally well with slices of eggplant and zucchini.

---

4 SERVINGS

EQUIPMENT: *4 warmed dinner plates.*

1 pound (500 g) skinless firm white-fleshed fish fillets, such as monkfish or halibut
2 large eggs, free-range and organic
1/2 cup (90 g) instant polenta
1/2 cup (50 g) freshly grated Parmigiano-Reggiano cheese
1/2 teaspoon fine sea salt
1/2 teaspoon ground Espelette pepper or other mild ground chile pepper
2 tablespoons Parsley and Garlic Butter (page 78), plus more for serving
1/4 cup (60 ml) capers in vinegar, drained
1/4 cup (60 ml) extra-virgin olive oil or Ghee (page 411)
A small handful of salad greens

1. Slice the fish into even strips about 1 inch (2.5 cm) by 4 inches (10 cm).

2. Place the eggs in a shallow bowl and whisk to blend. In another shallow bowl, combine the polenta, cheese, salt, and pepper and toss to blend.

3. In a small saucepan, melt the parsley and garlic butter over low heat. Add the capers and stir to combine. Cover to keep warm.

4. Dredge the fish strips first in the egg, shaking off any excess, then in the polenta mixture. Place on a large plate.

5. In a large skillet, heat the olive oil over medium heat until shimmering. Add the coated fish strips in a single layer and panfry until golden and cooked through, turning once, about 2 minutes per side. Divide the fish strips among the four plates and garnish with the caper butter. Serve immediately, with salad greens and extra parsley and garlic butter.

WINE MATCH: *I love this with a young, lemony Sauvignon Blanc from Philippe Gilbert's Domaine Gilbert Menetou-Salon from the Loire Valley. It's a wine rich in iodine minerality, flattering fish on all counts.*

Chickpea Crêpe with Fresh Goat Cheese, Zucchini Ribbons, and Toasted Pine Nuts

These earthy, full-flavored crêpes—made with wholesome chickpea flour—are a favorite lunchtime treat. Colorfully garnished with alabaster goat's milk cheese flecked with lemon zest, slim zucchini ribbons, and crunchy pine nuts, they're a festival on the plate and the palate. A few drops of basil oil and a showering of lemon thyme and parsley add their own bit of flavor and drama.

— **2 SERVINGS** ————————————————————————————

EQUIPMENT: *A mandoline; a 10-inch (25 cm) nonstick crêpe pan (see Note); a long-handled, flexible spatula.*

TOPPING

1 small zucchini, scrubbed and trimmed

2 teaspoons freshly squeezed lemon juice

1 tablespoon extra-virgin olive oil

Sea salt

4 ounces (125 g) fresh goat's milk cheese, crumbled

Grated zest of 1 organic lemon

Coarse, freshly ground black pepper

2 tablespoons pine nuts

1/4 red onion, thinly sliced and caramelized in Ghee (page 411; optional)

CRÊPES

1 scant cup (about 100 g) chickpea flour (garbanzo bean flour)

3/4 teaspoon fine sea salt

2 tablespoons extra-virgin olive oil or Ghee

Fresh lemon thyme leaves and parsley leaves, for garnish

Basil Oil (page 82), for garnish

1. PREPARE THE TOPPING: With the mandoline, slice the zucchini lengthwise into thin ribbons. Place in a bowl and toss with the lemon juice and olive oil. Season lightly with salt.

2. In a bowl, use a fork to mash together the goat's milk cheese and lemon zest. Season with salt and pepper.

3. In a small skillet, toast the pine nuts over medium heat, shaking the skillet to toast the nuts evenly until golden, about 2 minutes. Watch carefully; pine nuts can burn very quickly. Transfer to a plate to cool.

4. PREPARE THE CRÊPES: In a bowl, combine the flour, salt, and 1 cup (125 ml) water and, with a fork, whisk to blend. Heat 1 tablespoon of the olive oil in the pan over medium heat until shimmering. Pour half (3/4 cup/185 ml) of the batter into the pan, swirling to completely cover the bottom of the pan. Cook until the underside is golden, about 2 minutes. With the flexible spatula, very carefully flip the crêpe and cook the other side until the crêpe is cooked through, 1 to 2 minutes more. Transfer the first crêpe to a plate. Repeat to make the second crêpe.

5. Top each crêpe with half the goat cheese mixture, caramelized onions (if using), zucchini ribbons, pine nuts, and herbs. Drizzle with a touch of Basil oil. Serve.

NOTE: *Crêpe pans have a sloped edge. To determine the size of the pan, measure from lip to lip at the widest diameter at the top of the pan.*

DEEP-FRY

Deep-frying is the technique of submerging food in hot oil and cooking it until a crisp, golden outer layer forms but leaving a moist, tender interior. When food is dropped into very hot oil, steam escapes from the interior, shooting outward into the oil in tiny bubbles. This is why fried foods begin to fizz as they hit the hot oil. The high temperature of the oil forms a crust that immediately acts as a barrier to limit the amount of oil that is absorbed by the food, while the heat from the oil continues to cook the inside, causing starches and fibers to soften and proteins to denature. Herein lies the appeal of the perfect fried food: the contrast of crunch and softness that you find in a golden French fry, well-executed vegetable tempura, or crispy fried chicken.

Deep-frying is not complicated, but there are rules that are worth sticking with in order to get that perfect golden fry. (Here, we do take a diversion with our favorite "Cold-Fry" Frites [page 167], in which the potatoes and oil begin together at room temperature in a heavy-duty pot on top of a burner, with no need for a thermometer or a deep-fat fryer.)

Tips

~ I swear by my mini electric fryer. It's clean and simple, and with its built-in thermometer I don't have to worry about moderating the temperature of the oil. The next best thing is a heavy-duty pot made from a good-quality material that heats up at a moderate speed and distributes and maintains heat evenly, such as stainless steel or cast iron.

~ Getting the right oil temperature is essential. Too low a temperature means that a crust won't form immediately on the food or not enough steam will be ejected from the interior of the food, both of which result in overabsorption of oil. Too high a temperature causes the outside to cook too fast, while the inside remains undercooked. Deep-frying is best done at 340° to 375°F (170° to 190°C), depending upon the batter used and the food that you are frying. In my tests, the hotter end of that spectrum gives me the best results and I always fry at 375°C (190°C). If you do not have a deep-fry or candy thermometer, a wooden chopstick dipped into the hot oil will vigorously fizz with little air bubbles at around 350°F (180°C).

~ A neutral vegetable oil, such as sunflower oil, is best for deep-frying, as it won't impart any flavor to the final product. An exception can be made for tempura; you might want to add a bit of sesame oil to your base oil for additional flavor.

~ Food should be at room temperature and dry (unless it has a marinade on it) before frying.

~ Food items should be cut to similar sizes so that ingredients cook at the same rate.

~ Do not crowd the pot when frying, as it will lower the temperature of the oil too quickly. A good rule is never to cover more than one-third of the surface of the oil. Cook in batches, if necessary, either serving immediately or holding the finished items in a warm oven.

~ Adjust the heat during cooking if the temperature drops too low, and bring it back up to temperature between batches.

~ Always drain on paper towels after frying to absorb any oil.

~ Season immediately after frying so that the seasoning adheres quickly to the crust.

Crispy Golden Squid

I have lost count of the number of times I have ordered fried squid in restaurants, only to be served soggy, undercooked seafood. But this surefire method creates golden, crispy squid every time. Turmeric, an Indian spice, is responsible for the bright golden color of the batter and adds a gentle, exotic flavor to the crispy squid. When I can't find squid in the market, I prepare this with onions for a simple vegetarian variation.

When testing to find the ultimate batter recipe, I found that a beer-based batter consistently gave the best results. I am not a scientist, but modernist cuisine innovator and renowned food scientist Nathan Myhrvold offered compelling reasons for why beer makes the lightest, crispiest, and tastiest batter:

~ Beer brings three important components to a batter: carbon dioxide, foaming agents, and alcohol.

~ Gas dissolves in liquids at low temperatures, and reacts with it at higher temperatures. So when the carbon dioxide in beer comes into contact with the hot oil, the bubbles actually expand in the batter mix rather than dissolving (as, say, sugar would), resulting in a very light and lacy texture.

~ The foaming agents in beer also help to achieve a light and airy result by forming a protective casing around the bubbles that prevents them from popping too fast. They also act as a thermal insulator, heating up to 266°F (130°C; the point at which the Maillard reaction begins to work—see page 123) and effectively helping to create that perfectly deep golden crust while insulating the delicate food inside from overcooking.

~ While it may seem counterintuitive that a food submerged in oil dries as it cooks, that is basically what the crust is doing, as water evaporates from the batter and the food inside. Alcohol evaporates faster than water, so a beer batter does not have to cook as long as a batter prepared with water or milk, and the faster the batter dries, the less risk of overcooking the food it is surrounding.

~ Why cornstarch? Cornstarch, which is 100 percent starch and finely textured, seals the ingredients it coats, helping to promote crisp-textured fried foods. It also helps to prevent gluten from developing in the flour, too much of which can make batters puffy and heavy.

— 6 APPETIZER SERVINGS —

EQUIPMENT: *A 3-quart (3 l) heavy-duty saucepan or cast-iron pot or a deep-fat fryer fitted with a basket; a deep-fry thermometer or a wooden chopstick (optional); a frying screen (optional); a wire skimmer; a tray lined with paper towels.*

1 pound (500 g) small squid (2 to 3 inches/5 to 7 cm long)
5 tablespoons (50 g) unbleached, all-purpose flour
5 tablespoons (50 g) cornstarch
1/2 teaspoon fine sea salt, plus more for seasoning
1 teaspoon ground turmeric
2/3 cup (160 ml) beer
1 quart (1 l) vegetable oil, such as sunflower oil
A selection of sauces, such as Aïoli Piquant (page 94) or Chile-Lime Aïoli (page 97), Lime Mayonnaise (page 98), Harissa Yogurt Sauce (page 425), and infused salts (favorites for this dish are Piment d'Espelette Salt, page 84, and Saffron Salt, page 85), for serving

I. Rinse the squid and cut the bodies into 1-inch (2.5 cm) rings; halve the tentacles.

2. In a large bowl, combine the flour, cornstarch, salt, and turmeric. Set aside 1 tablespoon of the mixture to dust the squid later on. Add the beer to the dry ingredients in the bowl and whisk until the batter is smooth and lump-free.

3. Pour the oil into the saucepan or deep-fat fryer to a depth of at least 2 inches (5 cm). Heat the oil over medium heat to 375°F (190°C), or until a wooden chopstick inserted into the oil begins to fizz with bubbles. Do not be tempted to use too high a heat to bring the oil to temperature, as it will be harder to control and keep stable once you arrive at your goal temperature.

4. Dry the squid with paper towels. Dust the squid with the reserved flour mixture. Working in five or six batches, add the squid to the batter. Drag each piece against the side of the bowl to remove any excess batter, and drop gently into the hot oil, one at a time. Wait a few seconds before adding each piece, to prevent them from sticking together. Should they stick to the wire basket if using a fryer, dislodge them with the chopstick. If necessary, use a frying screen to keep the oil from spattering. Fry each piece until golden, about 2 minutes. Using the wire skimmer, transfer the squid to the paper-towel-lined tray to drain. Repeat with the rest of the squid. Season lightly with salt. Serve immediately, with a choice of sauces and salts.

MAKE-AHEAD NOTE: *In our tests we found that the batter can easily be made a day in advance and stored in an airtight container in the refrigerator. Whisk again before using to coat the squid.*

BEVERAGE MATCH: *Try this with a favorite chilled local artisanal beer.*

VARIATION

CRISPY GOLDEN ONION RINGS

Use 1 large onion in place of the squid, sliced crosswise into thin rings, then follow the remaining steps as above.

Mushroom, Seafood, and Shiso Tempura

Light and lacy tempura is one of the highlights of visiting a truly excellent Japanese restaurant. Much comes down to the treatment of the batter—keeping everything cold and working swiftly is key to slowing the gluten development in the batter, the culprit in a heavy, thick batter that absorbs too much oil. Low-protein flour such as cake flour is desirable, but the addition of cornstarch to all-purpose flour is remarkably effective in blocking gluten development.

As the batter warms up and is mixed around during the dredging process, the gluten develops further. To counter this, the batter is divided in two: One portion is refrigerated and used to coat the second half of the ingredients.

Serve this with soy-ginger dipping sauce and mushroom powders.

--- 4 SERVINGS ---

EQUIPMENT: *A 6-quart (6 l) cast-iron pot or an electric deep-fat fryer fitted with a basket; a deep-fry thermometer (optional); a wire skimmer; a pair of chopsticks; a tray lined with paper towels.*

1-1/2 cups (220 g) cake flour (not self-rising), plus more for dredging

1/2 cup (65 g) cornstarch

1 bunch enoki mushrooms, dirty roots trimmed, clean roots still attached, rinsed, divided into 8 small bunches

8 medium, flat shiitake mushrooms, wiped clean with a paper towel

8 to 12 oyster mushrooms, wiped clean with a paper towel, any dirt from the underside removed with the tip of a sharp knife

7 ounces (200 g) monkfish or other firm-fleshed white fish, cut into 1-1/2 × 2-inch (3 × 5 cm) pieces

4 ultra-fresh sea scallops, without roe

(Ingredients continue)

4 large shrimp, peeled and deveined but tail attached (reserve the heads and shells
   for Shellfish Stock, page 406, or another use)
2 small cleaned squid, bodies cut into 1 × 2-inch (2.5 × 5 cm) strips or sliced into
   1/2-inch (1.25 cm) rings, as preferred, tentacles halved
2 quarts (2 l) vegetable oil, such as sunflower oil
2 egg yolks, free-range and organic, chilled
2 cups ice water, plus 1/4 cup extra for thinning the batter, if necessary
1/4 cup (60 ml) toasted sesame oil
8 fresh shiso leaves
Soy-Ginger Dipping Sauce (page 429)
Mushroom Powders (page 432)
Fine sea salt or Dried Cèpe or Morel Salt (page 84), for dipping

1. Sift the flour and cornstarch together, or mix together in a bowl with a whisk, and place in the refrigerator to chill.

2. Prepare the mushrooms, fish, and shellfish in advance, making sure that they are all dry. Pat dry with paper towels, if necessary. Set aside on a tray at room temperature.

3. Pour the vegetable oil into the pot or deep-fat fryer to a depth of at least 2 inches (5 cm). If using a deep-fry thermometer to take the temperature of the oil, attach it to the side of the pot. Heat the oil over medium heat to 375°F (190°C), or until a wooden chopstick inserted into the oil begins to fizz with bubbles. Do not be tempted to use too high a heat to bring the oil to temperature, as it will be harder to control and keep stable once you arrive at your goal temperature.

4. While the oil is heating, place one of the egg yolks in a large bowl. Add the ice water and, using the chopsticks, mix together roughly. Add the sifted flour mixture and, again with the chopsticks, roughly mix together, six to ten strokes. The ingredients should not be well incorporated; there should remain a fair amount of unmixed flour. Divide the batter

evenly between two bowls. Cover one of the bowls with plastic wrap and refrigerate.

5. Just before you begin to fry, add the sesame oil to the hot vegetable oil. Working quickly with half the mushrooms, seafood, and *shiso* leaves, as you want the batter to remain as cold as possible to prevent gluten development, dredge four or five pieces in the extra flour, then, using the chopsticks, dip each quickly in the tempura batter, making sure that each piece is fully covered in batter (no need to dredge the *shiso* leaves in flour, they can be dipped directly into the batter). Drop the pieces into the hot oil and deep-fry until golden, 3 to 4 minutes. Using the wire skimmer, transfer the tempura to the paper-towel-lined tray to drain.

6. Using the skimmer, skim away any drops of batter that remain in the oil. Let the oil come back to temperature before continuing with four or five more pieces. Repeat until you have fried the remaining half of mushrooms, seafood, and *shiso* leaves, thinning the batter with the extra ice water as necessary.

7. Take the second batch of batter from the refrigerator and repeat the process to cook the remaining ingredients. This will make sure the second batch is just as lightly crisp as the first.

8. Serve with the dipping sauce, powders, and salt, dipping the tempura first in the sauce and then in one of the dipping powders or salt.

Oysters with Parmesan-Polenta Crust

I never realized fried oysters were such a uniquely American dish until
I served these one day to French friends in Provence. They are oyster
mavens and eat them regularly, raw on the half shell. This crunchy cooked
version was a revelation to them. The next Christmas, I gave our friends a
little deep-fat fryer as a gift, so they can now savor their own fried oysters
whenever they like. I love the crunch of the polenta, the richness of the
Parmesan, and the touch of spice from the ground red peppers. Serve this
with lemon wedges for a touch of acidity, and, if you like, a spicy *aïoli* or
vibrant lime mayonnaise.

--- 6 SERVINGS

EQUIPMENT: *A 3-quart (3 l) heavy-duty saucepan, cast-iron pot, or electric
deep-fat fryer fitted with a basket; a deep-fry thermometer or wooden chopstick
(optional); a wire skimmer; a tray lined with paper towels.*

4 large eggs, free-range and organic
1/2 cup (70 g) instant polenta
1/2 cup (50 g) freshly grated Parmigiano-Reggiano cheese
1/2 teaspoon fine sea salt
1/2 teaspoon ground Espelette pepper or other mild ground chile pepper
1 quart (1 l) vegetable oil, such as sunflower oil
12 freshly shucked oysters
Fresh lemon wedges, for garnish
Aïoli Piquant (page 94) or Lime Mayonnaise (page 98), for serving

1. Place the eggs in a shallow bowl and whisk to blend. In a second shallow
   bowl, combine the polenta, cheese, salt, and pepper.

2. Pour the oil into the saucepan or deep-fat fryer to a depth of at least
   2 inches (5 cm). If using a deep-fry thermometer to take the temperature of

the oil, attach it to the side of the saucepan. Heat the oil over medium heat to 375°F (190°C), or until a wooden chopstick inserted into the oil begins to fizz with bubbles. Do not be tempted to use too high a heat to bring the oil to temperature, as it will be harder to control and keep stable once you arrive at your goal temperature.

3. When the oil has come to temperature, coat the oysters: Dredge the oysters first in the eggs, allowing any excess to drip back into the bowl, then in the polenta mixture, shaking off any excess. Arrange on a platter. (The oysters should be fried within just a few moments of coating them.)

4. Fry the oysters in batches, about three at a time, until the breading is crisp, firm, and deep golden, 2 to 3 minutes. Remove with the wire skimmer and transfer to the paper towels to drain. Serve immediately with lemon wedges and *aioli* or lime mayonnaise.

WINE MATCH: *Sample these briny oysters with a Picpoul de Pinet, a favorite white from the Picpoul grape grown not far from the Mediterranean. The wine loves to partner with seafood, matching the iodine-rich flavors.*

Thai Crispy Chicken
with Kaffir Lime Rice

This spicy, flavorful fried chicken will transport you directly to the street-food stalls of Bangkok. Marinating the chicken overnight and particularly rubbing the marinade under the skin will help the flavors to penetrate deep into the flesh of the chicken. The rice flour gives it its distinct crispy crust. These two elements make for a winning combination that will surely make this a household favorite. A good accompaniment is jasmine rice, perfumed with several kaffir lime leaves in the cooking water.

--- 8 SERVINGS ---

EQUIPMENT: *A food processor, a blender, or an immersion blender; a 6-quart (6 l) heavy-duty saucepan, cast-iron pot, or electric deep-fat fryer fitted with a basket; a deep-fry thermometer (see Note) or a wooden chopstick (optional); an instant-read thermometer (optional); a tray lined with paper towels.*

MARINADE

2 tablespoons finely chopped fresh cilantro leaves

6 plump, fresh garlic cloves, peeled, halved, green germ removed if present, and coarsely chopped

3 lemongrass stalks (bottom third only), crushed, outer leaves removed, sliced paper-thin

6 tablespoons (90 ml) fish sauce

1/4 cup (60 ml) oyster sauce

2 teaspoons palm sugar, finely grated

30 white peppercorns, ground to a fine powder

2 teaspoons ground turmeric

5 green bird's-eye chiles, seeded

(Ingredients continue)

CHICKEN

8 chicken thighs and/or drumsticks (about 3 pounds/1.5 kg), free range
2 quarts (2 l) vegetable oil, such as sunflower oil
1-1/2 cups (225 g) rice flour

GARNISH

1/4 cup fresh cilantro leaves
5 scallions, white and greens parts, trimmed and sliced on the diagonal
3 bird's-eye chiles, seeded, sliced, and quickly fried in vegetable oil

1. In the food processor or blender or with the immersion blender, blend the marinade ingredients until you have a smooth mixture.

2. In a large dish, cover the chicken pieces with the marinade, rubbing it into the skin and between the skin and flesh. Cover the dish with plastic wrap and refrigerate for at least 4 hours, preferably overnight.

3. About 2 hours before cooking time, remove the chicken from the refrigerator, to allow it to come to room temperature.

4. At cooking time, pour the oil into the saucepan or deep-fat fryer to a depth of at least 2 inches (5 cm). If using a deep-fry thermometer to take the temperature of the oil, attach it to the side of the saucepan. Heat the oil over medium heat to 375°F (190°C), or until a wooden chopstick inserted into the oil begins to fizz with bubbles. Do not be tempted to use too high a heat to bring the oil to temperature, as it will be harder to control and keep stable once you arrive at your goal temperature.

5. When the oil is at temperature, dredge the chicken in the rice flour so it is completely covered.

6. Carefully drop the chicken pieces into the hot oil and fry until the skin is a deep golden color, 8 to 10 minutes, working in batches as needed so as

not to crowd the pot. You can test the doneness of the chicken by inserting a meat thermometer into the flesh, avoiding the bone. (The safe internal temperature for cooked chicken is 165°F/75°C.)

7. Place the chicken on the paper-towel-lined tray to drain. Garnish with the cilantro, scallions, and chiles and serve immediately.

NOTE: *A deep-fry thermometer is not essential but goes a long way in helping to achieve the perfect fry, since oil that is not hot enough will result in less crispy chicken that has absorbed more grease, and too high a temperature will burn the outside while leaving the inside raw.*

Falafel
(Crispy, Spicy Chickpea Balls)

These quick and easy spicy chickpea balls are a summertime family favorite. The healthy, hearty chickpeas require no cooking ahead—just an avalanche of spices and a fast deep-fry and you have an instant lunch or appetizer. Dip these in *hummus* for a traditional treat, or serve with roasted eggplant and garlic-yogurt sauce.

Note that you will need to soak the chickpeas 12 to 24 hours ahead of making the recipe.

— 4 SERVINGS ——————————————————————————

EQUIPMENT: *An electric spice mill; a food processor or blender; a 3-quart (3 l) heavy-duty saucepan, cast-iron pot, or electric deep-fat fryer fitted with a basket; a deep-fry thermometer or wooden chopstick (optional); a wire skimmer; a tray lined with paper towels.*

1-1/4 cups (200 g) dried chickpeas, rinsed

1-1/2 teaspoons cumin seeds

1/2 teaspoon coriander seeds

2 plump, fresh garlic cloves, peeled, halved, green germ removed if present, and minced

1 medium onion, peeled and finely chopped

1 cup minced fresh cilantro

1-1/2 teaspoons fine sea salt

1/2 teaspoon coarse, freshly ground black pepper

3/4 teaspoon cayenne pepper

1 quart (1 l) vegetable oil, such as sunflower oil

Lemon Salt (page 418), Hummus (page 418), Roasted Cubed Eggplant (page 202) and Garlic-Yogurt Sauce (page 425), for serving

1. At least 12 hours and up to 24 hours before preparing, soak the chickpeas at room temperature in at least 2 inches (5 cm) of cold water. Drain and rinse the chickpeas.

2. In a small skillet, toast the cumin and coriander seeds over medium heat, shaking the skillet to keep the seeds from burning, until fragrant, about 1 minute. Transfer to a plate to cool. In the spice mill, grind the cumin and coriander to a fine powder.

3. Place the chickpeas, ground cumin-coriander mixture, garlic, onion, cilantro, salt, black pepper, and cayenne in the food processor or blender and puree until as smooth as possible, about 2 minutes.

4. Pour the oil into the saucepan or the deep-fat fryer to a depth of at least 2 inches (5 cm). If using a deep-fry thermometer to take the temperature of the oil, attach it to the side of the saucepan. Heat the oil over medium heat to 375°F (190°C), or until a wooden chopstick inserted into the oil begins to fizz with bubbles. Do not be tempted to use too high a heat to bring the oil to temperature, as it will be harder to control and keep stable once you arrive at your goal temperature.

5. With your hands, carefully form the chickpea mixture into sixteen 1-inch (2.5 cm) balls. (This can be done several hours in advance. Arrange them on a tray, uncovered, at room temperature, and let them dry out slightly. If they are too wet, the oil will splatter when frying.)

6. At serving time, drop the chickpea balls into the hot oil and fry until firm and golden brown, about 3 minutes. Use the skimmer to transfer the falafel to the paper-towel-lined tray. Sprinkle with a touch of lemon salt, and serve with *hummus*, roasted eggplant, and garlic-yogurt sauce alongside.

Fried Green Tomatoes

My take on this popular summertime dish is inspired by a spectacular version I sampled at the restaurant 18 Seaboard in Raleigh, North Carolina. Use either firm, underripe tomatoes or heirloom varieties, such as Green Zebra or Evergreen. Do not peel the tomatoes: The skin helps the tomatoes retain their shape. Serve as an appetizer, first course, or vegetable side dish.

— 16 SERVINGS —

EQUIPMENT: *A sugar duster or small sieve; a 3-quart (3 l) heavy-duty saucepan, cast-iron pot, or electric deep-fat fryer fitted with a basket; a deep-fry thermometer or a wooden chopstick (optional); a wire skimmer; a tray lined with paper towels.*

1/4 cup (60 ml) buttermilk, shaken to blend
1/2 cup (125 ml) whole milk
1/2 cup (70 g) unbleached all-purpose flour
1/2 cup (75 g) cornmeal or instant polenta
1/2 cup (50 g) dried plain bread crumbs
1 teaspoon fine sea salt, plus more for seasoning
1 teaspoon fresh thyme leaves
1 quart (1 l) vegetable oil, such as sunflower oil
About 4 medium green tomatoes, sliced 1/2 inch (1.25 cm) thick
Spicy Tomato Marmalade (page 422), for serving (optional)
Lime wedges, for serving

1. In a shallow bowl, combine the buttermilk and milk and whisk to blend. Place the flour in a sugar duster or have a small sieve at hand. In another bowl, combine the polenta, bread crumbs, salt, and thyme and toss with a fork to blend.

2. Pour the oil into the saucepan or deep-fat fryer to a depth of at least 2 inches (5 cm). If using a deep-fry thermometer to take the temperature of the oil, attach it to the side of the saucepan. Heat the oil over medium heat to 375°F (190°C), or until a wooden chopstick inserted into the oil begins to fizz with bubbles. Do not be tempted to use too high a heat to bring the oil to temperature, as it will be harder to control and keep stable once you arrive at your goal temperature.

3. Dredge a tomato slice in the buttermilk-milk mixture, shaking to remove excess liquid, then dust with the flour, shaking to remove excess. Repeat the steps, dredging in the liquid, then dusting with the flour. Finally, dredge the slice in the bread crumb mixture, shaking to remove any excess. Set aside on a tray and repeat with the rest of the tomato slices.

4. Fry the tomato slices in batches, about four at a time, until the breading is crisp, firm, and deep golden, 3 to 4 minutes. Remove with the wire skimmer and transfer to the paper-towel-lined tray to drain. Season with salt. Serve immediately, with spicy tomato marmalade and lime wedges.

BEVERAGE MATCH: *Instead of wine here, I see a nice, chilled beer. Choose your local favorite.*

"Cold-Fry" Frites

This "revolutionary" method of making French fries at home is neither brand-new nor unique, but it is the best, easiest, most foolproof method I can imagine. This master has no offspring—it is a recipe that stands all on its own. My friend Jeffrey Bergman introduced me to this totally miraculous procedure, historically credited to chef Joël Robuchon.

Traditional fries are prepared by tossing potatoes in hot oil, usually cooking them twice: first poaching them once in a not-too-hot oil and then finishing them off in hotter oil. Not simple.

In this method, the potatoes and oil begin cooking together at room temperature, totally defying all the rules of deep-frying. The potatoes cook in a large pot, eventually reaching high heat, emerging golden and greaseless in less than 30 minutes. One pot, one cooking session, no blanching, no double frying, no electric deep-fat fryer, no thermometer. All you need is a good, large, heavy-duty cast-iron or stainless steel pot. And my experience suggests that with this method, the potatoes absorb almost no oil at all.

Best of all, you end up with fries with a moist, creamy interior, an intense potato flavor, and a perfectly crisp, golden, non-oily exterior that sends all of us into ecstasy.

The science behind this method is simple: When boiling potatoes, starting in cold water and bringing

them to a boil, the potatoes cook from the inside out. The same happens with this "cold" pan method, as the potatoes make friends with the oil and cook in unison, in the end, basically "poaching" in the fat. The potatoes do not absorb oil as they are heating up, since the oil is heating in unison with the potatoes. Culinary magic! And we are the beneficiaries! What's also great about this method is that the potatoes stay crisp for a good 20 minutes after cooking. Note: Do not try these with other potatoes, such as sweet potatoes; they will not crisp up but rather turn soggy once cooked.

Tips

~ Use firm, fresh potatoes. Rinse and soak them well to rid them of starch. The less starch in the potatoes, the crispier the fries will be.

~ To keep the oil well contained in the pot, make sure there is at least 2 inches (5 cm) of room from the top of the oil to the rim of the pot.

~ We have made these fries in varied quantities with proportionate quantities of oil and pot size:
   1 pound (500 g) potatoes/1-1/2 quarts (1.5 l) oil/4-quart (4 l) pot
   2 pounds (1 kg) potatoes/2-1/2 quarts (2.5 l) oil/5- to 7-quart (5 to 7 l) pot
   3 pounds (1.5 kg) potatoes/3 quarts (3 l) oil/7-quart (7 l) pot
   4 pounds (2 kg) potatoes/4 quarts (4 l) oil/8- to 9-quart (8 to 9 l) pot

~ Do not use an aluminum pot; it will not hold the heat in the same manner as a heavy cast-iron or stainless steel pot, and the results may not be satisfactory.

~ After frying, let the oil cool and strain it through cheesecloth into the original containers. Store in the refrigerator and reuse up to five times. Mark the bottles as to number of uses and sniff the oil before reusing; if there is any scent of rancidity, toss. Each time the oil is reused, add about 1 cup (250 ml) fresh, new oil to the mix.

EQUIPMENT: *A French-fry cutter (optional); 2 thick, clean kitchen towels; a 4- to 9-quart (4 to 9 l) heavy-duty saucepan or cast-iron pot; a kitchen timer; a wire skimmer or slotted metal spoon; 2 trays lined with paper towels; a warmed platter.*

2 pounds (1 kg/about 4 large) russet potatoes
2-1/2 quarts (2.5 l) vegetable oil, such as sunflower oil, at room temperature
Fine sea salt

1. Rinse the potatoes, peel them, rinse again, and cut lengthwise into 3/8-inch (10 mm) fries. (Precision is not essential here: I love the tiny, crunchy, almost-burned bits that emerge from the fryer.)

2. Soak the potatoes in a bowl of cold water for about 5 minutes, changing the water when it becomes cloudy (at least twice), until the water remains clear. (Soaking releases the starch in potatoes, making them less rigid and less likely to stick together while cooking.)

3. Drain the potatoes and wrap them in the kitchen towels to dry. (Removing the excess liquid will speed up the cooking time and reduce the likelihood of the potatoes splattering once the oil is hot.)

4. Transfer the potatoes to the saucepan and set it over the stove. Pour the oil over the potatoes. Do not cover the pot. Set the heat to high, stirring the potatoes gently with a metal spoon to distribute and prevent sticking. (A metal spoon lets you feel if any potato bits are stuck to the bottom of the pan and scrape them up.)

5. The oil should move from a peppy simmer to a boil in about 9 minutes. When the oil starts to boil, set a timer for 17 minutes. Stir the potatoes very gently every 3 to 4 minutes to prevent sticking and ensure even

cooking. Don't worry about overboiling—the oil should boil rapidly and evenly with no need to adjust the heat throughout the entire process.

6. When the timer rings, the potatoes should have begun to take on color, turning from white to slightly golden, but will still have about 4 minutes remaining until they are fully cooked. For these last few minutes, watch them closely, stirring gently. When the fries are a deep golden brown, taste one to make sure they are truly crisp and firm on the outside with a creamy interior. They should not be the least bit soggy, so resist the urge to remove them from the oil too soon. When you are happy with the consistency, carefully transfer the rest of the fries with the wire skimmer or slotted spoon to the paper-towel-lined trays to drain. Season with salt and serve immediately on the warmed platter.

Grilled Eggplant Slices with Asian Sauce
and Scallions (page 184)

GRILL

Cooking directly on a grill, whether gas, electric, charcoal, or under the broiler, is a favorite technique for flash-cooking very tender cuts of meat, seafood, and vegetables. The wood-fired bread oven and gas-fired outdoor grill at our Provence farmhouse are two of my cooking treasures; just the aroma of the grill heating evokes memories standing around with friends and students, grilling lamb—infused with its own smoky cooking aroma—on warm summer evenings. Of course if you don't have access to an outdoor grill, stovetop gas or electric grills, cast-iron stovetop grills, and oven broilers are worthy substitutes. Even a panini grill can create perfect, quick-grilled delights.

It is impossible to be encyclopedic here, but there are myriad grill books, websites, and experts out there to tell you what to do and what not to do when grilling any ingredient. For best results, I advise students to begin with a small list of foods they love to grill and work with them over and over again using their favorite grilling method and surfaces until they reach desired results. Here we offer a whole chicken, a lamb shoulder, and scallops grilled over an outdoor gas grill, and eggplant and asparagus grilled on a panini grill, to give a taste of the range of grilling possibilities at your disposal.

Grilled Scallops in Their Shells with Caper, Cornichon, Mustard, and Parsley Butter

In the wintertime in Provence, when scallops are at their finest and the weather in Provence allows for outdoor grilling, I turn to this dish when I am in the mood for elegant fare with a touch of the dramatic. Branches of juniper and rosemary add to the theater when grilling outdoors but are less practical on an indoor grill. You may not always find scallops on the half shell at all fish markets, but you can order empty shells on the Internet. And you can still achieve great results without the shells and in a standard oven or with a home indoor grill with a few adjustments.

6 SERVINGS

EQUIPMENT: *A gas grill with a lid; a baking rack from the oven.*

About 8 ounces (250 g) coarse sea salt
6 tablespoons (90 g) Caper, Cornichon, Mustard, and Parsley Butter (page 78)
6 scallop shells, top and bottom, well cleaned (optional; see Notes)
12 ultra-fresh sea scallops (with or without the roe), cleaned and side muscle
    detached from the shell
Coarse, freshly ground black pepper
6 teaspoons freshly squeezed lemon juice
Several handfuls of fresh juniper or rosemary branches (optional)
6 caper berries, for garnish

1. Preheat the grill to its highest heat (650°F/345°C).

2. Divide the salt among six salad plates, spreading it in an even layer to create a stable bed for the scallop shells at serving time.

3. Place a tablespoon of melted caper, cornichon, mustard and parsley butter in the bottom half of each of the scallop shells. Arrange scallops, with or without the roe, in each of the shells. Season liberally with pepper and drizzle each with 1 teaspoon of the lemon juice. Set the top shell on top of each prepared shell, like a lid, wrap the shells in aluminum foil to keep the liquid in, and place them side by side on the baking rack.

4. Arrange the juniper or rosemary branches (if using) on top of the grill. Place the baking rack on top of the branches. Close the grill lid and grill for 10 minutes at high heat for well-cooked scallops. (To check for scallop doneness, pierce the center of a scallop with the tip of a knife. The scallop meat should come apart easily.) Remove the baking rack from the grill.

5. Carefully arrange one scallop shell, with the top shell still in place, on each of the salt-covered plates. Carefully remove the top lid and top each with a caper berry. Return the top shell to its place. Serve immediately.

NOTES

~ Some fish markets sell scallops in the shell, and your fishmonger may be able to order them specially. Scallop shells can be reused indefinitely. I scrub them well after use and wash them in the dishwasher.

~ If scallop shells are not available, I set the scallops and butter in an ovenproof container (such as a heatproof porcelain dish, or I make a small boat out of aluminum foil), then wrap the container and prepared scallops in foil.

~ If there's no outdoor grill at hand, I use a stovetop grill or roast in the oven at high heat (450°F/230°C) until cooked to desired doneness, about 10 minutes.

Grilled Chicken Under a Brick

The Italian classic chicken cooked under a brick—*pollo al mattone*—spawned the inspiration for my fifth cookbook, *Trattoria*. It is simply a recipe for a whole chicken, split down the back and pressed flat, cooked whole, and pressed tight to the skillet, held down by a heavy weight, usually bricks, or *mattone*. The result is a super-crispy, moist, and tender bird that requires little tending and no more seasoning than salt and pepper. The chicken can be cooked on a gas or charcoal grill with a lid or on top of the stove in a skillet. Whichever way you prepare the bird, it's easy, quick, and totally rustic and satisfying. Seared Eggplant Caponata (page 129), Green Bean and Artichoke Salad with Hazelnut Vinaigrette (page 3), or Roasted Heirloom Carrots and Scallions with Cumin-Yogurt Dressing (page 191) make excellent sides for this chicken.

— 4 TO 6 SERVINGS ———————————————————

EQUIPMENT: *Poultry shears; a gas grill with a lid; a flat, cast-iron grill, skillet, or 2 bricks; an instant-read thermometer (optional); a warmed serving platter.*

1 chicken (about 3-1/2 pounds/1.6 kg), free-range, at room temperature
Extra-virgin olive oil
Fine sea salt
Coarse, freshly ground black pepper

1. Preheat the grill to its highest heat (650°F/345°C).

2. Place the bird, breast side down, on a flat surface. With the poultry shears, cut the bird lengthwise along the backbone. Open it flat, pressing down with the heel of your hand to flatten the carcass completely. The bird should be as flat as possible to ensure even cooking.

3. Rub the chicken all over with olive oil and season with salt and pepper. Place the bird, breast side down, on the grill. Place the grill, skillet, or bricks on top to weigh down the bird. Close the lid. Grill until the underside is golden brown, about 15 minutes. Remove the lid and weights. Using tongs so that you do not pierce the bird, turn the chicken over. Replace the weights, close the lid, and grill for 15 minutes more. To test for doneness, pierce the thigh with the tip of a knife to make sure that the juices run clear, or use the instant-read thermometer to check that the internal temperature of the flesh has reached 165°F (75°C).

4. Arrange the chicken at an angle against an inverted shallow bowl set on a cutting board, to allow the juices to flow down into the breast meat, giving a juicier and more flavorful result. Season again with salt and pepper. Tent the chicken lightly with aluminum foil and leave to rest for at least 10 minutes and up to 30 minutes.

5. Carve the chicken and arrange it on the warmed platter. Serve with a vegetable side dish.

NOTE: *To cook the chicken in a skillet, use a vessel large enough to hold the chicken flat (about a 12-inch/30 cm skillet), heat about 1/2 cup (125 ml) olive oil in the skillet until shimmering, then cook the chicken according to the instructions above.*
WINE MATCH: *I love to serve chicken with a light and fruity red. Try a Morgon from the Beaujolais region of France.*

Grilled Leg of Lamb with Fresh Herbs

Inspired by an incredible lamb I savored at the Parisian restaurant Hexagone, I now make this grilled lamb preparation often in Provence. This recipe is a simple blueprint for how to use a mix of fresh herbs as a flavorful and colorful garnish for any cooked meat, poultry, fish, or vegetable. Let your creativity and imagination run wild, and your palate will be rewarded. Fried Green Tomatoes (page 165), Roasted Eggplant with Harissa, Fennel Seeds, and Honey (page 195), or Spring Pea and Mint Salad (page 14) are good accompaniments for the lamb.

— 8 TO 12 SERVINGS —

EQUIPMENT: *A gas grill with a lid; an instant-read thermometer; a warmed platter.*

1 boneless leg of lamb (about 3 pounds/1.5 kg), butterflied and trimmed of excess fat
Fine sea salt
Coarse, freshly ground black pepper
Several handfuls of fresh herbs, such as a mix of cilantro, tarragon, and oregano, stemmed
Several tablespoons Classic Vinaigrette (recipe follows)

1. Preheat the grill to medium heat (350° to 450°F/175° to 230°C). Brush the cooking grates clean.

2. Sear the lamb directly on the grill grates, with the lid closed, until nicely browned, 10 to 15 minutes. Season with salt and pepper and turn, grilling until well seared on the other side, 10 to 15 minutes. Slide the lamb over to indirect medium heat, close the lid, and continue cooking to the desired doneness, or until an instant-read thermometer inserted into the thickest

part reads 130° to 135°F (54° to 57°C) for medium rare, about 20 minutes. Transfer the lamb to the platter and season once again with salt and pepper. Lightly tent with aluminum foil and let rest for at least 10 minutes and up to 30 minutes.

3. While the lamb is resting, toss the herbs with the vinaigrette. Cut the lamb crosswise into thick slices and arrange on the platter. Shower the lamb with the vinaigrette and herbs and serve with a vegetable side dish.

WINE MATCH: *Go for a big and meaty red here, like a Châteauneuf-du-Pape from our winemaker, Yves Gras. His Habemus Papem ("We have a pope") is ruby red and spicy.*

Classic Vinaigrette

The secret to this vinaigrette is to use two kinds of vinegar to create a more complex and well-balanced dressing.

— MAKES 1-1/4 CUPS (310 ML) —

EQUIPMENT: *A small jar with a lid.*

2 tablespoons sherry wine vinegar
2 tablespoons red wine vinegar
1/2 teaspoon fine sea salt
1 cup (250 ml) extra-virgin olive oil

In the jar, combine the vinegars and salt to taste. Cover with the lid and shake to dissolve the salt. Add the oil and shake to blend. Taste for seasoning. The dressing can be used immediately.

MAKE-AHEAD NOTE: *The vinaigrette can be prepared several weeks in advance. Store in an airtight container at room temperature or in the refrigerator. Shake to blend again before using.*

Blanched and Grilled Asparagus
with Chives and Chive Oil

Here, two techniques come into play, as seasonal fresh green asparagus are both blanched and grilled. Blanching precooks the vegetable and helps maintain its brilliant green color, while grilling brings out its earthy flavors and imparts a smoky note. The panini grill is ideal for simple preparations such as this. If you don't have a panini maker, use the baking parchment technique described in step 3 with a stovetop grill plate, weighing down the asparagus with a heavy skillet. You will need to turn the vegetables during cooking, however, to achieve the grill marks on all sides.

— 4 SERVINGS

EQUIPMENT: *A 5-quart (5 l) pasta pot fitted with a colander; a thick, clean kitchen towel; baking parchment; a panini grill.*

16 thin, fresh asparagus spears, woody ends trimmed
3 tablespoons coarse sea salt
Fine sea salt
Chive Oil (page 83)
Finely minced fresh chives, for garnish

1. To create an attractive presentation and allow for a convenient "handle" for picking up the asparagus with the fingers, lightly make a thin cut, or marker, into the flesh of the asparagus stalk with a sharp knife, about 1 inch from the bottom. Using the blade of the knife, carefully cut away the thick outer layer from the incision to the end of the stalk, to create a small handle.

2. Prepare a bowl of ice water. Fill the pasta pot with 3 quarts (3 l) water and bring to a rolling boil over high heat. Add the coarse sea salt and the asparagus and blanch, uncovered, for 2 minutes, counting from when the water comes back to a boil. Drain well. Immediately plunge the asparagus into the ice water for a minute or two to stop the cooking process. When the asparagus is chilled, transfer it to the kitchen towel to drain.

3. Cut off two pieces of baking parchment about the size of the panini grill. Place one piece of parchment on the bottom plate of the grill. Place the asparagus on top of the parchment and cover the asparagus with the second piece of parchment. Turn the grill to its highest setting, close the lid, and grill the asparagus until it begins to soften, and clear, golden grill marks are visible, about 3 minutes.

4. Remove the asparagus from the grill, transfer to salad plates, and season with fine sea salt and a showering of chive oil and minced chives. Serve.

Grilled Eggplant Slices
with Asian Sauce and Scallions

Years ago I traded my classic toaster for a panini grill, a super-user-friendly and versatile kitchen tool now on my list of essential kitchen equipment that I could not do without! I use it daily for grilling breads, sandwiches, and vegetables, such as eggplant and asparagus. Grilling on one of these machines adds that hint of charcoal or perfectly toasted crust without all the fuss of an outdoor or stovetop grill, and without the extra fat. Plus, with the clever trick of sandwiching the grilled item in baking parchment, cleanup is a cinch. If you don't have a panini maker, use the baking parchment technique described below with a stovetop grill plate, weighing down the food with a heavy skillet. You will need to turn the vegetables during cooking, however, to achieve the grill marks on all sides.

— 4 SERVINGS

EQUIPMENT: *Baking parchment; a panini grill.*

1 medium eggplant, rinsed
1 tablespoon Sweet and Spicy Dipping Sauce (page 430)
Fine sea salt
1 scallion, sliced on the diagonal

1. Cut the eggplant lengthwise into 1/4-inch (5 mm) slices.

2. Cut off two pieces of baking parchment about the size of the panini grill. Place one piece of the parchment on the bottom plate of the grill. Place the eggplant slices on top of the parchment. Cover with the second piece of parchment. Turn the grill to its highest setting and close the lid. Grill the

eggplant until it is softened, and clear, golden grill marks are visible, about 3 minutes.

3. Remove from the grill, transfer to salad plates, and season with salt and a splash of sweet and spicy dipping sauce. Sprinkle with the scallions and serve.

ROAST

Roasting is a dry, high-heat method of cooking in an oven. I differentiate between roasting and baking in part because roasting generally employs slightly higher oven temperatures, but also because it is a method applied to large cuts of meat, coated in oil, butter, or *ghee,* then deliciously caramelized as they cook.

Roasted vegetables take on a distinctive caramelized personality when cooked in this way, bringing out the natural sweetness of winter squash and carrots, dampening the sulfurous personality of broccoli and cauliflower, and transforming the flesh of eggplant into silk.

Anytime of year, but especially in the autumn and winter, I love roasted fruits: Their mild sweetness calls out for spices and a touch of honey. Favorites noted here include fresh figs, apples, pears, and plums.

Roasting Vegetables

There is no great secret to roasting vegetables; simply cut them into equal-size pieces for even cooking, toss in *ghee* or oil, season with sea salt, and roast in a tray that is not too crowded, at a temperature high enough to caramelize the sugars (over 330°F/165°C) until crispy edged and golden. The trick is to choose your vegetables wisely, those that can be transformed by the intense heat of a high-temperature oven: Brussels sprouts, broccoli, and cauliflower all become more nutty and sweet; the sweetness of caramelized beets and carrots blends perfectly with their earthy nature.

Roasted Autumn Rainbow Vegetables

4 TO 6 SIDE SERVINGS

EQUIPMENT: *2 roasting pans or rimmed baking sheets.*

2 pounds (1 kg) mixed autumn vegetables, such as:
> *Small heirloom beets (chiogga, yellow, or red), ends trimmed, greens and peel removed, quartered*
> *Winter squash, such as kabocha or acorn, peeled, seeded, and cut into 2-inch (5 cm) slices*
> *Heirloom carrots (yellow, orange, or Purple Haze), with green tops if organic, peeled or scrubbed, halved lengthways*
> *Turnips, with green tops if organic, halved or quartered*
> *Scallions or small whole spring onions, peeled*
> *Jerusalem artichokes, scrubbed and halved*

2 tablespoons Ghee (page 411), melted, or extra-virgin olive oil
Fine sea salt
6 Swiss chard leaves and stems
Lime Mayonnaise (page 98) and Tarragon Chimichurri Sauce (page 424), for serving

1. Evenly center two racks in the oven. Preheat the oven to 400°F (200°C).

2. Toss the vegetables with the *ghee* and season with salt. Set the Swiss chard aside.

3. Divide the vegetables (except the Swiss chard) evenly between the two roasting pans. (Avoid overcrowding the pan, as this creates moisture and

steams the vegetables rather than roasting them.) Roast for 25 minutes, stirring and turning the vegetables once or twice during cooking.

4. Add the Swiss chard and roast for 5 to 10 minutes, or until the vegetables are tender, caramelized, and brown on all sides and the Swiss chard is wilted. Serve with lime mayonnaise and tarragon chimichurri sauce.

Roasted Heirloom Carrots and Scallions with Cumin-Yogurt Dressing

We modern-day cooks are so very fortunate. With such an incredible abundance of vegetables within easy reach—especially the avalanche of colorful heirloom varieties—we have no excuse for not honoring these treasures. Here, those healthy, beautiful yellow, orange, and red rainbow carrots are slow-roasted in a not-too-hot oven, teamed up with baby spring onions or scallions and garlic, and tossed with the intense, rich flavor of *ghee*. A cumin-and-yogurt sauce helps boost flavors to their highest.

4 TO 6 SIDE SERVINGS

EQUIPMENT: *An electric spice mill; a large roasting pan or 2 rimmed baking sheets.*

12 medium carrots of various varieties, peeled and halved or quartered lengthwise, plus green tops for garnish (see Note)
12 scallions, including greens, outer layer removed
2 tablespoons Ghee (page 411), melted
Fine sea salt

CUMIN AND YOGURT DRESSING
1/4 cup plain, full-fat yogurt
1 plump, fresh garlic clove, halved, green germ removed if present, and finely minced
1/2 teaspoon fine sea salt
1 teaspoon cumin seeds

1. Center a rack in the oven. Preheat the oven to 325°F (165°C).

2. In a bowl, toss the carrots and scallions in the *ghee*. Arrange the vegetables in a single layer in the roasting pan or on the baking sheets. Season lightly

with salt. Roast the vegetables for about 45 minutes, turning the carrots over from time to time, until they are soft and golden and can be easily pierced with the tip of a knife.

3. PREPARE THE CUMIN AND YOGURT DRESSING: While the vegetables are roasting, combine the yogurt, garlic, and salt in a small bowl. Thin the mixture into a dressing with 3 to 4 tablespoons water. Refrigerate until serving time. Thin with more water at serving time if needed.

4. In a small saucepan, toast the cumin seeds over medium heat until fragrant, about 2 minutes. Transfer to a dish to cool, then grind to a fine powder in the spice mill.

5. Arrange the vegetables on a serving platter and scatter with the carrot tops. Serve with the dressing sprinkled with the toasted cumin.

NOTE: *Carrots are nutritionally robust, but a lot of their goodness can be found in or just under the skin, so if buying organic carrots, use a vegetable brush to clean the carrot's surface rather than peeling with a vegetable peeler.*

Roasted Broccoli with Lemon, Mustard, Garlic, and Chile Butter

Broccoli can often be a hard sell, especially when it's cooked to within an inch of its life, served soggy as a halfhearted attempt to add green to the plate. But with a little love and some strong heat, broccoli can be completely transformed, its sulfurous personality subdued as the sugars caramelize and the tips of the florets become golden and crispy. I once heard a Michelin-starred chef refer to the inner stalk of a broccoli as the *moelle*, or "marrow," of the broccoli, the most delicious part that should never be thrown away, and I couldn't agree more. The leaves, too, are quite delicious and should be cooked along with the florets.

— 4 SIDE SERVINGS ————————————————————————

EQUIPMENT: *A rimmed baking sheet.*

1 small broccoli head (about 1 pound/500 g)
4 tablespoons (60 g) Ghee (page 411), melted, or toasted sesame oil
Fine sea salt
1/4 cup (2 ounces/60 g) Lemon, Mustard, Garlic, and Chile Butter (page 77)
Hot red pepper flakes, for garnish

1. Center a rack in the oven. Preheat the oven to 400°F (200°C).

2. Trim the broccoli florets at the base of their stem and halve them lengthwise. Peel the large stem and slice it into 2 × 1/2-inch (5 × 1 cm) pieces. In a large bowl, toss the broccoli florets, stems, and leaves in the *ghee* until evenly coated and season with salt.

3. Spread the broccoli out onto the baking sheet, taking care not to overcrowd the pan, as this will cause the broccoli to steam and not roast.

4. Roast the broccoli until it is cooked through but gives some resistance when speared with a knife, 20 to 25 minutes, turning once during cooking. The broccoli should be golden and the edges of the stems and florets beginning to crisp.

5. Toss the broccoli with the lemon, mustard, garlic, and chile butter and garnish with hot red pepper flakes.

VARIATION: *For a different umami hit, drizzle with 2 tablespoons Anchoïade (page 100) or even a splash of fish sauce.*

Roasted Eggplant with Harissa, Fennel Seeds, and Honey

I find eggplant endlessly elegant and full of possibility, with its burnished purple skin, and creamy, meaty flesh. It grows in abundance in my garden in Provence, so I am always looking for new ways to bring out its best qualities. I find that eggplant responds excellently to intense heat, setting off its naturally smoky, earthy flavors. This version with *harissa*, fennel seeds, and honey is all at once heady, spicy, sweet, and aromatic, a worthy accompaniment for Grilled Leg of Lamb with Fresh Herbs (page 179), with perhaps a cooling splash of Garlic-Yogurt Sauce (page 425).

— 4 TO 6 SERVINGS ————————————————

EQUIPMENT: *An electric spice grinder; a roasting pan or a rimmed baking sheet.*

1-1/2 teaspoons fennel seeds
1-1/2 teaspoons Harissa (page 417)
1 plump, fresh garlic clove, halved lengthwise, green germ removed if present, and finely minced
1/2 teaspoon sea salt
1-1/2 teaspoons intensely flavored honey, such as mountain or buckwheat
6 tablespoons (100 ml) extra-virgin olive oil
1 large eggplant or 2 small, slender ones (about 1 pound/500 g)
Minced fresh flat-leaf parsley or mint, for garnish

1. Center a rack in the oven. Preheat the oven to 400°F (200°C).

2. In a small saucepan, toast the fennel seeds over medium heat until fragrant, about 2 minutes. Transfer to a dish to cool, then grind to a fine powder in the spice grinder.

3. In a large bowl, whisk the ground fennel seeds, *harissa*, garlic, salt, honey, and olive oil until well combined.

4. Trim the ends of the eggplant but do not peel. Slice in half lengthwise. Slice each half lengthwise into 5 slices, then crosswise into 4, to make bite-size pieces (remembering that they will reduce in size when they lose moisture during roasting). In a large bowl, combine the eggplant and the *harissa* dressing and toss to coat evenly.

5. Spread the dressed eggplant mixture evenly on the baking sheet, taking care not to crowd the pan, and roast until golden brown, 25 to 30 minutes. For even browning, toss the eggplant once or twice during roasting. Serve warm, garnished with parsley.

Honey-Roasted Squash with Mozzarella, Arugula Salad, and Tarragon Chimichurri

A touch of honey, the wholesome goodness of winter squash, a nice hit of pungent arugula, the sweet lactic flavors of mozzarella, and an exclamation point of tarragon *chimichurri* make this dish a winter winner. Acorn squash and the soft-skinned Japanese kabocha squash are ideal here, but butternut squash also works well.

— 4 SERVINGS ————————————————————————

EQUIPMENT: *A roasting pan or rimmed baking sheet.*

1 tablespoon extra-virgin olive oil, plus more as needed for the dressing
2 teaspoons honey
1 teaspoon balsamic vinegar
1/4 teaspoon sea salt, plus more as needed for the dressing
1 pound (500 g) winter squash, such as kabocha, acorn, or butternut, skins scrubbed (and peeled, if using acorn or butternut), cut into 1-inch (2.5 cm) slices
8 ounces (250 g) Italian buffalo-milk mozzarella
4 handfuls (about 2.5 ounces/75 g) fresh arugula
Tarragon Chimichurri Sauce (page 424), for serving

1. Center a rack in the oven. Preheat the oven to 400°F (200°C).

2. In a large bowl, mix together the olive oil, honey, vinegar, and salt. Add the squash and toss to coat.

3. Spread the squash on the roasting pan or baking sheet, making sure not to overcrowd the pan, as this steams the vegetables rather than roasting them. Roast for about 20 minutes, or until the squash is soft, turning it once during cooking.

4. Tear the mozzarella into bite-size pieces. Dress the arugula lightly with olive oil and season with salt.

5. Assemble as a platter or on individual dishes, starting with a bed of arugula, then slices of roasted squash, mozzarella bites, and generous dollops of tarragon chimichurri sauce.

Whole Roasted Cauliflower
with Tarragon and Lime Butter

Ever since I began roasting this favorite wintertime vegetable whole, I don't want to eat it any other way. Flavors here are earthy, smoky, and well developed, taking well to the forward, vibrant flavors of tarragon and lime.

— 6 TO 8 SERVINGS

EQUIPMENT: *An 8-quart (8 l) pasta pot fitted with a colander; a small roasting pan.*

3 tablespoons coarse sea salt
1 medium cauliflower head (under 2 pounds/1 kg), including leaves and stalks
Extra-virgin olive oil
Fine sea salt
Coarse, freshly ground black pepper
Minced fresh parsley, for garnish
Tarragon and Lime Butter (page 78), for serving

1. Center a rack in the oven. Preheat the oven to 450°F (230°C).

2. In the pasta pot, bring 6 quarts (6 l) water to a rolling boil over high heat. Add the coarse sea salt. Place the whole cauliflower in the colander, insert into the boiling water, and blanch, uncovered, for 5 to 6 minutes, or until a sharp knife easily pierces the cauliflower. Remove the colander from the pasta pot, set in a sink, and rinse under cold running water for several minutes to stop the cooking process. (This can be done several hours in advance.)

3. Pat the cauliflower dry with paper towels or a clean kitchen towel and place it in the roasting pan. Drizzle lightly with olive oil, season with fine sea salt

and pepper, and roast until the cauliflower is nicely browned all over, 40 to 50 minutes.

4. Transfer the cauliflower to a serving platter, garnish with parsley, and cut into wedges. Serve with tarragon and lime butter.

Roasted Cubed Eggplant

When roasted, eggplant expresses an entirely new personality, bringing out its rich, smoky flavors and silken texture. This summertime favorite is a key element in the dish Chicken with Eggplant, Chickpeas, Pine Nuts, and Garlic-Yogurt Sauce (page 232) or can be served simply with garlic-yogurt sauce, an asian dipping sauce, or hummus.

— 6 SERVINGS —

EQUIPMENT: *A large roasting pan or 2 rimmed baking sheets.*

2 medium eggplants (about 1-1/2 pounds/750 g total)
3 tablespoons extra-virgin olive oil
1 teaspoon fine sea salt
Garlic-Yogurt Sauce (page 232), Asian Dipping Sauce (pages 428–431), or
  Hummus (page 418; optional)

1. Evenly center two racks in the oven. Preheat the oven to 400°F (200°C).

2. Trim the ends of each eggplant but do not peel them. Cut each eggplant lengthwise in half. Cut each half into 4 lengthwise pieces, then cut each of the 8 pieces crosswise to create 2-inch (5 cm) cubes.

3. In a large bowl, toss the eggplant with the olive oil and salt until well coated. Arrange the eggplant in a single layer in the roasting pan or divide between two if using two smaller baking sheets, leaving space between each cube to make sure the eggplant roasts rather than steams. Roast until the white flesh of the eggplant is golden, 25 to 30 minutes, swapping the baking sheet from top to bottom and back to front, if necessary, for even roasting.

4. Serve immediately on its own or accompanied by garlic-yogurt sauce, an asian dipping sauce, or *hummus*.

Roasting Poultry and Meat

As a general rule, meat should be seared first, either on the stovetop or for a short time at a very high temperature in the oven, then left to roast in its own juices. Poultry, which already has a nice layer of fat beneath its skin, does not need to be seared before roasting. See the tips below for more specifics.

Tips

~ Bring poultry and meat to room temperature before putting them in the oven.

~ Never season poultry or meat in the roasting pan, as excess salt can make the meat juices overly salty.

~ Searing meat at a very high oven temperature for 10 to 20 minutes (depending on the size of the meat) at the beginning of the cooking time will brown the meat, caramelizing the sugars and amino acids.

~ Rotate the meat during roasting to encourage juices and for even cooking.

~ It is worth using an instant-read thermometer to measure the internal temperature of the poultry and meat. There is nothing more frustrating than cutting into a piece of poultry or meat and having to return it to the oven, or more disappointing than discovering that it is dried out or overcooked.

~ DEGLAZING THE PAN: When your poultry or meat has finished roasting and has been removed from the heat and covered to rest, place the roasting pan with the meat juices over medium heat, scraping up any caramelized bits that cling to the bottom. Cook for 2 to 3 minutes (depending on the amount of cooking juices you have), scraping and stirring until the liquid is almost caramelized. Do not let it burn. Spoon off and discard any excess fat. Add several tablespoons cold water to deglaze (hot water will cloud the sauce). Bring to a boil. Reduce the heat to low and simmer until thickened, about 5 minutes. Transfer to a sauce boat for serving or pour directly over the meat or poultry.

~ An instant-read thermometer can be helpful. Though I do not like to rely on it exclusively, I use temperature as a doneness guideline. But nothing can replace past experience, which is why I like to make the recipes in my repertoire over and over again, perfecting them.

Roasted Lemon and Thyme Chicken

Ask twenty cooks how they roast a chicken and you are likely to get twenty different answers. Brine it, marinate it, salt it days before, don't season it at all before cooking, turn it, don't turn it, season it after cooking, let it rest, start it in a cold oven, roast at very high heat, and so on, and so on. For decades, I have been very happy with the method shared with me by chef Joël Robuchon when we were working on the book *Simply French*.

Tips

Here are some of Joël Robuchon's tips, keeping in mind that the most important tip is top-quality free-range poultry, the best you can find:

~ Roast in a fairly hot oven, 425°F (220°C). Any hotter, and the chicken could dry out. Any cooler, and the skin may not crisp up properly.

~ Just before roasting, rub the skin with butter, then season inside and out with salt and pepper. (Chef Robuchon did say it was even better to salt and pepper after about 10 minutes in the oven—when the skin was beginning to seize and brown and thus would most benefit from seasoning—but admitted that most cooks would forget to do this!)

~ Truss the bird so it roasts evenly. Trussing makes for a moister bird.

~ Begin roasting the chicken on one side for 20 minutes, turn to the other side for 20 minutes, then roast breast side up for the final 20 minutes. This ensures an evenly moist bird.

~ Remove the finished bird from the oven and let it rest upside down, with its tail in the air. This lets the flavorful juices flow back into the chicken.

EQUIPMENT: *Kitchen twine; an oval roasting pan, just slightly larger than the chicken (about 9 × 13 inches/23 × 33 cm) fitted with a roasting rack; a fine-mesh sieve; an ovenproof platter; a warmed platter.*

1 chicken (about 5 pounds/2.5 kg), with giblets, free-range
Fine sea salt
Coarse, freshly ground black pepper
2 organic lemons, scrubbed, dried, and quartered lengthwise
A bunch of fresh thyme
2 tablespoons unsalted butter, at room temperature
6 onions, halved (do not peel)

1. Center a rack in the oven. Preheat the oven to 425°F (220°C).

2. Generously season the cavity of the chicken with salt and pepper. Place the gizzard in the cavity. (Reserve the heart and liver for Seared Chicken Hearts and Livers with Fresh Thyme, page 128.) Squeeze the lemons, adding the juice and the squeezed rinds to the cavity. Add the thyme to the cavity as well. Truss the bird with kitchen twine (see sidebar, page 208). Rub the skin of the chicken with the butter. Season all over with salt and pepper.

3. Place the onions, cut side down, in the roasting pan.

4. Insert the roasting rack into the pan over the onions, arranging the chicken on its side on the rack. Pour 1 cup (250 ml) water into the bottom of the pan to help create a rich and pleasing sauce. (Check the pan from time to time during cooking and replenish the water if it begins to dry out.)

5. Place the pan in the oven and roast, uncovered, for a total of about 1 hour, 15 minutes. During this time, rotate the chicken at 20-minute intervals,

first turning the chicken onto its other side, then breast side up. By this time, the skin should be a deep golden color.

6. After 1 hour of total cooking time, reduce the oven temperature to 375°F (190°C) and roast until the juices run clear when you pierce a thigh with a skewer, or an instant-read thermometer inserted into the thickest part of the thigh but not touching the bone reads 165°F (74°C), about 15 minutes more.

7. Remove the chicken from the oven and generously season it with salt and pepper. Transfer it to an ovenproof platter and arrange at an angle against the edge of an inverted shallow bowl, with its head down and tail in the air, to let the juices flow toward the breast meat, giving a more juicy and flavorful result. Tent loosely with aluminum foil. Turn off the oven and place the overproof platter in the oven with the door open. Let rest for at least 10 minutes and up to 30 minutes. The chicken will continue to cook during this resting time.

8. Meanwhile, prepare the sauce: Place the roasting pan over medium heat, scraping up any bits that cling to the bottom. Cook for 2 to 3 minutes, scraping and stirring until the liquid is almost caramelized, but do not let it burn. Spoon off and discard any excess fat. Add several tablespoons cold water to deglaze (hot water will cloud the sauce). Bring to a boil, reduce the heat to low, and simmer until thickened, about 5 minutes.

9. After the chicken has rested and the sauce is cooking, snip away the kitchen twine with scissors and remove the lemons from the cavity. Carve the chicken into serving pieces and transfer to the warmed platter. Squeeze the remaining juice from the lemons over the pieces of poultry, extracting as much juice as possible.

10. Strain the pan sauce through a fine-mesh sieve and pour half over the platter of chicken. Pour the rest into a sauceboat for serving. Serve immediately.

Trussing Poultry

I find that students are always amazed and intrigued as I demonstrate the art of trussing poultry. The fact that most of our farm-fresh chickens in France come with the head and feet intact also shocks most. Keeping the head and feet intact assures the freshness of the poultry, and though the head has no culinary appeal, carefully manicured feet (I give them a pedicure) have a great deal of gelatin and help make delicious, gelatinous stocks.

All that aside, the art of trussing is simple, and once mastered, will ensure that your roasted birds cook evenly, and that the meat, breast meat especially, remains moist and does not dry out. To me, even more important is that a trussed bird simply has greater visual appeal over an untrussed bird that looks as though its legs are flailing in the air.

There are many trussing methods, and here is mine:

1. Clear a counter space and set it up with the utensils you will need: a piece of kitchen twine about 5 feet (150 cm) long, salt, pepper, and any ingredients needed for stuffing the bird. Season and stuff the bird as directed in the recipe.
2. Place the bird on the counter with the legs facing you. Tuck the wings behind the bird's back.
3. Bring the bird's legs together and, using the center of the twine, wrap the twine twice around the bird's ankles, binding them tightly.
4. Drape the ends of the twine over the bird where the thighs meet the breast. Flip the bird over and crisscross the twine on the bird's back, tying the wings. Make a double knot and cut off any excess string. Flip the bird again and continue with the recipe.

Roasted Turkey, French-Style

I love my Parisian butcher, Antoine Guilhien of Boucherie du Bac in the 7th *arrondissement,* for he never, ever lets me down with the quality of his meat and poultry or with his cooking and roasting advice. One Christmas I ordered a smallish turkey from him (it weighed just under 10 pounds, or 4.3 kg, to be exact) and followed his advice to the letter, resulting in one of the best-cooked festive birds I've ever had. Here are some tips. (The same procedure can be used for a larger turkey.)

Tips

~ Be sure to cover the breast portion of the turkey with caul fat, so the breast does not dry out in roasting. (Caul fat can be purchased from most butchers, though it may need to be ordered in advance.)

~ Preheat the oven to the highest possible temperature. Mine will soar to 500°F (260°C). This will help create a good crust on the skin of the bird and help it remain moist when it later roasts at a lower temperature.

~ After 30 minutes of roasting at the highest temperature, reduce the oven temperature to 350°F (180°C) and continue roasting for 15 minutes per pound (500 g).

— 6 TO 8 SERVINGS —————————————————————————

EQUIPMENT: *Kitchen twine; an oval roasting pan just slightly larger than the turkey (about 9 × 13 inches; 23 × 33 cm) fitted with a roasting rack; a fine-mesh sieve.*

1 turkey (about 10 pounds/4.3 kg), with giblets, free-range
Fine sea salt
Coarse, freshly ground black pepper

(Ingredients continue)

2 organic lemons, halved crosswise

1 bunch fresh thyme

1 piece caul fat large enough to cover the breast of the turkey

2 tablespoons unsalted butter, at room temperature

10 shallots, umpeeled, halved lengthwise

1 bunch fresh parsley

4 bay leaves

1. Center a rack in the bottom third of the oven. Preheat the oven to its highest possible temperature, ideally 500°F (260°C).

2. Generously season the cavity of the turkey with salt and pepper. Place the giblets, lemons, and thyme in the cavity. Truss the turkey with kitchen twine (see sidebar, page 208). Also using the kitchen twine, tie the caul fat to the bird, covering the breast. Rub the caul fat and the remaining exposed skin of the turkey with the butter. Season all over with salt and pepper.

3. Place the shallots cut side down in the roasting pan. Add the parsley and bay leaves.

4. Set the roasting rack in the roasting pan, over the shallots, and place the turkey breast side up on the roasting rack. Pour 2 cups (500 ml) water into the bottom of the pan to help create a rich and pleasing sauce.

5. Roast, uncovered, for 30 minutes. Reduce the oven temperature to 350°F (180°C) and roast for a further 15 minutes per pound (500 g), for a total roasting time of 2-1/2 hours for a 10-pound (4.3 kg) bird, or until the juices run clear when a thigh is pierced with a sharp knife or skewer, or an instant-read thermometer inserted into the thickest part of the thigh, but not touching the bone, reaches 165°F (75°C).

6. Season the turkey generously with salt and pepper. Remove and discard the twine. Transfer the turkey to a platter and tent it loosely with foil. Let the

bird rest at least 10 minutes and up to 30 minutes. The turkey will continue to cook during this resting time.

7. Meanwhile, prepare the sauce: Place the roasting pan over medium heat, scraping up any bits that cling to the bottom. Cook for 2 to 3 minutes, scraping and stirring until the liquid is almost caramelized, but do not let it burn. Spoon off and discard any excess fat. Add several tablespoons cold water to deglaze (hot water will cloud the sauce). Bring to a boil, reduce the heat to low, and simmer until thickened, about 5 minutes.

8. While the sauce is cooking, carve the turkey into serving pieces and transfer to a warmed platter. Strain the sauce through a fine-mesh sieve and pour half over the turkey. Transfer the rest to a sauceboat for serving. Serve immediately.

WINE MATCH: *Any young "GS" (Grenache, Syrah) wine from the southern Rhône is my choice here. Try the Vacqueyras from Famille Perrin, a dazzling red that's 75 percent Grenache, 25 percent Syrah—a winning combination.*

Roasted Beef Rib-Eye Steak
with Tarragon Chimichurri

Johan Neveux is a young and energetic butcher whose extraordinary selection of meat, especially beef, at Paris's President Wilson market, is one I have admired for years. During one market visit I simply could not resist a thick, gorgeous, well-marbled *côte de boeuf*. Johan insisted that the best way to cook the beef was to simply sear it, then roast it. I followed his instructions diligently and did not regret it.

— 4 TO 6 SERVINGS

EQUIPMENT: *A seasoned cast-iron skillet with ovenproof handles or a roasting pan, both large enough to snugly hold the meat; an instant-read thermometer (optional).*

1 bone-in beef rib-eye steak (about 2 pounds/1 kg), about 1-1/2 inches (3 cm) thick
Coarse sea salt
Coarse, freshly ground black pepper
Lemon wedges, Tarragon Chimichurri Sauce (page 424), or compound butters (pages 77–80), for serving
"Cold-Fry" Frites (page 167), for serving

1. Remove the meat from the refrigerator at least 4 hours before cooking. This will help it cook more evenly and prevent the meat from steaming as it roasts.

2. Center a rack in the oven. Preheat the oven 475°F (245°C).

3. Dry the meat with paper towels to prevent it from sticking to the pan and to maximize the Maillard reaction (see page 123). Generously season the

meat on both sides with coarse sea salt. Preheat the skillet over high heat for 2 minutes. Add the meat and sear for about 4 minutes on each side. Be patient; do not turn the meat too early, as it will actually stick until the Maillard reaction kicks in.

4. Just before placing the meat in the oven, reduce the oven temperature to 400°F (200°C).

5. Place the skillet in the oven (or if the skillet does not have ovenproof handles, transfer the meat to a roasting pan). Roast the meat for 15 minutes per pound (500 g) for rare, and 20 minutes per pound (500 g) for medium-rare. (If you use an instant-read thermometer, the temperature should range from 125°F/55°C for rare to 155°F/68°C for well-done.)

6. Remove the meat from the oven. To prevent the steak from stewing in its own juices, arrange the meat against an inverted shallow bowl on a cutting board. Season both sides once again with salt and pepper. Set the steak at an angle against the inverted bowl to rest and tent very loosely with foil to prevent the surface from cooling off too quickly. As the muscle fibers relax they reabsorb the juices expelled during the cooking process, resulting in a much juicier and flavorful steak. The angle of the steak helps to retain the juices while protecting the seared crust from becoming soggy. Let the meat rest for 10 minutes.

7. To serve, carefully cut away the bone and carve against the grain into thick slices. Serve with lemon wedges, tarragon chimichurri sauce, or the compound butter of your choice, and "cold-fry" frites.

WINE MATCH: *Dig into your cellar to find a big red to serve here—a 100 percent Syrah should do the trick!*

Roasting Fruit

Roasting caramelizes the sugars in fruits as it does with vegetables, making this a great technique to draw out sweeter flavors when nature falls short. Sweet, sticky roasted summer fruits like apricots, plums, and peaches are easily paired with a fragrant sorbet for a homely but rewarding dessert.

Roasted Thyme-Infused Figs
with Roasted Fig Sorbet

One day as I was creating a roasted fig sorbet, I lifted the colorful, fragrant whole figs from the oven and realized that the perfect accompaniment to this soon-to-be-frozen dessert would be the whole roasted fruits themselves, served warm alongside the sorbet. The contrasting temperatures bring out such different notes in the fruit, providing a sort of fig flavor spectrum.

Figs are not the only fruit that works beautifully with this master preparation. Try also red and purple plums, a mix of winter fruits that might include sliced apples, pears, and quince, or peaches and apricots in the summer months.

— 6 SERVINGS

EQUIPMENT: *A rectangular porcelain baking dish, about 8 × 12 inches (20 × 30 cm); a blender or a food processor; an ice cream maker; 6 ice cream bowls, chilled in the freezer.*

2 pounds (1 kg) fresh figs, stems trimmed
6 tablespoons (75 g) vanilla-scented unrefined cane sugar (see page 441)
Grated zest of 1 organic lemon
1 teaspoon fresh thyme leaves
2 tablespoons sweet red wine, such as port or a vin doux naturel from Rasteau
1 cup (250 g) plain Greek-style whole-milk yogurt
2 tablespoons Invert Sugar Syrup (page 438) or light corn syrup

I. Center a rack in the oven. Preheat the oven to 400°F (200°C).

2. Cut an X in the top of each fig and gently squeeze from the bottom to open the fruit like a flower. Arrange the figs, cut side up and side by side, in the baking dish. Scatter the sugar, lemon zest, thyme, and wine over the figs.

3. Roast, uncovered, until hot and bubbling, about 30 minutes.

4. Set aside half the figs to serve whole. Transfer the other half to a container and refrigerate until thoroughly chilled.

5. At serving time, combine the chilled roasted figs and their liquid, the yogurt, and the syrup in the blender or food processor and puree. Transfer the mixture to the ice cream maker and freeze according to the manufacturer's instructions. For best results, serve the sorbet in well-chilled ice cream bowls as soon as it is frozen. Do not refreeze. Warm the whole figs and their juices and serve in shallow bowls with a generous scoop of the sorbet.

VARIATIONS

ROASTED PLUMS WITH VANILLA AND STAR ANISE

In place of the figs, use 10 red plums and 10 purple plums (about 2 pounds or 1 kg of each), halved, pitted, and roasted as directed, seasoning the plums lightly with Vanilla Powder (page 442), 2 whole star anise, grated zest of half an organic orange, and 2 tablespoons crème de cassis (blackcurrant liqueur). From step 3, follow the instructions for the sorbet and serving.

ROASTED APPLES AND PEARS WITH BEAUMES-DE-VENISE AND HONEY

In place of the figs, use 2 red winter apples (cored and cut into 8 wedges), 4 red pears (quartered lengthwise, cored, and each quarter halved), the grated zest of 2 organic oranges, 6 tablespoons honey, and 2 tablespoons Beaumes-de-Venise or other sweet wine. From step 3, follow the instructions for the sorbet and serving.

Chicken with Eggplant, Chickpeas, Pine Nuts,
and Garlic-Yogurt Sauce (page 232)

BRAISE

Braise, stew, *fricassée, daube*—these are all slight variations on a theme, which is, at its most essential, cooking at a low temperature in liquid for long periods of time (except for chicken and very tender cuts, which dry out with long cooking times).

Braising meat, poultry, and fish involves searing over high heat to create a flavorful caramelized crust (traditionally this is not always called for in braising recipes, but I never braise without searing first; food simply tastes better that way). Dishes are often set over a bed of diced vegetables, covered (partially or in the case of stews fully) with liquid (usually strong stock, sometimes with wine or tomato sauce added), and cooked over a low heat until tender. It is slow cooking at its best, a wonderful technique to master for the short days and long nights of winter, allowing your meat to tenderize over several hours in a flavorful broth, until it falls off the bone. It's a fabulous way to feed lots of people—after the initial attention to detail of searing, the liquid does all the work as it bubbles away, so you can make large quantities to feed big families and lots of friends without having to spend hours over the stove. And cheaper cuts of meat lend themselves best to slow cooking, so feeding the hordes does not break the bank.

Tips

~ The key to braising meat is the liquefying of the collagen in the meat, adding flavor and a silky texture. This happens at about 160°F

(70°C), but it's a slow process—time, patience, and a low temperature yield the best results.

~ Look for meat and poultry cuts with lots of collagen-containing connective tissue. Bone-in is also most desirable, for it gives the most flavor.
    PORK: Shoulder, picnic ham, bone-in pork loin
    BEEF: Shoulder or "chuck," brisket, rump
    LAMB: Shoulder
    CHICKEN: Thighs and drumsticks or whole chickens, cut up

~ The ideal braising vessel is a cast-iron pot in which the ingredients fit snugly (you cannot go wrong with Le Creuset).

~ Sear the meat or poultry before braising in a pot with a little fat or oil. Make sure the pot is hot before the meat goes in. Work in batches so as not to crowd the pot, and do not move the ingredients around too much, letting the meat and poultry form a nice, dark, uniform crust.

~ Cooking bone side down helps stabilize the position of the meat, and fat side up allows the fat to evenly melt into the meat and the sauce, effectively self-basting.

~ The braising liquid gives a good deal of flavor to a braise, so it is important to pay attention to the quality of the liquid—usually wine or stock—that you use.

~ Particularly for meat, a low heat is essential, and enough time to let the meat slowly tenderize to the point where it can almost be cut with a spoon.

~ Never allow the liquid to boil, as this will toughen the fibers of the meat: Start the braise off at a gentle simmer, with the lid off. Then cover with the lid. Beginning the braise at a low temperature will help retain the color of the ingredients, even after they have finished cooking.

~ Keep an eye on the amount of cooking liquid and top it off if it gets too low. Having the proper-size vessel, in which the braising food is snug, will help retain the cooking liquid. Too large a pot will encourage the cooking liquid to evaporate too quickly, totally negating the technique.

~ Always let the meat rest for at least 10 to 15 minutes before serving to allow the braising liquids to be reabsorbed into the meat.

~ In some cases, once the meat or poultry has finished braising, the cooking liquid may need to be reduced into a thicker sauce.

~ Braised dishes benefit from being prepared in advance—flavors can develop nicely over a day or two—and the dish can easily be reheated at serving time. Remove the solidified fat from the sauce before reheating.

~ Do as all good cooks do: Taste, taste, taste along the way. This is particularly important when cooking any ingredient for a long time, since the provenance and quality of an ingredient can vastly affect the perfect cooking time. Let your palate be the judge, not a kitchen timer.

Braised Meats

Four-Hour Aromatic Braised Pork

This is a classic blueprint for braising a medium-size cut of meat. You can sub in pork, lamb, or beef shoulder here or any other bone-in meat cut with lots of connective tissue. This recipe has an Asian flair with the ginger, soy, sesame paste, and hint of spice, but really you can flavor the braising liquid any way you like, substituting wine, stock, or canned tomatoes; just keep the total amount of liquid relatively the same as in the master recipe. Swap the Asian ingredients for whatever spices take your fancy, such as lamb seasoned with cumin and cinnamon along with some preserved lemon for a Moroccan twist.

One could prepare this warming braised pork just to enjoy the spicy, fragrant aromas that fill the kitchen as it cooks. I love it right from the oven, and the fact that it usually leaves some welcome leftovers, giving me a day off in the kitchen!

8 SERVINGS

EQUIPMENT: *A 4-quart (4 l) cast-iron pot with a lid; a baster; a fine-mesh sieve; a warmed serving platter.*

3 pounds (1.5 kg) bone-in pork loin roast (do not trim off the fat), trussed in kitchen twine
Fine sea salt
Coarse, freshly ground black pepper
1/4 cup (60 ml) extra-virgin olive oil

(Ingredients continue)

3 tablespoons julienne of fresh ginger

12 large shallots, peeled but left whole

12 plump, fresh garlic cloves, peeled but left whole

3 whole star anise

1/4 cup (60 ml) organic soy sauce

2 teaspoons intensely flavored honey, such as mountain or buckwheat

2 tablespoons tahini (sesame paste) or peanut butter

1 tablespoon brown rice vinegar

1/2 teaspoon hot red pepper flakes

Crunchy Jasmine Rice (page 434), for serving

1. About 3 hours before cooking the pork, remove the meat from the refrigerator and let it come to room temperature. This will ensure more even cooking.

2. Position a rack in the bottom third of the oven. Preheat the oven to 275°F (135°C).

3. Generously season the pork all over with salt and pepper. In the pot, heat the olive oil over medium heat until shimmering. Add the pork and sear well on all sides, about 10 minutes total. Transfer the pork to a platter.

4. To the fat remaining in the pot, add the ginger, shallots, garlic, star anise, soy sauce, honey, tahini, vinegar, and red pepper flakes. Cook over low heat until fragrant, 3 to 4 minutes. Taste for seasoning. Add 1-1/3 cups (330 ml) water and cook for 2 minutes more. Return the pork to the pot with the fat side up and bone side down.

5. Cover the pot, place it in the oven, and braise, basting the pork with the braising liquid about every 30 minutes and rotating it from time to time, until the meat is just about falling off the bone, at least 4 hours and up to 8 hours.

6. Carefully transfer the meat to a carving board. Tent it loosely with aluminum foil and set it aside to rest for about 15 minutes.

7. While the pork is resting, strain the cooking juices through the fine-mesh sieve into a serving bowl, scooping off the fat that rises to the top. Discard the star anise but set aside the shallots and garlic to serve with the roast. Remove and discard the twine that was holding the pork together. With two forks, shred the meat and place on the warmed platter, passing the sauce. Serve with crunchy jasmine rice.

MAKE-AHEAD NOTE: *Make this a day or two in advance and store in the refrigerator or freeze for up to 1 month.*

WINE MATCH: *This spicy braise calls out for a sturdy white, such as a rare Châteauneuf-du-Pape. Favorites include offerings from Domaine Marcoux, Raymond Usseglio, and Patrice Magni.*

✦   What to Do with Leftovers?   ✦

Don't shy away from making this recipe if you are cooking for fewer than six people. The leftover pork can be transformed into all sorts of wonderful dishes, since it easily lends itself to reheating. Reserve some of the cooking juices, sear the pork over high heat for a minute on each side, add a few more tablespoons of the marinade, and cook until it has reduced to a thick sauce. Serve with Crunchy Jasmine Rice (page 434) and Roasted Cubed Eggplant (page 202), garnished with sliced scallions. Or serve reheated with steamed Chinese *bao* (buns) or Peking duck pancakes, Lime Mayonnaise (page 98), pickled carrots, and fresh mint leaves.

Four-Hour Citrus-Braised Lamb Shoulder with Star Anise and Cumin

I sampled this unforgettable braised lamb shoulder on my first visit to the ultra-popular Parisian brasserie Lazare. At home, it's become a favorite: The lamb is boldly seasoned with star anise, lemon, oranges, garlic, and toasted cumin, then braised until it's super tender and falling off the bone. I often serve it with a giant bowl of *épeautre* (Provençal wheat berries).

Note that the lamb marinates for 24 hours before braising, so plan accordingly.

— 8 SERVINGS

EQUIPMENT: *A 6-quart (6 l) cast-iron pot with a lid; 8 warmed dinner plates.*

MARINADE

2 teaspoons cumin seeds

2 onions, peeled, halved lengthwise, and cut into thin half-moons

2 organic lemons, ends trimmed and discarded, cut crosswise into thin slices

2 organic oranges, ends trimmed and discarded, cut crosswise into thin slices

2 garlic heads, cloves peeled but left whole

4 bay leaves, crushed

10 whole star anise

1 cup (250 ml) extra-virgin olive oil

1 quart (1 l) Chicken Stock (page 402)

LAMB

1 bone-in lamb shoulder (about 4 pounds/2 kg), trimmed of fat, at room temperature

Fine sea salt

Coarse, freshly ground black pepper

Cooked épeautre *(Provençal wheat berries), for serving*

1. PREPARE THE MARINADE: In a small skillet, toast the cumin seeds over medium heat until fragrant, about 2 minutes. Transfer to a dish to cool.

2. In a large bowl, combine the marinade ingredients. Place the lamb in a bowl large enough to hold it easily. Pour the marinade over the lamb, turning the meat over to distribute the marinade evenly. Cover the bowl and refrigerate for 24 hours, turning the lamb at least once.

3. Remove the lamb from the marinade and transfer it to a platter. Season the meat all over with salt and pepper. Pour several tablespoons of the marinade into the pot. Heat the liquid over medium heat until hot but not smoking. Add the lamb and sear well on both sides, 3 to 4 minutes per side. Transfer the lamb to the platter and season it liberally with salt and pepper.

4. Return the lamb and the marinade to the pot, cover, and place over the lowest possible heat, braising until the meat is tender and falling off the bone, about 4 hours. Baste the lamb with the braising liquid about every 30 minutes, turning the meat each time.

5. When the lamb is very tender and falling off the bone, taste the liquid for seasoning and add salt or pepper as needed. Remove and discard the bay leaves and star anise. Transfer the lamb to a platter and cut into thick slices. Serve on the warmed dinner plates dressing with the sauce, citrus, onions, and garlic, with the *épeautre* alongside.

MAKE-AHEAD NOTE: *The lamb can be prepared up to 3 days in advance and stored in an airtight container in the refrigerator.*

WINE MATCH: *Red, red, and more red, such as a simple Côtes-du-Rhône from the very serious and talented winemaker Gilles Ferran. His showstopping Rasteau Heritage 1924 (from grenache grapes planted—guess when—in 1924) loves to be paired with this spicy, warming lamb daube.*

Provençal Lamb Daube
with Olives, Mushrooms, and Tomatoes

Stéphane Raymond, our butcher in Provence, offered this *daube* in his prepared foods case one winter weekend. It looked delicious, and having no time to prepare dinner that evening, I took home a portion. It was so fantastic that I begged for the recipe the next day, and now I can share it with you. Make this a few days in advance for a deeply flavorful braise that can be served with rice or *èpeautre (*Provençal wheat berries) and shared among friends. It can also be prepared with beef, using two or three different cuts of meat, choosing from the top or bottom round, head of round, shoulder, or shoulder blade, neck, or short ribs.

—— 8 SERVINGS ——————————————————————————————

EQUIPMENT: *A 6-quart (6 l) cast-iron pot with a lid; 6 warmed bowls.*

3 tablespoons extra-virgin olive oil

About 4 pounds (2 kg) boneless lamb shoulder (see Note), cut into 3-ounce (90 g) pieces (about 2 x 3 inches/5 x 7.5 cm), at room temperature

Fine sea salt

Coarse, freshly ground black pepper

2 bottles (750 ml each) dry white wine (such as a young Chardonnay)

Several fresh oregano, rosemary, and thyme sprigs

Several bay leaves

Two 14-ounce (400 g) cans diced Italian tomatoes in their juice

1 pound (500 g) fresh mushrooms, rinsed, trimmed, and cut lengthwise into thick slices

1/2 cup (125 ml) best-quality cured black olives, pitted and halved

Fresh herbs, such as minced parsley, rosemary, or oregano, for garnish

Cooked rice or épeautre (Provençal wheat berries), for serving (optional)

1. In the pot, heat the olive oil over medium-high heat until shimmering. Reduce the heat to medium and add several pieces of the lamb, searing on all sides. Do not crowd the pan, and be patient: Good browning is essential to achieve depth of flavor. Continue to sear the meat in batches, about 5 minutes per batch. Use tongs (to avoid piercing the meat) to transfer the seared lamb to a platter. Immediately season generously with salt and pepper.

2. Return all the lamb to the pot. Add the wine, herbs, bay leaves, tomatoes, mushrooms, and olives, cover, and braise at a gentle simmer over low heat until the meat is very tender, 1 to 1-1/2 hours. Taste the *daube* from time to time; adjust the seasoning and check the doneness of the meat. Braise too briefly and the meat will be tough; too long, and the meat could become oversaturated and watery. Let your palate be your guide.

3. Serve in the warmed bowls, garnish with herbs, and accompany, if desired, by rice or grains such as *èpeautre*.

MAKE-AHEAD NOTE: *Like all braised meat dishes, this one actually benefits from being prepared a day or two in advance and then refrigerated. Before reheating, skim off and discard any fat that may have risen to the surface.*
WINE MATCH: *Why not try our very own peppery red Côtes-du-Rhône, Clos Chanteduc? It's largely a blend of Grenache and Syrah, with many of the vines dating from the 1950s.*

Provençal Beef Daube

This is my classic winter Provençal beef *daube,* one I make when the sun is shining in December and I can relax by a roaring fire in the kitchen fireplace as the fragrant *daube* quietly works its magic. And when a local hunter supplies the meat, I also prepare this *daube* with tender baby boar known as *marcassin.* (We have lots on our property that are constantly trying to raid my vegetable garden!). Use at least three cuts of meat for greater depth of flavor and varied textures. Another trick is to flame the wine once the meat is browned and the wine has been added. Flaming creates the Maillard reaction (see page 123) and will help intensify the final flavors.

──── 8 TO 12 SERVINGS ────────────────────────

EQUIPMENT: *A 6 quart (6 l) cast-iron pot with a lid; matches.*

1/4 cup (60 ml) extra-virgin olive oil
4 pounds (2 kg) varied cuts of beef (see Note), cut into 3-ounce (90 g) pieces (about
  2 × 3 inches/5 × 7.5 cm), at room temperature
Fine sea salt
Coarse, freshly ground black pepper
2 bottles (750 ml each) hearty red wine, such as a Côtes-du-Rhône
1-1/2 quarts (1.5 l) Chicken Stock (page 402)
4 large onions, peeled, halved crosswise, and cut into thin rings
1 plump, fresh garlic head, peeled, halved, green germ removed if present
6 carrots, peeled and cut into thick rounds
4 bay leaves, crushed
1/4 cup (60 ml) Italian tomato paste
Several strips of caul fat (optional)
Several marrow bones (optional)
Rice or pasta, for serving
Fresh parsley leaves, for garnish

1. In the pot, heat the olive oil over medium-high heat until shimmering. Reduce the heat to medium and add several pieces of meat, searing on all sides. Do not crowd the pan, and be patient: Good browning is essential to achieve depth of flavor. Continue to sear the meat in batches, about 5 minutes per batch. Use tongs (to avoid piercing the meat) to transfer the seared beef to a platter. Immediately season generously with salt and pepper.

2. Return all the meat to the pot. Add the wine and bring to a simmer over medium heat. Remove from the heat and carefully set a match to the wine in the pot, letting it flame to burn off the alcohol and enrich the flavors. Take care that there is nothing flammable nearby. It can take 2 to 3 minutes of flaming to burn off the alcohol.

3. Return the pot to medium heat. Add the stock, onions, garlic, carrots, bay leaves, and tomato paste, stirring to combine the paste into the liquid. If using, add the caul fat and marrow bones. Cover and bring to a very gentle simmer over low heat. Braise until the meat is very tender, 3 to 4 hours. Stir from time to time to coat the meat with the liquid. Taste for seasoning as well as doneness. The sauce should be thick and glossy.

4. Reheat at serving time, and serve accompanied by rice or pasta and garnished with fresh parsley.

NOTE: *If your butcher can supply some beef cheeks, this is a great cut of meat for this dish; when cooked long and slow, the result is much like the texture of pulled pork. Other more common cuts to try include short ribs, top or bottom round, heel of round, shoulder arm, or shoulder blade. Marrow bones and caul fat help add a remarkably silken texture to the sauce.*

MAKE-AHEAD NOTE: *The* daube *benefits from being prepared at least 1 day and up to 3 days in advance. Flavors will have time to meld and develop. Store, well covered, in the refrigerator. Reheat at serving time.*

WINE MATCH: *Any red from Provençal winemaker Isabel Ferrando at Domaine Saint Préfert in Châteaneuf-du-Pape would make a fine accompaniment to this dish.*

Chicken Stews

Chicken with Eggplant, Chickpeas, Pine Nuts, and Garlic-Yogurt Sauce

This is a streamlined adaptation of a favorite Lebanese dish, the chicken *fattee*. The dish is a complete meal on its own, no sides necessary, and a great recipe to have up your sleeve when feeding large groups, as you can make it in advance and reheat at serving time. The finished product, served assembled on one large platter, is a dramatic work of art.

— 6 SERVINGS —————————————————————————

EQUIPMENT: *A 6-quart (6 l) cast-iron pot with a lid; a large serving platter.*

6 bone-in chicken thighs and drumsticks, free-range, at room temperature
Fine sea salt
Coarse, freshly ground black pepper
1/4 cup (60 ml) extra-virgin olive oil
1 onion, peeled, trimmed, halved lengthwise, and sliced into thin half-moons
1 teaspoon fennel seeds
1 cup (250 ml) Chicken Stock (page 402)
One 28-ounce (794 g) can diced Italian tomatoes in juice
2 cups (250 g) home-cooked or drained and rinsed canned chickpeas
1 cinnamon stick
1/3 cup (60 g) pine nuts, for garnish
Crunchy Jasmine Rice (page 434), for serving

1 recipe Roasted Cubed Eggplant (page 202)
Garlic-Yogurt Sauce (page 000)
Fresh parsley leaves, for garnish

1. Liberally season the chicken on all sides with salt and pepper.

2. In the pot, heat the olive oil over medium heat until shimmering. Add the chicken pieces in two batches, and sear on all sides until they turn an even golden color, about 10 minutes per batch. Do not crowd the pan, and be patient: Good browning is essential to achieve depth of flavor. Carefully regulate the heat to avoid scorching the skin. Use tongs (to avoid piercing the poultry) to transfer the chicken to a platter.

3. Reduce the heat to low, and to the fat remaining in the pot, add the onions and 1/8 teaspoon salt and sweat—cook, covered, over low heat—until soft but not browned, about 5 minutes. Add the fennel seeds and cook for 2 to 3 minutes more. Return the chicken to the pot. Add the stock, tomatoes (with juices), chickpeas, and cinnamon stick. Cover and simmer gently over low heat until you have a unified, glossy sauce and the chicken is cooked through, about 30 minutes. Taste for seasoning.

4. While the chicken is cooking, toast the pine nuts in a small skillet over medium heat, shaking to toast the nuts evenly and keep them from burning, until golden, about 2 minutes. Transfer to a plate to cool.

5. At serving time, assemble the ingredients on the large serving platter, beginning with the cooked rice in a layer at the bottom. Arrange the chicken on top of the rice, spooning the pan sauce over all. Scatter the roasted eggplant on top. Garnish with garlic-yogurt sauce, the toasted pine nuts, and a shower of parsley. Serve hot, warm, or at room temperature.

WINE MATCH: *I love the festive nature of simple whites from the Mâcon region of Burgundy: Try the noble Chardonnay offering from Domaine des Comtes Lafon.*

Chicken with Tarragon and Cream

This is right out of France's 100 greatest hits of home-style recipes. A classic of the housewife's kitchen, it is justifiably made over and over again, and is a dish that I find guests adore.

— 6 SERVINGS ——————————————————————

EQUIPMENT: *Kitchen twine; a 6-quart (6 l) cast-iron pot with a lid; a warmed platter; 6 warmed dinner plates.*

1 large bunch fresh tarragon
1 cup (250 ml) heavy cream
1 chicken (3 to 4 pounds/1.5 to 2 kg), free-range, cut into 8 serving pieces, at room temperature
Fine sea salt
Coarse, freshly ground black pepper
2 tablespoons (30 g) unsalted butter, Clarified Butter (page 411), or Ghee (page 411)
1/4 cup (60 ml) extra-virgin olive oil
2 onions, peeled, halved lengthwise, and cut into thin half-moons
4 plump, fresh garlic cloves, peeled, quartered, green germ removed if present
1/4 (60 ml) dry white wine, such as a young Chardonnay
2 cups (500 ml) Chicken Stock (page 402)
Cooked rice or fresh pasta, for serving

1. Tie half of the tarragon in a bunch with kitchen twine. Set aside the remaining tarragon. In a small saucepan, combine the cream and the tied tarragon and bring just to a boil over medium heat. Remove from the heat, cover, and set aside to infuse the cream.

2. Generously season the chicken on all sides with salt and pepper.

3. In the pot, combine the butter and olive oil and heat over medium heat until shimmering. Add the chicken, skin side down, and sear until it turns an even golden color, about 5 minutes, working in batches if necessary. Using tongs (to avoid piercing the skin), turn the pieces and sear them on the other side, 5 minutes more. Carefully regulate the heat to avoid scorching the skin. Transfer the browned chicken to a platter and season once again with salt and pepper.

4. Add the onions and garlic to the fat in the pot and sweat—cook, covered, over low heat—until soft but not browned, about 5 minutes. Transfer the onions and garlic to a platter. Deglaze the pot with the white wine, scraping up any browned bits from the bottom of the pot. Simmer for 2 minutes to burn off the alcohol. Return the chicken and any cooking juices to the pot. Add the stock.

5. Cover and simmer gently over low heat, turning the chicken in the sauce once or twice, until the chicken is cooked through and has thoroughly absorbed the sauce, about 20 minutes more. The breast meat will cook faster than the dark meat, so check during the cooking time for when it is cooked through and tender. Look for juices that run clear when pierced with the tip of a knife in the thickest part of breast, or until an instant-read thermometer inserted into the flesh, avoiding the bone, reads 165°F (74°C). Transfer to a platter and tent with aluminum foil. Continue to simmer the remaining meat gently for about 15 minutes more, or until the dark meat is cooked through and the juices run clear when pierced with the tip of a knife. Return the breast meat to the pot to warm through. Taste for seasoning.

6. Meanwhile, strip the leaves from the remaining tarragon stems, discarding the stems, and finely chop the leaves.

7. With tongs, transfer the chicken pieces to the warmed platter. Remove and discard the tarragon bundle from the cream. Stir the cream and the

chopped tarragon into the sauce in the saucepan to combine. Taste for seasoning. Pour the sauce over the chicken and serve immediately on the warmed dinner plates with rice or fresh pasta.

WINE MATCH: *This calls for a white that can stand up to the carefully infused tarragon cream: A lively Viognier-based wine from the Northern or Southern Rhône would be right at home here.*

Chicken with Morels

Fragrant, wild morels are a perfect match for a farm-fresh chicken, teamed up with a rich poultry stock and a touch of cream and garnished with a shower of mixed fresh herbs. This dish often appears on the menu the opening night of my truffle cooking class in Provence, embellished with fresh truffle matchsticks, of course!

6 SERVINGS

EQUIPMENT: *Dampened cheesecloth; a 6-quart (6 l) cast-iron pot with a lid; 6 warmed dinner plates.*

1 cup (2 ounces/60 g) dried morel mushrooms
1 chicken (3 to 4 pounds/1.5 to 2 kg), free-range, cut into 8 pieces, at room temperature
Fine sea salt
Coarse, freshly ground black pepper
3 tablespoons extra-virgin olive oil
4 shallots, peeled, trimmed, halved lengthwise, and thinly sliced
1 cup (250 ml) dry white wine, such as a young Chardonnay
1 cup (250 ml) Chicken Stock (page 402)
1 cup (250 ml) heavy cream
Crunchy Jasmine Rice (page 434), for serving
Minced fresh herbs, such as tarragon, chives, parsley, or a mix, for garnish

1. In a colander, rinse the morels under cold running water to rid them of any grit. Transfer them to a heatproof bowl and top with 2 cups (500 ml) hottest possible tap water. Set aside for 15 minutes to plump up the mushrooms. With a slotted spoon, carefully remove the mushrooms from the liquid, leaving behind any grit that may have fallen to the bottom, and set aside.

2. Place the dampened cheesecloth in a colander set over a large bowl. Carefully spoon the soaking liquid into the colander, leaving behind any grit at the bottom of the measuring cup. You should have 1-1/2 cups (375 ml) liquid.

3. Generously season the chicken pieces on all sides with salt and pepper.

4. In the pot, heat the olive oil over medium heat until shimmering. Add the chicken, in batches, if necessary, and sear until it turns an even golden color, about 5 minutes. Turn the pieces (using tongs, to avoid piercing the skin) and brown them on the other side, 5 minutes more. Carefully regulate the heat to avoid scorching the skin. When the pieces are browned, transfer them to a platter.

5. Reduce the heat to low, add the shallots and 1/8 teaspoon salt to the pot, and sweat—cook, covered, over low heat—until softened but not browned, about 5 minutes. Return the chicken to the pot. Add the wine, deglaze the pot, scraping up any browned bits that have stuck to the bottom, and simmer for several minutes to burn off the alcohol. Add the morels, morel soaking liquid, and stock.

6. Cover and simmer gently over low heat for about 20 minutes. The breast meat will cook faster than the dark meat, so check during the cooking time for when it is cooked through and tender. Look for juices that run clear when pierced with the tip of a knife in the thickest part of breast, or until an instant-read thermometer inserted into the flesh, avoiding the bone, reads 165°F (74°C). Transfer to a platter and tent with aluminum foil. Continue to simmer the remaining meat gently for about 15 minutes more, or until the dark meat is cooked through and the juices run clear when pierced with the tip of a knife. Return the breast meat to the pot to warm through. Taste for seasoning.

7. About 10 minutes before serving, add the cream to the pot and stir to blend it in. Taste for seasoning.

8. To serve, arrange a serving of rice on each of the warmed dinner plates. Spoon a piece of chicken and some morel sauce over the rice. Garnish with herbs and serve.

WINE MATCH: *I pull out all the stops here and open a white Châteauneuf-du-Pape. A favorite is the nuanced, balanced 100 percent Roussanne from Patrice Magni.*

Chicken with Vinegar Sauce

Eyes light up when I simply mention "chicken with vinegar." The lovely fragrant aroma of vinegar and homemade tomato sauce fills the air as this *fricassée* simmers away on the stove, the promise of a homely, satisfying meal soon to be set on the table.

--- 6 SERVINGS ---

EQUIPMENT: *A 6-quart (6 l) cast-iron pot with a lid; 6 warmed dinner plates.*

4 tablespoons (60 g) unsalted butter, Clarified Butter (page 411), or Ghee (page 411)
2 medium onions, peeled, halved lengthwise, and cut into thin half-moons
Fine sea salt
1 chicken (3 to 4 pounds/1.5 to 2 kg), free-range, cut into 8 serving pieces, at room temperature
Coarse, freshly ground black pepper
2/3 cup (160 ml) best-quality red wine vinegar
1 cup (250 ml) tomato sauce
1 cup (250 ml) Chicken Stock (page 402)
Cooked rice or fresh pasta, for serving

1. In the pot, combine 2 tablespoons of the butter, the onions, and 1/2 teaspoon fine sea salt. Sweat—cook, covered, over low heat—until softened but not browned, about 5 minutes. Transfer the onions to a platter.

2. Liberally season the chicken on all sides with salt and pepper.

3. Add the remaining 2 tablespoons butter to the pot and heat until it shimmers. Add the chicken, skin side down, and sear until the skin turns an even golden color, about 5 minutes, working in batches as needed so

as not to crowd the pot. Turn the chicken (using tongs, so as not to pierce the skin) and brown on the other side, 5 minutes more. Carefully regulate the heat to avoid scorching the skin. When all the pieces are browned, transfer them to a platter.

4. Off the heat, deglaze the pot with the vinegar. Add the tomato sauce and stock and stir to blend. Return the chicken to the pot. Cover and simmer over low heat for 20 minutes. During that time, check to see that the breast meat is cooked through and tender: Pierce the thickest part of breast with a knife to see that it is cooked through. Transfer to a platter and tent with aluminum foil. Continue to simmer gently for about 15 minutes more, or until the dark meat is cooked through. Return the breast meat to the pot to warm through.

5. Taste the sauce for seasoning. If you want a thicker sauce, transfer the chicken to a large, warmed platter and tent lightly with foil to keep warm. Over medium heat, reduce the sauce to the desired consistency. Return the chicken to the pot, cover, and warm over low heat, turning the chicken from time to time to absorb the sauce, about 5 minutes more. Taste for seasoning. Serve on the warmed dinner plates with rice or fresh pasta.

WINE MATCH: *Chicken makes me think of the Bresse region of France, home to France's most prized poultry. Beaujolais is nearby, so go for a fruity Morgon.*

RISE

Baking with Baking Powder, Yeast, and Sourdough Starter

THE BASICS OF LEAVENING AGENTS

Baking Powder

Baking powder, a dry leavening agent added to flour-based cake, cookie, and quick bread mixtures, releases carbon dioxide in the mixture when wet, expanding the air pockets that already exist and causing the mixture to rise. In double-acting baking powders, the most commonly available type, a second heat-activated rise will happen once the dough or batter goes in the oven.

~ Many bakers advise against buying baking powders with aluminum in them, as it can give a metallic taste to your baking. Rumford brand does not contain aluminum. Or you can follow baking specialist Shirley Corriher's recipe for making a batch of homemade baking powder: Combine 1 tablespoon baking soda, 2 tablespoons cream of tartar, and 1-1/2 tablespoons cornstarch. Replace commercial baking powder 1:1 with this mixture.

~ Use the exact amount of baking powder indicated in the recipe, as overleavening can cause too many carbon dioxide bubbles to form together, creating large bubbles that cause the baking batter to sink.

Yeast

Working with students at my cooking school over the past twenty years, I've found that the idea of working with yeast instills more fear than possibly any other ingredient. The first time they make a brioche from scratch, however, not only do they realize that their fears were completely unfounded, but they beam with pride when they pull their puffy, golden loaves out of the oven.

When flour comes into contact with water, two proteins—glutenin and gliadin—bond together to form another protein: gluten. Protein is what gives bread its structure, and kneading bread helps to further develop the gluten. Yeast's main mission in life is to eat the sugars (in this case, the flour) in the dough, in the process releasing carbon dioxide, first as the dough rises and then later as it bakes. The gassy bubbles become trapped in the dough, helping the rise and creating the lacy structure we associate with bread.

Types of Yeast

There are several types of yeast, some of which can be used interchangeably. My go-to yeast for making brioche is traditional active dry yeast. I like the drama of proofing the tiny pellets in warm milk and watching them bubble up, and it gives my students confidence to see the chemical reactions at work. However, my tests show that instant yeast works just as well and can be added directly to the flour without the need to proof in liquid. Instant yeast is my go-to yeast for instant no-knead pizza dough; its quick and easy character seems to suit this dough best. But don't let the various options put you off baking with yeast—just buy whatever yeast is most readily available near you.

~ TRADITIONAL ACTIVE DRY YEAST: 100 percent yeast that comes in packets in small, dry pellet form. This yeast needs to be proofed in a warm liquid in order to activate it and so that it can be seamlessly incorporated into the dough.

~ INSTANT YEAST: This kind is not always 100 percent yeast and may have some additives, such as the mysterious E491 and ascorbic acid. Instant yeast has smaller grains than active dry yeast and can be added directly to the flour in the mix. There is no need to proof instant yeast.

~ FRESH YEAST: This is 100 percent yeast and comes in a claylike block. It can be crumbled and used like active dry yeast. This yeast needs to be proofed

Tips

~ Be vigilant about the "use by" date. Old yeast may not work, which you might not discover until much later in the baking process, and what a waste of good ingredients that is!

~ All sorts of factors can contribute to how quickly a dough will rise, including the temperature of the room, so let visual cues be at least as much a guide as any time given in a recipe.

~ Yeast loves heat, so if your dough is failing to rise, place it in a warm place, such as next to a radiator, near a stove with a pilot light, or in a warming drawer.

Sourdough Starter

A starter is simply a dough made from flour and water, left out on the counter at room temperature to harvest the natural yeast in the air. With a little love and attention, in just a few days you will have a bubbling starter, alive with natural yeast, that will give your sourdough a flavor and texture impossible to achieve with commercially bought yeasts.

Creating, nurturing, and developing a starter or natural yeast to make your own bread is admittedly more complicated, challenging, and time-consuming than using commercial yeast, but the rewards and satisfaction are immeasurable. The process is not complicated, but it does require attention—and a little corner of your work top reserved for it.

I have been making homemade sourdough—one loaf at a time—for nearly forty years. I have baked in gas ovens, electric ovens, and my own wood-fired bread oven, all to great success (and, yes, occasional total failures, too—I simply call them sourdough bread pancakes). Always curious and eager to improve any cooking technique, I signed up for two separate bread-baking classes at the San Francisco Baking Institute. The first class on sourdough bread was amazing, but I did return home more confused than ever, and with trial and error created the sourdough recipe I use to this day (page 293). I also attended their wood oven class with friends and learned to create an entire parade of breads for the oven. The one major tip I took away was using an infrared thermometer (see page xxviii) to gauge the exact temperature of the oven; I now use this tool every day to check the oven temperature or even the temperature in the refrigerator or freezer.

I have learned—and also know from artisanal bakers—that the environment matters. In Provence, my bubbling starter has an extra boost of life during the grape harvest in September and October from the sheer amount of yeast in the air from the many local wineries.

Tips

~ Use the least-processed flour you can find. Best choices include organic unbleached flours or those from King Arthur flour.

~ The starter should always have a fresh, yeasty, faintly acidic aroma and be full of lively bubbles. If it discolors or develops a foul aroma, discard it and start over.

~ Always shape the dough after mixing, and bake after only one rise. Most starters are not strong enough to undergo a second rise.

Quick Breads:
No Rise, Quick and Easy

Does your quick bread batter need to rest? Many quick bread recipes suggest you leave the batter to rest before baking. Always curious about the chemistry of baking, I wanted to see if letting a baking powder batter rest for the prescribed 15 minutes before baking would result in a better-textured bread, with a better rise.

I tried a no-rest version of the batter, baked immediately; a second version rested in the pan for 15 minutes, then baked; and a third test rested in the bowl for 15 minutes, then poured into the pan and baked. There was no discernible difference in texture or rise among any of them. So save yourself 15 minutes and bake the bread as soon as the batter is mixed.

NOTE: When making quick breads, if you do not have an electric mixer, the wet and dry ingredients can be beaten by hand in a large bowl. The end result will most certainly be denser but no less delicious.

Polenta, Jalapeño, and Fresh Corn Quick Bread with Spicy Tomato Marmalade

I am not sure where I would be without the bright, vibrant heat of pickled jalapeño peppers. I toss them in my leftover mixes of rice, chicken, and stock; in omelets and scrambled eggs; and here, in this heavenly bread paired with fresh corn and crunchy polenta.

MAKES 1 LOAF (12 SLICES)

EQUIPMENT: *A 1-quart (1 l) rectangular nonstick loaf pan; a heavy-duty mixer fitted with a whisk (optional); a baking rack.*

Vegetable oil, for oiling the pan
1-1/4 cups (180 g) unbleached, all-purpose flour
1/2 cup (70 g) instant polenta
2 teaspoons baking powder
3/4 teaspoon fine sea salt
1/3 cup (45 g) sliced pickled jalapeño peppers, minced
1 cup (125 g) fresh or frozen corn kernels (from about 1 ear of corn)
3 large eggs, free-range and organic, lightly beaten
1/3 cup (80 ml) vegetable oil, such as sunflower oil
1/3 cup (80 ml) whole milk

Spicy Tomato Marmalade (page 422), for serving

1. Center a rack in the oven. Preheat the oven to 400°F (200°C). Lightly oil the loaf pan.

2. In a large bowl, combine the flour, polenta, baking powder, and salt and toss to blend. Add the peppers and corn and toss to coat the vegetables.

3. In the bowl of the heavy-duty mixer, whisk together the eggs, oil, and milk at high speed until the mixture is light and frothy, about 3 minutes. On low speed, mix in the dry ingredients until just combined. The batter should be quite thick.

4. Pour the batter into the prepared pan and bake until the bread is well risen, firm, and golden, 25 to 30 minutes. Remove the bread from the pan and place it on the baking rack to cool. Serve sliced, fresh or toasted, with spicy tomato marmalade.

MAKE-AHEAD NOTE: *Store, carefully wrapped, in a cool, dry place for up to 3 days or in the freezer for up to 1 month.*

Candied Lemon Quick Bread
with Candied Lemon and Ginger Butter

Candied lemon zest (a staple item in my refrigerator) turns this savory bread into a semisweet dessert. Toasted and spread with a touch of candied lemon and ginger butter, this bread makes a bright and zesty breakfast with a brisk cup of espresso.

— MAKES 1 LOAF (12 SLICES) ————————————————————————

EQUIPMENT: *A 1-quart (1 l) rectangular nonstick loaf pan; a heavy-duty mixer fitted with a whisk (optional); a baking rack.*

Vegetable oil, for oiling the pan
1-1/4 cups (180 g) unbleached, all-purpose flour
2 teaspoons baking powder
3/4 teaspoon fine sea salt
1/4 cup (75 g) Candied Lemon and Syrup (page 414), syrup reserved for later use
3 large eggs, free-range and organic, lightly beaten
1/3 cup (80 ml) vegetable oil, such as sunflower oil
1/3 cup (80 ml) whole milk
3 tablespoons syrup from Candied Lemon and Syrup (page 414) or mild honey,
    such as clover
Candied Lemon and Ginger Butter (page 80), for serving
Candied Citrus pieces (page 414), for garnish (optional)

1. Center a rack in the oven. Preheat the oven to 400°F (200°C). Lightly oil the loaf pan.

2. In a large bowl, combine the flour, baking powder, salt, and candied lemon. Toss to mix the dry ingredients and coat the lemon.

3. In the bowl of the heavy-duty mixer, whisk together the eggs, oil, milk, and syrup at high speed until the mixture is light and frothy, about 3 minutes. On low speed, mix in the dry ingredients until just combined. The batter will be quite thick.

4. Pour the batter into the prepared pan and bake until the bread is well risen, firm, and golden, 25 to 30 minutes. Remove the bread from the pan and place it on the baking rack to cool. Serve sliced, fresh or toasted, with candied lemon and ginger butter and extra candied citrus pieces.

MAKE-AHEAD NOTE: *Store, carefully wrapped, in a cool, dry place for up to 3 days or in the freezer for up to 1 month.*

Walnut-Cheddar Quick Bread

During my vegetarian days in the 1970s, one of my favorite recipes was a walnut-cheddar loaf that must have had a kilo (2 pounds!) of mixed cheese and nuts in it—it could have sunk a ship! Back then, I just thought more was better. Today I make a much lighter version, flecked with a more modest amount of cheese and just a handful of those earthy, nutritious nuts.

— MAKES 1 LOAF (12 SLICES) ————————————————

EQUIPMENT: *A 1-quart (1 l) rectangular nonstick loaf pan; a heavy-duty mixer fitted with a whisk (optional); a baking rack.*

Vegetable oil, for oiling the pan
1-1/4 cups (180 g) unbleached, all-purpose flour
2 teaspoons baking powder
1 teaspoon fine sea salt
3 large eggs, free-range and organic, lightly beaten
1/3 cup (80 ml) vegetable oil, such as sunflower oil
1/3 cup (80 ml) whole milk
2 cups (250 g) grated cheddar cheese
1 cup (125 g) walnut halves

1. Center a rack in the oven. Preheat the oven to 400°F (200°C). Lightly oil the loaf pan.

2. In a large bowl, combine the flour, baking powder, and salt and mix to blend.

3. In the bowl of the heavy-duty mixer, whisk together the eggs, oil, and milk at high speed until the mixture is light and frothy, about 3 minutes. On low speed, mix in the dry ingredients until just combined. The batter will be quite thick. Stir in the cheese and walnuts by hand.

4. Pour the batter into the prepared pan and bake until the bread is well risen, firm, and golden, 25 to 30 minutes. Remove the bread from the pan and place it on the baking rack to cool. Serve sliced, fresh or toasted.

MAKE-AHEAD NOTE: *Store, carefully wrapped, in a cool, dry place for up to 3 days or in the freezer for up to 1 month.*

Multigrain Quick Bread

This multigrain version is truly satisfying and versatile. I love to toast it on the panini grill; top it with a thick layer of sliced cheese and a slathering of Spicy Tomato Marmalade (page 422), and I'm in heaven.

— MAKES 1 LOAF (12 SLICES) ————————————————

EQUIPMENT: *A 1-quart (1 l) rectangular nonstick loaf pan; a heavy-duty mixer fitted with a whisk (optional); a baking rack.*

Vegetable oil, for oiling the pan
1-1/4 cups (180 g) unbleached, all-purpose flour
2 teaspoons baking powder
3/4 teaspoon fine sea salt
1/4 cup (30 g) sunflower seeds
1/4 cup (30 g) sesame seeds
1/4 cup (30 g) flaxseeds
3 large eggs, free-range and organic, lightly beaten
1/3 cup (80 ml) vegetable oil, such as sunflower oil
1/3 cup (80 ml) whole milk

1. Center a rack in the oven. Preheat the oven to 400°F (200°C). Lightly oil the loaf pan.

2. In a large bowl, combine the flour, baking powder, salt, and seeds. Toss to mix the dry ingredients and seeds.

3. In the bowl of the heavy-duty mixer, whisk together the eggs, oil, and milk at high speed until the mixture is light and frothy, about 3 minutes. On low speed, mix in the dry ingredients until just combined. The batter will be quite thick.

4. Pour the batter into the prepared pan and bake until the bread is well risen, firm, and golden, 25 to 30 minutes. Remove the bread from the pan and place it on the baking rack to cool. Serve sliced, fresh or toasted.

MAKE-AHEAD NOTE: *Store, carefully wrapped, in a cool, dry place for up to 3 days or in the freezer for up to 1 month.*

Seaweed Quick Bread

In our house, we love thin slices of smoked salmon and freshly shucked oysters, and this recipe, with a touch of Seaweed Butter (page 79), goes fantastically with both. Since this bread freezes so well, we slice it, freeze it, and have it at the ready for spontaneous moments of decadence.

— MAKES 1 LOAF (12 SLICES) —

EQUIPMENT: *A 1-quart (1 l) rectangular nonstick loaf pan; a heavy-duty mixer fitted with a whisk (optional); a baking rack.*

Vegetable oil, for oiling the pan
1-1/4 cups (180 g) unbleached, all-purpose flour
2 teaspoons baking powder
1/2 teaspoon fine sea salt
1/2 cup (15 g) dehydrated wakame seaweed flakes
3 large eggs, free-range and organic, lightly beaten
1/3 cup (80 ml) vegetable oil, such as sunflower oil
1/3 cup (80 ml) whole milk

1. Center a rack in the oven. Preheat the oven to 400°F (200°C). Lightly oil the loaf pan.

2. In a large bowl, combine the flour, baking powder, salt, and seaweed flakes. Toss to blend.

3. In the bowl of the heavy-duty mixer, whisk together the eggs, oil, and milk at high speed until the mixture is light and frothy, about 3 minutes. On low speed, mix in the dry ingredients until just combined. The batter will be quite thick.

4. Pour the batter into the prepared pan and bake until the bread is well risen, firm, and golden, 25 to 30 minutes. Remove the bread from the pan and place it on the baking rack to cool. Serve sliced, fresh or toasted.

Yeasted Breads

Most students arrive at my class believing that making brioche from scratch is an impossible task for the home cook and should be left to professional bakers. But when they produce airy golden loaves completely made from scratch, they swell with pride and exclaim how easy it is to get such impressive results. It's true that there are several steps to follow to allow the dough to rise, but it's not complicated, and the results are truly worth it.

You will need a heavy-duty mixer for these recipes as the dough requires heavy beating and I do not recommend attempting this by hand. Note also that you'll need to start the brioche several hours or the day before you plan to bake it.

Honey Brioche

This is my foolproof classic brioche, one that students prepare and bake with awesome pride. Make it as a whole loaf or turn it into rolls; any way you bake it, it's a winner, and you can use this method to create all sorts of variations in the recipes to follow.

MAKES 2 LOAVES (ABOUT 16 SLICES EACH)

EQUIPMENT: *A heavy-duty mixer fitted with a flat paddle; a pastry scraper; a kitchen scale; 2 nonstick 1-quart (1 l) rectangular bread pans; a baking rack.*

SPONGE

1/3 cup (80 ml) whole milk, lukewarm
1 package (about 2 teaspoons) active dry yeast or instant yeast
1 tablespoon mild, fragrant honey, such as lavender
1 large egg, free-range and organic, lightly beaten
2 cups (280 g) unbleached, all-purpose flour

DOUGH

1/3 cup (80 ml) mild, fragrant honey, such as lavender
1 teaspoon fine sea salt
4 large eggs, free-range and organic, lightly beaten
1-1/2 cups (210 g) unbleached, all purpose-flour
3/4 cup (6 ounces/180 g) unsalted butter, at room temperature

EGG WASH

1 large egg, free-range and organic, lightly beaten

1. PREPARE THE SPONGE: In the bowl of the heavy-duty mixer, combine the milk, yeast (see Note if using instant yeast), and honey and stir to blend. Let stand until foamy, about 5 minutes. Add the egg and half the flour and stir to blend. The sponge will be soft and sticky. Sprinkle with the remaining flour, to cover the sponge dough, but don't mix it in. Set aside to rest, uncovered, for 30 minutes. The sponge should erupt slightly, cracking the layer of flour. This indicates that the yeast is live and doing its job.

2. PREPARE THE DOUGH: Add the honey, salt, eggs, and flour to the sponge. Mix at low speed just until the ingredients come together, about 1 minute. Increase the mixer speed to medium and beat for 5 minutes.

3. When the butter is incorporated, it should be the same consistency as the dough. To prepare the butter, place it on a flat work surface, and with the pastry scraper, smear it bit by bit across the surface. (If you do not have a pastry scraper, use the back of a large metal spoon.) When it is ready, the butter should be smooth, soft, but still cool—not warm, oily, or greasy.

4. With the mixer on medium-low speed, add the butter a few tablespoons at a time. When all the butter has been added, increase the mixer speed to medium-high for 1 minute, then reduce the speed to medium and continue to beat for 5 minutes more. The dough will be soft and pliable but shouldn't stick to your hands.

5. FIRST RISE: Cover the bowl tightly with plastic wrap. Let the dough rise at room temperature until doubled in bulk, about 2 hours.

6. CHILLING AND SECOND RISE: Punch down the dough. Cover the bowl tightly with plastic wrap and refrigerate the dough overnight, or for at least 4 hours, during which time it should double in size again.

7. TO FORM THE BRIOCHE: Divide the dough into 12 equal pieces, each weighing about 2-1/2 ounces (75 g). Roll each piece of dough tightly into a ball and place 6 pieces in each bread pan, staggering them in two rows of 3;

there will be some space left at either end of the loaf but it will fill up when the dough rises again. Cover the pans with a clean cloth and let the dough rise at room temperature until doubled in bulk, 1 to 1-1/2 hours.

8. Center a rack in the oven. Preheat the oven to 375°F (190°C).

9. Lightly brush the dough with the beaten egg. Working quickly, using the tip of a pair of sharp scissors, snip a cross on the top of each ball of dough; this will help the brioche rise evenly as it bakes. Bake until the loaves are puffed and deeply golden, 30 to 35 minutes. Place the pans on the baking rack to cool. Turn the loaves out after they have cooled.

NOTES

~ When using instant yeast, there is no need to let the yeast proof in warm milk; it can be added directly to the flour. Don't omit the milk, however, as this will change the balance of liquid to dry ingredients in the recipe. Instant yeast and active dry yeast can be used interchangeably in the same quantities.

~ Honey both enriches the flavor of this brioche and helps keep it moist. Top-quality honey makes all the difference here.

~ The brioche is best eaten the day it is baked, although it can be tightly wrapped and stored for a day or two or frozen for up to 1 month. Thaw, still wrapped, at room temperature.

Blueberry and Orange Blossom Brioche

This dreamy breakfast brioche with blueberries and a delicate hint of orange blossom water is ideal for making French toast (page 268) but equally as good eaten warm straight from the oven, smeared with Lemon Curd or Orange Curd (page 415) or Honey and Orange Butter (page 80). And with dried blueberries, you can make this at any time of year.

Note that you'll need to start the brioche several hours or the day before you plan to bake it.

MAKES 2 LOAVES, ABOUT 16 SLICES EACH

EQUIPMENT: *A heavy-duty mixer fitted with a flat paddle; a dough scraper; 2 nonstick 1-quart (1 l) rectangular bread pans.*

SPONGE

1/4 cup (60 ml) whole milk, lukewarm

1 package (about 2 teaspoons) active dry yeast or instant yeast

2 tablespoons orange blossom water

1 tablespoon mild, fragrant honey, such as lavender

1 large egg, free-range and organic, lightly beaten

2 cups (280 g) unbleached, all-purpose flour

DOUGH

1/3 cup (80 ml) mild, fragrant honey, such as lavender

1 teaspoon fine sea salt

4 large eggs, free-range and organic, lightly beaten

1-1/2 cups (210 g) unbleached, all purpose-flour

3/4 cup (4 ounces/125 g) dried blueberries

3/4 cup (6 ounces/180 g) unsalted butter, at room temperature

(Ingredients continue)

EGG WASH

1 large egg, free-range and organic, lightly beaten

1. **PREPARE THE SPONGE:** In the bowl of the heavy-duty mixer, combine the milk, yeast (see Notes on page 264 if using instant yeast), orange blossom water, and honey and stir to blend. Let stand until foamy, about 5 minutes. Add the egg and half the flour and stir to blend. The sponge will be soft and sticky. Sprinkle with the remaining flour, to cover the sponge dough, but don't mix it in. Set aside to rest, uncovered, for 30 minutes. The sponge should erupt slightly, cracking the layer of flour. This indicates that the yeast is live and doing its job.

2. **PREPARE THE DOUGH:** Add the honey, salt, eggs, and flour to the sponge. Mix at low speed just until the ingredients come together, about 1 minute. Increase the mixer speed to medium and beat for 5 minutes. Add the blueberries and mix for 1 minute more.

3. When the butter is incorporated, it should be the same consistency as the dough. To prepare the butter, place it on a flat work surface, and with the pastry scraper, smear it bit by bit across the surface. (If you do not have a pastry scraper, use the back of a large metal spoon.) When it is ready, the butter should be smooth, soft, and still cool—not warm, oily, or greasy.

4. With the mixer on medium-low speed, add the butter a few tablespoons at a time. When all the butter has been added, increase the mixer speed to medium-high for 1 minute, then reduce the speed to medium and continue to beat the dough for 5 minutes more. The dough will be soft and pliable but should not stick to your hands.

5. **FIRST RISE:** Cover the bowl tightly with plastic wrap. Let the dough rise at room temperature until doubled in bulk, about 2 hours.

6. CHILLING AND SECOND RISE: Punch down the dough. Cover the bowl tightly with plastic wrap and refrigerate the dough overnight, or for at least 4 hours, during which time it should double in size again.

7. TO FORM THE BRIOCHE: Divide the dough into 12 equal pieces, each weighing about 2-1/2 ounces (75 g). Roll each piece of dough tightly into a ball and place 6 pieces in each bread pan, staggering them in two rows of 3; there will be some space left at either end of the loaf but it will fill up when the dough rises again. Cover the pans with a clean cloth and let the dough rise at room temperature until doubled in bulk, 1 to 1-1/2 hours.

8. Center a rack in the oven. Preheat the oven to 375°F (190°C).

9. Lightly brush the dough with the beaten egg. Working quickly, using the tip of a pair of sharp scissors, snip a cross on the top of each ball of dough; this will help the brioche rise evenly as it bakes. Bake until the loaves are puffed and deeply golden, 30 to 35 minutes. Place on the baking rack to cool. Turn the loaves out after they have cooled.

Blueberry and Orange Blossom French Toast

What's better than breakfast brioche pulled straight from the oven? One that's thickly sliced and panfried in *ghee* to make French toast! Orange blossom and blueberries make for a bright, aromatic partnership here, boosted by a zesty Honey and Orange Butter and a slathering of blueberry jam. Weekend brunches just got a lot more exciting!

Using *ghee* or clarified butter will allow you to panfry the brioche at a high temperature without burning the milk solids in the butter. Alternatively, use a mildly flavored vegetable oil such as sunflower oil.

— 8 SERVINGS —

3/4 cup (190 ml) whole milk
3 large eggs, free-range and organic
1 teaspoon orange blossom water (optional)
2 tablespoons Ghee (page 411) or Clarified Butter (page 411)
1 Blueberry and Orange Blossom Brioche (page 265), cut into 8 slices
Honey and Orange Butter (page 80) and blueberry jam, for serving

1. In a bowl, whisk together the milk, eggs, and orange blossom water until well combined.

2. In a large skillet, heat the *ghee* over medium-high heat. Dredge the slices of brioche in the egg-milk mixture and panfry until golden brown and cooked through, about 2 minutes on each side. If needed, panfry in batches and keep warm in an oven set to 215°F (100°C). Serve with honey and orange butter and blueberry jam.

Lemon Curd and Candied Lemon Brioche Cake

Candied lemon has to be one of my favorite refrigerator condiments to keep on hand, lending an uplifting citrusy zing to cakes and desserts. Here it is paired with lemon curd to make a brioche cake that is a burst of sunshine at any time of the day.

Note that you'll need to start the brioche several hours or the day before you plan to bake it.

MAKES ONE 10-INCH BRIOCHE CAKE/7 SERVINGS

EQUIPMENT: *A heavy-duty mixer fitted with a flat paddle; a pastry scraper; a 10-inch (25 cm) round cake pan or metal cake ring; a baking sheet lined with baking parchment; a baking rack.*

SPONGE

1/3 cup (80 ml) whole milk, lukewarm

1 package (about 2 teaspoons) active dry yeast or instant yeast

1 tablespoon mild, fragrant honey, such as lavender

1 large egg, free-range and organic, lightly beaten

2 cups (280 g) unbleached, all-purpose flour

DOUGH

1/3 cup (80 ml) mild, fragrant honey, such as lavender

1 teaspoon fine sea salt

4 large eggs, free-range and organic, lightly beaten

1-1/2 cups (210 g) unbleached, all purpose-flour

3/4 cup (6 ounces/180 g) unsalted butter, at room temperature

LEMON FILLING

5 tablespoons Lemon Curd (page 415)

(Ingredients continue)

1/2 cup (125 ml) Candied Lemon and Syrup (page 414), drained of syrup, finely chopped

1 large egg, free-range and organic, lightly beaten
Confectioners' sugar, for dusting

1. PREPARE THE SPONGE: In the bowl of the heavy-duty mixer, combine the milk, yeast (see Notes on page 264 if using instant yeast), and honey, and stir to blend. Let stand until foamy, about 5 minutes. Add the egg and half the flour and stir to blend. The sponge will be wet and sticky, like cake batter. Sprinkle with the remaining flour, to cover the sponge dough, but don't mix it in. Set aside to rest, uncovered, for 30 minutes. The sponge should erupt slightly, cracking the layer of flour. This indicates that the yeast is live and doing its job.

2. PREPARE THE DOUGH: Add the honey, salt, eggs, and flour to the sponge. Mix at low speed just until the ingredients come together, about 1 minute. Increase the mixer speed to medium and beat for 5 minutes.

3. When the butter is incorporated, it should be the same consistency as the dough. To prepare the butter, place it on a flat work surface, and with the pastry scraper, smear it bit by bit across the surface. (If you do not have a pastry scraper, use the back of a large metal spoon.) When it is ready, the butter should be smooth, soft, but still cool—not warm, oily, or greasy.

4. With the mixer on medium-low speed, add the butter a few tablespoons at a time. When all the butter has been added, increase the mixer speed to medium-high for 1 minute, then reduce the speed to medium and continue to beat the dough for 5 minutes more. The dough will be soft and pliable but should not stick to your hands.

5. FIRST RISE: Cover the bowl tightly with plastic wrap. Let the dough rise at room temperature until doubled in bulk, about 2 hours.

6. CHILLING AND SECOND RISE: Punch down the dough. Cover the bowl tightly with plastic wrap and refrigerate the dough overnight or for at least 4 hours, during which time it should double in size again.

7. TO FORM THE BRIOCHE: On a lightly floured surface, roll the dough out into a 10 x 14-inch (25 x 35 cm) rectangle. Turn the dough so the longer edge of the dough is closest to you. Spoon the lemon curd onto the dough and spread it evenly over the surface, keeping a 1/2-inch (1.25 cm) border clean. Spoon the candied lemon evenly over the curd. Starting with the side closest to you, roll the dough into a log. Cut the log crosswise into seven 2-inch (5 cm) slices. With the spiral facing upward, place 6 of the slices in a circle around the outer edge of the cake pan or metal ring, reserving the last slice for the center. The dough slices should be touching but the dough will not fill the entire pan.

8. Cover the pan with a clean kitchen towel and let the dough rise at room temperature until doubled in bulk, 1 to 1-1/2 hours. The dough should have expanded to almost fill the pan.

9. Center a rack in the oven. Preheat the oven to 375°F (190°C).

10. Lightly brush the dough with the beaten egg. Bake until the brioche is puffed and deeply golden, 30 to 35 minutes. Place the pan on a rack to cool. Remove the cake from the pan, and, leaving it right side up, transfer to a serving platter and dust the top with confectioners' sugar.

11. Serve by pulling the cake apart into 7 buns.

Mushroom Brioche Rolls

For years I have been taking my Paris cooking class students to experience the exquisite cuisine of the Michelin three-star chef Guy Savoy. For years, he has served an earthy mushroom puff-pastry roll with his artichoke soup. Always inspired by his creations, I developed this yeasted variation to serve at dinner parties with a touch of Dried Cèpe Butter (page 79) or Truffle Butter (page 79) alongside my Magic Cèpe Mushroom Soup (page 69) or Artichoke Soup (page 104), or simply to take along on hikes or picnics.

Note that you'll need to start the brioche rolls several hours or the day before you plan to bake them.

MAKES 12 ROLLS

EQUIPMENT: *A heavy-duty mixer fitted with a flat paddle; a pastry scraper; a standard 12-well nonstick muffin tin.*

SPONGE

1/3 cup (80 ml) whole milk, lukewarm

1 package (about 2 teaspoons) active dry yeast or instant yeast

1 teaspoon mild, fragrant honey, such as lavender

1 large egg, free-range and organic, lightly beaten

2 cups (280 g) unbleached, all-purpose flour

MUSHROOMS

2 tablespoons (1-1/2 ounces/30 g) unsalted butter

14 ounces (400 g) button mushrooms, halved lengthwise and thinly sliced

1/4 cup finely sliced fresh chives

1/4 teaspoon fine sea salt

2 plump, fresh garlic cloves, green germ removed if present, finely minced

(Ingredients continue)

DOUGH

2 tablespoons Cèpe Mushroom Powder (page 432; optional)
1-1/2 cups (210 g) unbleached, all purpose-flour
1-1/2 teaspoons fine sea salt
4 large eggs, free-range and organic, lightly beaten
3/4 cup (6 ounces/180 g) unsalted butter, at room temperature

EGG WASH

1 large egg, free-range and organic, lightly beaten

1. PREPARE THE SPONGE: In the bowl of the heavy-duty mixer, combine the milk, yeast (see Notes on page 264 if using instant yeast), and honey and stir to blend. Let stand until foamy, about 5 minutes. Add the egg and half the flour and stir to blend. The sponge will be soft and sticky. Sprinkle with the remaining flour, to cover the sponge dough, but don't mix it in. Set aside to rest, uncovered, for 30 minutes. The sponge should erupt slightly, cracking the layer of flour. This indicates that the yeast is live and doing its job.

2. PREPARE THE MUSHROOMS: In a large skillet, melt 1 tablespoon of the butter over medium heat. As the butter begins to foam, add half the mushrooms and mix to coat evenly with the butter. Sear gently until all the mushroom liquid that is released has evaporated. The mushrooms should have reduced significantly in size and be nicely browned on the exterior. Set aside the cooked mushrooms in a bowl and repeat the process with the remaining butter and mushrooms. Return the first batch of mushrooms to the skillet, add the chives, salt, and garlic, and cook for 1 minute more. Remove from the heat and set aside to cool.

3. PREPARE THE DOUGH: Add the *cèpe* powder (if using) to the flour and whisk to combine. Add the salt, eggs, and flour mixture to the sponge. With the paddle attached, mix at low speed just until the ingredients come

together, about 1 minute. Increase the mixer speed to medium and beat for 5 minutes.

4. When the butter is incorporated, it should be the same consistency as the dough. To prepare the butter, place it on a flat work surface, and with the pastry scraper, smear it bit by bit across the surface. (If you don't have a pastry scraper, use the back of a large metal spoon.) When it is ready, the butter should be smooth, soft, but still cool—not warm, oily, or greasy.

5. With the mixer on medium-low speed, add the butter a few tablespoons at a time. When all the butter has been added, increase the mixer speed to medium-high for 1 minute. Add the mushroom mixture, then reduce the speed to medium and continue to beat the dough for 2 minutes more. The dough will be soft and pliable but shouldn't stick to your hands.

6. FIRST RISE: Cover the bowl tightly with plastic wrap. Let the dough rise at room temperature until doubled in bulk, about 2 hours.

7. CHILLING AND SECOND RISE: Punch down the dough. Cover the bowl tightly with plastic wrap and refrigerate the dough overnight, or for at least 4 hours, during which time it should double in size again.

8. TO FORM THE ROLLS: Divide the dough into 12 equal pieces, each weighing about 2-1/2 ounces (75 g). Roll each piece of dough tightly into a ball and place one ball in each of the muffin cups. Cover the pan with a clean kitchen towel and let the dough rise at room temperature until doubled in bulk, 1 to 1-1/2 hours.

9. Center a rack in the oven. Preheat the oven to 375°F (190°C).

10. Lightly brush the dough with the beaten egg. Working quickly, using the tip of a pair of sharp scissors, snip a cross on the top of each ball of dough. (This will help the brioche rise evenly as it bakes.) Bake until the rolls are puffed and deeply golden, 30 to 35 minutes. Place the pan on the baking rack to cool. Turn the rolls out when they have cooled.

Comté and Paprika Brioche

Switch most of the honey for some aged Comté cheese and smoked paprika, and you have a winning savory version of my classic brioche. I love this sliced and grilled with extra cheese for a quick snack, with sautéed mushrooms, chile ricotta, and a poached egg for a decadent brunch (page 46), or as the "bun" for my Duck Breast Burgers (page 118).

Note that you'll need to start the brioche several hours or the day before you plan to bake it.

MAKES 2 LOAVES (ABOUT 16 SLICES EACH)

EQUIPMENT: *A heavy-duty mixer fitted with a flat paddle; a pastry scraper; 2 nonstick 1-quart (1 l) rectangular bread pans; a baking rack.*

SPONGE

1/3 cup (80 ml) whole milk, lukewarm
1 package (about 2 teaspoons) active dry yeast or instant yeast
1 teaspoon mild, fragrant honey, such as lavender
1 large egg, free-range and organic, lightly beaten
2 cups (280 g) unbleached, all-purpose flour

DOUGH

1-1/2 teaspoons fine sea salt
4 large eggs, free-range and organic, lightly beaten
2 teaspoons Spanish smoked paprika
1-1/2 cups (210 g) unbleached, all-purpose flour
3/4 cup (6 ounces/180 g) unsalted butter, at room temperature
1 cup (4 ounces/125 g) grated aged Comté or Gruyère cheese

EGG WASH AND TOPPING

1 large egg, free-range and organic, lightly beaten
1/4 cup (1 ounce/30 g) grated aged Comté or Gruyère cheese
1/4 teaspoon Spanish smoked paprika

1. PREPARE THE SPONGE: In the bowl of the heavy-duty mixer, combine the milk, yeast (see Notes on page 264 if using instant yeast), and honey and stir to blend. Let stand until foamy, about 5 minutes. Add the egg and half the flour and stir to blend. The sponge will be soft and sticky. Sprinkle with the remaining flour, to cover the sponge dough, but do not mix it in. Set aside to rest, uncovered, for 30 minutes. The sponge should erupt slightly, cracking the layer of flour. This indicates that the yeast is live and doing its job.

2. PREPARE THE DOUGH: Add the salt, eggs, paprika, and flour to the sponge. Mix on low speed just until the ingredients come together, about 1 minute. Increase the mixer speed to medium and beat for 5 minutes.

3. When the butter is incorporated, it should be the same consistency as the dough. To prepare the butter, place it on a flat work surface, and with the pastry scraper, smear it bit by bit across the surface. (If you do not have a pastry scraper, use the back of a large metal spoon.) When it is ready, the butter should be smooth, soft, but still cool—not warm, oily, or greasy.

4. With the mixer on medium-low speed, add the butter a few tablespoons at a time. When all the butter has been added, increase the mixer speed to medium-high for 1 minute. Add the cheese, then reduce the speed to medium and beat the dough for 5 minutes more. The dough will be soft and pliable but shouldn't stick to your hands.

5. FIRST RISE: Cover the bowl tightly with plastic wrap. Let the dough rise at room temperature until doubled in bulk, about 2 hours.

6. CHILLING AND SECOND RISE: Punch down the dough. Cover the bowl tightly with plastic wrap and refrigerate the dough overnight, or for at least 4 hours, during which time it should double in size again.

7. TO FORM THE BRIOCHE: Divide the dough into 12 equal pieces, each weighing about 2-1/2 ounces (75 g). Roll each piece of dough tightly into a ball and place 6 pieces side by side in each bread pan, staggering them in two rows of 3; there will be some space left at either end of the loaf but it will fill up when the dough rises again. Cover the pans with a clean kitchen towel and let the dough rise at room temperature until doubled in bulk, 1 to 1-1/2 hours.

8. Center a rack in the oven. Preheat the oven to 375°F (190°C.)

9. Lightly brush the dough with the beaten egg. Working quickly, using the tip of a pair of sharp scissors, snip a cross on the top of each ball of dough; this will help the brioche rise evenly as it bakes. Sprinkle the cheese evenly across the top of the brioche and dust with the paprika. Bake until the brioche loaves are puffed and deeply golden, 30 to 35 minutes. Place the pans on the baking rack to cool and turn the loaves out when they have cooled.

Instant No-Knead Pizza and Bread Dough

This instant no-knead dough is a wondrous, versatile thing: Rolled out immediately, it is ideal for pizza bases; left for a short rise, it is the base for a satisfying pinwheel loaf recipe. My preference is usually for active dry yeast, which I always use for recipes that call for a serious rise: I love the ritual and assurance of watching the fragrant yeast bubbling away as it proofs. But because the pizza base makes a fairly thin crust, there is no need for it to rise, so I go for instant yeast that can be added directly to the flour for that essential yeasty flavor, and a small rise activated in the heat of the oven that gives a little flexibility to the cooked base. The dough can of course be set to rise for breads or thicker pizza bases or stored in the refrigerator for up to 5 days to create a dough with a great deal of character, almost mimicking a sourdough bread, with that welcoming, lactic, fermented aroma and more developed yeast flavor.

Instant No-Knead Dough

This foolproof, totally versatile no-knead dough is a staple in my kitchen. It can be made a few minutes ahead or days before. Made quickly in the food processor with instant yeast, it requires no kneading and is ready to use immediately for a rustic family pizza or, with just a quick rise, for pinwheels and *focaccia*, fresh from your own oven!

MAKES TWO 13-INCH (33 CM) PIZZAS, 2 PINWHEEL LOAVES, OR 1 *FOCACCIA*

EQUIPMENT: *A measuring cup with a pouring spout; a food processor.*

1 cup (250 ml) lukewarm water
2 tablespoons extra-virgin olive oil
3 cups (420 g) unbleached, all-purpose flour
1 package (about 2 teaspoons) instant yeast
21/4 teaspoons fine sea salt

1. In a cup with a pouring spout, combine the water and olive oil.

2. In the food processor, combine the flour, yeast, and salt. Pulse to blend. Add the liquid slowly through the feed tube, pulsing just before the dough forms a ball, 15 to 20 seconds. You may not need all the liquid. (If the dough is too wet, add a bit more flour. If it is too dry, add a bit more liquid.)

3. Transfer the dough to a clean work surface and form it into a ball. The dough should be soft. Divide the dough into two equal balls. The dough can be used immediately or can be stored in an airtight container in the refrigerator for up to 5 days. Punch down the dough as necessary.

~ I have found that in home ovens a flat, cast-iron grill or a baking steel will get hotter than a classic baking stone, so that is what I prefer to use.

~ Lining a pizza peel with baking parchment makes it easier to transfer the dough to the baking surface, preventing it from sticking to the peel.

~ If you do not have a pizza peel, use a parchment-lined flat ovenproof plate or a wooden cutting board to slide the pizza onto the baking stone or baking steel.

~ I hate kitchen waste and so have gotten into the habit of saving the liquid that comes with fresh mozzarella. When preparing the dough, I use it in place of water, either all or in part. I cannot say scientifically that it makes a huge difference but I do find that it adds a pleasant and faintly acidic flavor to the dough.

Thin Crust Pizza with Mozzarella, Capers, and Basil Oil

We make this quick, foolproof pizza dough every Thursday in my cooking classes in Provence, heating the wood-fired oven up to a blasting 700°F (370°C), and topping with creamy fresh buffalo *burrata* or mozzarella cheese, infused oil made from fresh fragrant basil from the garden, and plenty of love. For a meat lover's version, my Pork and Fennel Sausage (page 113) is unbeatable. In my home ovens, I bake the pizzas on a baking steel or baking stone, heating the oven to as hot as it will go, which is normally around 500°F (260°C). I also use this dough for pinwheel loaves (page 285) and *focaccia* (page 289).

MAKES 1 PIZZA

EQUIPMENT: *A flat cast-iron grill pan or baking steel; a pizza peel lined with baking parchment; a pastry brush.*

One 14-ounce (400 g) can diced Italian tomatoes in juice
1 ball (1/2 recipe) Instant No-Knead Dough (page 280)
8 ounces (250 g) Italian burrata or Italian buffalo-milk mozzarella cheese, torn into bite-size pieces
1 tablespoon capers in vinegar, drained
Basil Oil (page 82)
About 10 fresh basil leaves, torn
Hot red pepper flakes, for serving

1. Place the flat cast-iron grill plate or baking steel on the bottom rack of the oven. Preheat the oven to its highest temperature, around 500°F (260°C).

2. Pour the tomatoes through a fine-mesh sieve set over a bowl. Crush the tomatoes with a fork. (Reserve the drained tomato juice for another use.)

3. On a lightly floured surface, roll or stretch the dough ball into a 13-inch (33 cm) round. Fold the dough in half and carefully transfer it to the parchment-lined pizza peel. Unfold the dough.

4. Evenly spread the crushed tomatoes over the dough. Scatter with the mozzarella pieces (if using *burrata*, wait for step 4) and capers. Brush the rim of the dough with the basil oil.

5. Transfer the pizza, still on the parchment, to the baking sheet or baking stone and bake until the dough is firm and crisp and the top is bubbling, 8 to 10 minutes. Check the bottom of the dough: It should be very crispy and well cooked, dotted with bubbles and with sections that are almost blackened. Remove from the oven. If using *burrata*, scatter it over the topping, letting the cream drizzle over the pizza.

6. Drizzle the surface of the pizza lightly with the basil oil, and scatter with the basil leaves. Cut into 8 equal wedges and serve immediately, passing the hot red pepper flakes at the table.

VARIATION

THIN CRUST PIZZA WITH PORK AND FENNEL SAUSAGE
Replace the capers with 8 ounces (250 g) cooked Pork and Fennel Sausage (page 113), scattering it over the crushed tomatoes in step 3.

40-Minute Cheese Pinwheel Loaf

I am an early riser, almost always hours before anyone else stirs in the house or apartment. This gives me a wonderful stretch of private time. In Paris as well as Provence, the first thing I do is turn on the coffee machine, and next, if it is chilly, I light a fire in the fireplace. In the quiet and peace of the early morning I attend to my kitchen tasks, like feeding my sourdough starter. This is also the perfect time to make my Instant No-Knead Dough, so that when the rest of the house rises, I can pull a warm loaf from the oven in time to serve with the morning coffee.

The inspiration for this loaf came from French baker Eric Kayser's cheese bread, and I have varied it, endlessly, to great enjoyment. I roll and stretch the dough, fill it with what is on hand, roll it up, let it rise, drizzle it with olive oil for color and flavor, and let it bake! Here's the master recipe, with several variations. No need to leave the house to buy a loaf of bread for breakfast! Use either freshly made dough or dough taken from the refrigerator.

MAKES 1 BAGUETTE-SIZE LOAF

EQUIPMENT: *A flat cast-iron grill pan or baking steel; a pizza peel covered with baking parchment; a razor blade; a baking rack.*

Flour, for dusting
1 ball (1/2 recipe) Instant No-Knead Dough (page 280)
Extra-virgin olive oil spray or Basil Oil (page 82)
About 3/4 cup (3 ounces/90 g) freshly grated Gruyère cheese
Several teaspoons finely minced fresh rosemary leaves (optional)

1. Place the flat cast-iron grill pan or baking steel on the bottom rack of the oven. Preheat the oven to 425°F (220°C.)

2. On a lightly floured surface, roll or stretch the dough into a 7 x 10-inch (18 x 25 cm) rectangle. Using the tips of your fingers, press down to dimple the dough all over. Sprinkle with two-thirds of the cheese and half the rosemary (if using). Working from the longest side, roll the dough into a long log.

3. Carefully transfer the dough, without stretching, to the parchment-lined pizza peel. Let the dough rise for 20 minutes.

4. At baking time, use the razor blade to score five shallow diagonal incisions into the top of the log. Spray with olive oil. Shower with the rest of the cheese and rosemary, if using.

5. Transfer the bread, still on the parchment, to the baking steel or baking stone and bake until the dough is firm and golden, about 20 minutes. The bread may not rise dramatically but should have a crisp, golden crust. Remove from the oven.

6. Immediately transfer the loaf to a baking rack to cool. Or, if you simply cannot wait to slice the bread, use a bread knife to cut the warm bread into thin crosswise slices. I like to toast it on a panini grill, anointed with a touch of salted butter.

VARIATIONS

In place of the freshly grated cheese (or a mix of hard cheeses one might have on hand), try these fillings:

ROSEMARY PINWHEEL LOAF
Sprinkle the dimpled dough with 2 teaspoons minced fresh rosemary leaves and drizzle with 1 teaspoon extra-virgin olive oil. Before baking, score, then sprinkle

with an additional 2 teaspoons minced fresh rosemary leaves and 1 teaspoon olive oil.

GOLDEN TURMERIC PINWHEEL LOAF

Sprinkle the dimpled dough with 1/2 teaspoon ground turmeric and drizzle with 1 teaspoon extra-virgin olive oil. Before baking, score, then sprinkle with an additional 1/2 teaspoon turmeric and 1 teaspoon olive oil.

PESTO PINWHEEL LOAF

Spread 3 tablespoons fresh basil pesto over the dimpled dough. Before baking, score, then carefully spread with an additional 1 tablespoon pesto.

MUSHROOM POWDER PINWHEEL LOAF

Sprinkle the dimpled dough with 1 teaspoon of Cèpe Mushroom Powder (page 432) and drizzle with 1 teaspoon extra-virgin olive oil. Before baking, score, then sprinkle with an additional 1 teaspoon mushroom powder and 1 teaspoon olive oil.

Rosemary and Lemon Focaccia

When I don't have time to make sourdough and want a quick yeasted loaf, I turn to the crowd-pleasing flatbread known as *focaccia*. My favorite is topped with rosemary and lemon, but here you can let your imagination run wild, varying the herbs and toppings according to the season and your mood.

— MAKES ONE 7 X 10-INCH (18 X 25 CM) LOAF

EQUIPMENT: *A baking sheet lined with baking parchment; a baking rack.*

Flour, for dusting
1 recipe Instant No-Knead Dough (page 280)
3 tablespoons extra-virgin olive oil
1/2 teaspoon flaky sea salt
Coarsely grated zest of 2 organic lemons
3 tablespoons finely minced fresh rosemary

1. Preheat the oven to 400°F (200°C).

2. On a lightly floured surface, roll or stretch the dough into a 7 x 10-inch (18 x 25 cm) rectangle. Carefully transfer to the parchment-lined baking sheet. Cover lightly with a clean kitchen towel and set aside to rise for 1 hour.

3. Using the tips of your fingers, press down to dimple the dough all over. Drizzle with the olive oil and sprinkle with the salt, lemon zest, and rosemary.

4. Place the baking sheet in the oven and bake until the *focaccia* is firm and golden, about 20 minutes. Immediately transfer the *focaccia* to the baking rack to cool. Serve warm or at room temperature, cut into slices or squares.

Sourdough Bread

Tips

~ There is no getting away from it: Sourdough is a messy affair, with dough that wants to stick to everything in sight, including the bowls, the spatulas, your clothes, and your arms. Before you begin, have all your equipment and ingredients carefully organized: measure out all the flours, have a clean container ready for your starter and a dough scraper handy. Be sure to dust your bowl or your linen-lined basket (*banneton*) with plenty of flour. Your hands get very sticky when making bread, so the more you organize in advance, the better! I clean up immediately after preparing the dough, making sure nothing has time to dry too much. I also reserve a sponge just for cleaning up, since it usually gets matted with bits of dough.

~ Be sure to keep your starter pure: nothing but water and flour. If your last loaf did not rise as you want, boost the yeast content by adding 1 teaspoon active dry yeast when adding water to the starter, until it is lively and bubbling. (As an insurance policy, I often add a touch of yeast to the dough when I thaw a batch of frozen starter.)

~ Your first several loaves may not rise very much. Do not be discouraged—just forge on ahead! At the beginning, you may need to adjust the rising time, from 6 hours to anywhere up to 24 hours, depending on your schedule and the vitality of the starter. The more bread you make, the more active your starter will become, shortening the rising time and resulting in lighter bread.

~ I have found that I can keep my starters virtually forever. While there are reportedly ancient sourdough starters floating around the world, passed down from generation to generation, one of my bread professors told me: "It doesn't matter if your starter is a thousand years old, or you made it yesterday. Your starter doesn't know how old it is!" When I am baking bread almost daily, as I do in Provence, I keep the starter on the counter, in a securely covered bowl, at room temperature. If I am not going to make bread for several days, I refrigerate it in a covered container. If I am not going to make bread for several weeks, I freeze the starter in a covered container, then thaw it in the refrigerator.

~ We consume a good deal of mozzarella in our house, and since I hate to discard any food product that might be of use, I reserve the liquid that comes in the package of mozzarella. The liquid should be used within 1 day or frozen in an airtight container for up to 1 month. Its faintly lactic (think of the aroma of yogurt) flavor adds a special touch to the final loaf. Combine it with water to make the 3 cups (750 ml) liquid needed for a loaf, but do not use 100 percent mozzarella liquid—I found that it creates a rather funky-tasting bread!

Pain au Levain (Classic Sourdough Bread)

Nothing makes me prouder than slipping a thin metal paddle into the oven to extract a golden brown, crusty, fragrant loaf of homemade sourdough bread. It's magic, it's religion, it's a thrill. Not every loaf gives me that "pat on the back" happiness; succeeding at sourdough bread is tricky, and just when you feel you have solved all the possible issues (the starter, your environment, your oven, your flour, your own mood), something new comes into play. Volumes have been written about sourdough bread, and will continue to be written. Here is my very personal contribution to creating sourdough alchemy.

Using standard bread flour results in a very basic white sourdough. When I use top-quality organic flour, however, I get a loaf with a glowing, golden interior. Note the multiple variations on this classic loaf. Once you have mastered the basic concept, let your imagination run wild—add seeds, nuts, or dried fruits.

Makes one 3-pound (1.5 kg) loaf

EQUIPMENT: *A 1-quart (1 l) airtight container; a dough scraper; a large bowl or linen-lined basket* (banneton); *a shaker filled with flour for dusting; a heavy-duty mixer fitted with a flat paddle (not the dough hook); a kitchen scale; a flat cast-iron grill pan or baking steel; a baking peel lined with baking parchment; a razor blade; an instant-read thermometer; a baking rack.*

STARTER (LEVAIN)
2 cups (280 g) white bread flour

(Ingredients continue)

BREAD

Flour, for dusting
1 pound (500 g) sourdough starter (levain)
7 cups (980 g) white bread flour
2 tablespoons malt flakes or malt powder (optional)
1 tablespoon plus 1 teaspoon coarse sea salt

1. PREPARE THE STARTER: In the airtight container, combine 1/4 cup (60 ml) room-temperature water and 1/2 cup (70 g) of the flour and stir until the flour absorbs all the water and forms a soft dough. Cover loosely with a clean kitchen towel and set aside at room temperature for 24 hours. The mixture should rise slightly and take on a faintly acidic aroma. Repeat this for 3 days more, each day feeding your starter by adding an additional 1/4 cup (60 ml) water and 1/2 cup (70 g) of the flour to the dough and mixing to combine. Each day the starter should rise slightly and should become more acidic in aroma. By day 5 you should have 1 pound (500 g) of bubbling, lively starter. If in doubt about its liveliness, add 1 teaspoon dry active yeast when preparing the bread and combining the starter and water.

2. On the day you want to bake your bread, line the bowl with a clean kitchen towel or use the *banneton*. Dust the towel or lining generously with flour.

3. In the bowl of the heavy-duty mixer, combine the starter and 3 cups (750 ml) room-temperature water and mix on low speed to dissolve the starter. Add the flour, cup by cup, mixing just until the dough is hydrated. This should take 1 to 2 minutes. The dough should be sticky, thicker than a batter but not so dense that the dough could easily be kneaded. Mix at the lowest speed for 5 minutes. The dough should be extremely sticky and wet, with web-like, visible strands of gluten.

4. Wash and dry the airtight container. Remove 1 pound (500 g) of the dough and transfer it to the container to reserve as a starter for your next

loaf. (There is no need to feed the starter from this point on, simply store it, refrigerated in the airtight container, for up to 3 days. It can also be frozen almost indefinitely. Thaw at room temperature for 24 hours before the next baking.)

5. Add the malt flakes and salt to the dough in the mixer and mix at low speed just until all the ingredients are well incorporated, 1 to 2 minutes. The dough will be sticky.

6. Carefully transfer the dough to the flour-dusted basket. Cover until the dough has risen slightly, about 6 hours. (To gauge how the dough is rising, leave the starter on the counter in its airtight container. If the starter is rising nicely—with big air bubbles throughout—you can be assured that your bread dough is rising as well.)

7. About 20 minutes before baking the bread, place the baking steel or baking stone on a rack in the lower third of the oven and preheat the oven to 425°F (220°C).

8. Carefully turn the dough out onto the parchment-lined pizza peel. Score the top of the loaf with a razor blade. Carefully slip the dough (still on the baking parchment) onto the flat cast-iron grill pan or baking steel and bake for about 25 minutes, or until the loaf is evenly browned. Continue baking until the bread reaches an interior temperature of 200°F (93°C), 20 minutes more. Check the temperature by piercing the center of the loaf with the thermometer. Watch carefully, since ovens vary: If the bread seems to be browning too quickly, reduce the heat.

9. Transfer the bread to the baking rack to cool. The bread continues to bake as it cools, so resist the temptation to cut the bread before it is thoroughly cooled, at least 4 hours. (If you do, it may tear, with an uneven texture.) Store the bread at room temperature in a cloth towel or cloth bag, slicing off only as much as you need at a time (sliced bread will go stale much faster). The loaf will stay fresh for 1 week.

LIGHT WHOLE WHEAT SOURDOUGH LOAF

For a heartier loaf, substitute 3 cups (420 g) of the following for the white flour:

1 cup (140 g) light whole wheat bread flour
1 cup (140 g) rye flour
1 cup (140 g) spelt flour

MULTIGRAIN SOURDOUGH LOAF

For a multigrain loaf with whole-grain goodness, add 1-1/2 cups (about 200 g) mixed seeds (equal parts sesame, flax, and sunflower seeds).

CRANBERRY, PISTACHIO, AND ALMOND SOURDOUGH LOAF

For a festive touch of color and sweetness, add about 3/4 cup (4 ounces/125 g) dried cranberries, 1 cup (4 ounces/125 g) slivered almonds, and 1/3 cup (4 ounces/125 g) pistachios at the same time as the coarse sea salt.

BAKE

Sweet and Savory

Baking is the dry-heat oven cooking of delicately structured foods that begin life as a batter or dough (as opposed to heavy, dense foods such as meat and vegetables that are covered in the Roast chapter).

The sugars in the batters and doughs (from cane sugar, honey, and milk lactose) caramelize when heated to create an appealing, browned crust on the outside of the food, and, in the case of batters, a soft, moist interior. The recipes here are the core of my baked-goods repertoire, ones that, once mastered, give endless options for reinvention and playfulness.

They say baking is a science. And while not all baking recipes call for absolute technical precision, there are practices worth adopting to ensure the best possible outcome. Stick with these rules and you're on your way to becoming a baking champion.

~ *MISE EN PLACE*: As described on page xxvi, it's a French culinary term that translates as "put in place," and it's your best friend when baking. Weigh or measure out your ingredients and prep any equipment necessary for the recipe, such as lining a baking sheet or oiling a dish, before starting to combine your ingredients. There's nothing worse than getting halfway through a recipe and finding you are a cup short on flour or that your ingredients are not at the right temperature. Doing your *mise en place* first means you're more likely to be accurate with your measurements and less likely to leave out an ingredient, and you can keep the kitchen tidy while working—all things that are key to successful baking.

~ BAKING PANS AND SHEETS: As with saucepans and skillets, the quality of baking pans and sheets can drastically affect the outcome of your baking. Chose good-quality, heavy, metal pans and sheets for baking, as they heat evenly and encourage even browning, producing a crispier pastry than glass or ceramic tins. Cheap baking sheets can heat too quickly and unevenly, leading to uneven baking and possible burning.

Measure your baking pans! Having the wrong size pan can result in your baked item turning out a lot thinner or thicker than the recipe intended and will most likely have a significant effect on the cooking time. Try to get as close to the recommended size as possible. You can swap out a square pan for a round one or vice versa, but make sure the quantities they hold are relative. For example, an 8-inch (20 cm) round pan is roughly the equivalent of a 7-inch (18 cm) square one. (Note that some, but not all pans, come with dimensions marked on the bottom.)

~ TIMERS AND COOKING TIMES: Use a timer! Most smartphones come with a built-in timer; you can also pick up a digital timer for next to nothing, and it's worth it. I have multiple timers in my kitchen, not only to service the students who cook with me, but so I can work on a couple of things at once without worrying that I will forget something in the oven or on the stovetop. They rank high on my essential kitchen items list (see page xxviii).

But do not rely solely on the baking times given in a recipe. Since ovens vary so much, what may work in our test kitchen may take 5 or 10 minutes more or less in your oven. Set your timer for 10 to 15 minutes (for baking times over 20 minutes) before the stated baking time is up and check on how the baking is coming along. For shorter cooking times, check 5 minutes before the stated time is up. This will also help you get to know your oven better and calculate more accurate cooking times in the future.

~ KNOW YOUR OVEN: Every oven has its own personalities, kinks, and oddities. Maybe an old oven heats unevenly, baking things faster on one side than the other, or heats more from the top. Almost all my baking recipes (except for pizzas and sourdough breads) call for the oven rack to be positioned in the center of the oven, as it is the most reliable position for even baking.

   Try to compensate for idiosyncrasies in your oven by turning the baking sheet around during cooking, and have some aluminum foil at the ready to place on top of your baked goods if they are not fully cooked but the heat from above threatens to burn the top. If you have a very hot top element, place the oven rack one level down from center, but avoid doing this during baking, as a sudden drop in oven temperature can cause some batters to sink.

~ BAKING TEMPERATURES: An oven thermometer is a worthy investment, as oven temperatures can be off by 10 to 20 degrees. It will help you understand your oven and even out any differences between your oven and that of the recipe tester, allowing you to get the most accurate oven temperature every time.

~ ADDING SALT: Most baking recipes call for a bit of salt: Don't skip it! Salt added to sweet batters and doughs helps to balance sweetness and enhance other flavors during baking.

Almond Bars

These recipes were first inspired by a bewitching pastry square I tried at a Moulin de la Vierge bakery on rue Saint Dominique in Paris. The pastry was a modest-looking thing, dotted with dried fruits, often overlooked in favor of the more spectacular-looking pastries. But one bite and I was truly addicted. I developed a version for my students as a kind of entry-level introduction to baking, showing how with just a simple dough and topping, you can create a truly impressive dessert. Now my students are hooked, too!

I have been tinkering with it over the years, and my most recent version is a gluten-free variation using just ground almonds in the pastry, no flour. The honey and almond slices in the topping are more or less fundamental elements to the recipe (it's the honey that caramelizes in the oven and makes it so addictive!), but the rest is open to experimentation: cinnamon, cardamom, ginger, candied orange, dried blueberries, lemon or orange zest—or a mixture of all—would make worthy versions!

Ginger and Almond Bars

This is a gluten-free version of the classic Chestnut Honey Squares (see Variations, page 303) I've been making for years, always to rave reviews from my students and friends. Here, fresh and candied ginger team up to make an uplifting, zesty treat that can be prepared in any season. This quick yet impressive dessert lends itself to endless reincarnations, using various dried fruits and citrus zests, or even cocoa for chocolate lovers—see the recipes that follow for ideas!

MAKES 16 BARS

EQUIPMENT: *A 9-1/2-inch (24 cm) square baking pan; baking parchment; a 2-quart (2 l) saucepan; a baking rack.*

BASE

3 tablespoons (45 g) unsalted butter

1-3/4 cups (165 g) almond meal (also called almond flour or almond powder)

2 tablespoons peeled and grated fresh ginger

3 tablespoons mild honey, such as clover

1 large egg, free-range and organic, lightly beaten

1/2 teaspoon fine sea salt

1 teaspoon Homemade Vanilla Extract (page 439) or pure vanilla extract

TOPPING

4 tablespoons (60 g) unsalted butter

1 cup (80 g) sliced almonds

1/3 cup (45 g) minced candied ginger

1/3 cup (80 ml) mild honey, such as clover

(Ingredients continue)

1/4 teaspoon fine sea salt

1 teaspoon Homemade Vanilla Extract (page 439) or pure vanilla extract

Fresh Thyme Sorbet (page 92) or Rosemary Sorbet (page 491), for serving (optional)

1. Center a rack in the oven. Preheat the oven to 400°F (200°C). Line the pan with baking parchment, letting the parchment hang over the sides. (This will make it easier to remove the dessert once baked.)

2. PREPARE THE BASE: In the saucepan, melt the butter. Add the almond meal, fresh ginger, honey, egg, salt, and vanilla. Stir until well combined. The mixture should be thick and sticky.

3. Turn the mixture out into the prepared pan. To help make a level and even base, place a piece of plastic wrap on top of the base. Using a flat-bottomed glass (or your fingers), smooth out the base by pressing gently to evenly cover the bottom of the pan. Remove and discard the plastic wrap. Bake until the base is slightly firm, 12 to 15 minutes.

4. MEANWHILE, PREPARE THE TOPPING: In the same saucepan, melt the butter over low heat. Add the almonds, candied ginger, honey, salt, and vanilla. Stir just until the ingredients are incorporated.

5. When the base is baked, spread the topping evenly over the base and bake until the topping is dark and sizzling, 12 to 15 minutes. Do not underbake.

6. Transfer the pan to the baking rack to cool. When the dessert is completely cool, remove it from the pan using the overhanging parchment as handles and cut it into 16 even squares. Serve with fresh thyme or rosemary sorbet.

MAKE-AHEAD NOTE: *Store in an airtight container at room temperature for up to 1 week.*

VARIATION

CHESTNUT HONEY SQUARES

For the base, replace 1 cup (90g) almond meal with 3/4 cup (120 g) unbleached, all-purpose flour and use a strong honey, such as chestnut, in place of the mild honey. For the topping, replace the candied ginger with organic candied orange or lemon peel, cut into tiny cubes.

Honey, Candied Lemon, and Almond Bars

A zesty hit of candied lemon gives this straightforward dessert a touch of class. Serve it with fresh lemon verbena sorbet for extra zing!

EQUIPMENT: *A 9-1/2-inch (24 cm) square baking pan; baking parchment; a 2-quart (2 l) saucepan; a baking rack.*

BASE

3 tablespoons (45 g) unsalted butter

1-3/4 cups (165 g) almond meal (also called almond flour or almond powder)

1/2 teaspoon fine sea salt

1 large egg, free-range and organic, lightly beaten

3 tablespoons intensely flavored honey, such as chestnut, buckwheat, or mountain

1 teaspoon Homemade Vanilla Extract (page 439) or pure vanilla extract

TOPPING

4 tablespoons (60 g) unsalted butter

1 cup (80 g) sliced almonds

1/3 cup (1 ounce/30 g) Candied Lemon Peel and Syrup (page 441), drained of syrup and finely cubed

1/3 cup (65 g) intensely flavored honey, such as chestnut, buckwheat, or mountain

1 teaspoon Homemade Vanilla Extract (page 439) or pure vanilla extract

Fresh Lemon Verbena Sorbet (page 92), for serving (optional)

1. Center a rack in the oven. Preheat the oven to 400°F (200°C). Line the baking pan with baking parchment, letting the parchment hang over the sides. (This will make it easier to remove the dessert once baked.)

2. PREPARE THE BASE: In the saucepan, melt the butter. Add the almond meal, salt, egg, honey, and vanilla. Stir until well combined. The mixture should be thick and sticky.

3. Turn the mixture out into the prepared baking pan. To help make for a level and even base, place a piece of plastic wrap on top of the base. Using a flat-bottomed glass (or your fingers), smooth out the base by pressing gently to evenly cover the bottom of the pan. Discard the plastic wrap. Bake until the base begins to brown around the edges, 12 to 15 minutes. Do not underbake.

4. MEANWHILE, PREPARE THE TOPPING: In the same saucepan, melt the butter over low heat. Add the almonds, candied peel, honey, and vanilla. Stir just until the ingredients are incorporated.

5. When the base is baked, spread the almond-honey mixture evenly over the base. Bake until the topping is dark and sizzling, 12 to 15 minutes. Do not underbake.

6. Transfer the pan to the rack to cool. When the dessert is completely cool, remove it from the pan using the overhanging parchment as handles, and cut it into 16 even squares. Serve with fresh lemon verbena sorbet.

VARIATIONS: *Swap the candied lemon for other candied citrus or dried fruit, such as candied orange, raisins, currants, or chopped dried blueberries or create a mixture, adding citrus zest for extra zing.*
MAKE-AHEAD NOTE: *Store in an airtight container at room temperature for up to 1 week.*

Cocoa and Almond Bars

This is a favored go-to dessert. It amazes me that just a few tablespoons of pure, unsweetened cocoa powder (no fat there!) can taste so rich and satisfying. I often make this ahead of time, before serving, and savor it over several days, if it lasts that long! Note that this cocoa version bakes at a lower temperature for less time than the other almond bars, since at higher temperatures the cocoa has a tendency to burn.

─── MAKES 16 BARS ───────────────────────────────

EQUIPMENT: *A 9-1/2-inch (24 cm) square baking pan; baking parchment; a 2-quart (2 l) saucepan; a baking rack.*

BASE

3 tablespoons (45 g) unsalted butter
1-3/4 cups (165 g) almond meal (also called almond flour or almond powder)
2 tablespoons unsweetened cocoa powder
3 tablespoons mild honey, such as clover
1 large egg, free-range and organic, lightly beaten
1/4 teaspoon fine sea salt
1 teaspoon Homemade Vanilla Extract (page 439) or pure vanilla extract

TOPPING

6 tablespoons (90 g) unsalted butter
1-1/2 cups (120 g) sliced almonds
2 tablespoons unsweetened cocoa powder
1/3 cup (80 ml) mild honey, such as clover
1/4 teaspoon fine sea salt
1 teaspoon Homemade Vanilla Extract (page 439) or pure vanilla extract

Fresh Rosemary Sorbet (page 91) or Lemon Verbena Sorbet (page 92), for serving (optional)

1. Center a rack in the oven. Preheat the oven to 375°F (190°C). Line the pan with baking parchment, letting the parchment hang over the sides. (This will make it easier to remove the dessert once baked.)

2. PREPARE THE BASE: In the saucepan, melt the butter. Add the almond meal, cocoa powder, honey, egg, salt, and vanilla. Stir until well combined. The mixture should be thick and sticky.

3. Turn the mixture out into the prepared pan. To help make for a level and even base, place a piece of plastic wrap on top of the base. Using a flat-bottomed glass (or your fingers), smooth the base by pressing gently to evenly cover the bottom of the pan. Discard the plastic wrap. Bake until the base is slightly firm, about 12 minutes.

4. MEANWHILE, PREPARE THE TOPPING: In the same saucepan, melt the butter over low heat. Add the almonds, cocoa powder, honey, salt, and vanilla. Stir just until the ingredients are incorporated.

5. When the base is baked, spread the topping evenly over the base. Bake until the topping is dark and sizzling, about 12 minutes.

6. Transfer the pan to the rack to cool. When the dessert is completely cool, remove it from the pan using the overhanging parchment as handles, and cut it into 16 even squares. Serve with fresh rosemary or lemon verbena sorbet.

MAKE-AHEAD NOTE: *Store in an airtight container at room temperature for up to 1 week.*

Madeleines:
Sweet and Savory

At least once a year, with a group of my cooking school students, I dine at the three-Michelin-star restaurant Astrance, by the ultra-talented chef Pascal Barbot. Under his creative hand, even the simplest dishes are transformative. I have never looked at a *madeleine* the same way since tasting his chestnut honey version that he serves at the end of the meal with coffee. His trick is to use *beurre noisette*, or brown butter, to add deep caramel notes, alongside an intensely flavored honey. The use of ground almonds likens this recipe more to that of a *financier* than the traditional, lighter *madeleine*. Inspired, I created my own version of that unforgettable treat. With just a few adjustments, the batter is made truly versatile as the base for shell-shaped *madeleines:* it becomes Walnut Cake (page 313); in a savory twist, as Rosemary, Parmesan, and Sun-Dried Tomato Muffins (page 316).

Chestnut Honey Madeleines

I guarantee these *madeleines* are like none you have ever tasted before: dense, rich, and sumptuous from ground almonds, *beurre noisette* (brown butter), and an intensely flavored honey. For this recipe, stay away from light-colored, overly sweet honeys such as acacia and go for one that is dark in color with deep, nuanced flavors that will stand up to the nutty aroma of the brown butter.

MAKES 24 *MADELEINES*

EQUIPMENT: *A fine-mesh sieve; a pastry brush; two 12-cavity 2 x 3-inch (5 x 7.5 cm) madeleine mold tins; a baking sheet.*

3/4 cup (6 ounces/180 g) unsalted butter
3 tablespoons intensely flavored honey, such as chestnut, buckwheat, or mountain
1-1/2 cups (165 g) almond meal (also called almond flour or almond powder)
1 cup plus 2 tablespoons (140g) confectioners' sugar
1/2 cup plus 2 tablespoons (90 g) unbleached, all-purpose flour
1/2 teaspoon fine sea salt
6 large egg whites, free-range and organic

1. Preheat the oven to 350°F (175°C).

2. In a small, heavy-duty saucepan, melt the butter over medium heat, stirring as it melts. Turn the heat to low and simmer the butter until the milk solids begin to brown and smell warm and nutty. Be careful, as the milk solids can burn quickly at this stage. The butter should have no specks of dark brown or black. Remove from the heat and strain through a fine-mesh sieve

into a bowl to stop the cooking process. Whisk the honey into the brown butter. Set aside to cool.

3. With the pastry brush, use some of the butter mixture to thoroughly butter the *madeleine* molds. Place the *madeleine* pan on the baking sheet.

4. In a large bowl, combine the almond meal, sugar, flour, and salt. Mix to blend. Add the egg whites and mix until thoroughly blended. Add the slightly cooled brown butter mixture and mix until well incorporated. The mixture should be like a thin, pourable cake batter.

5. Spoon the batter into the molds, filling them almost to the rim. Bake until the *madeleines* are golden brown and spring back when pressed with a finger, 15 to 20 minutes.

6. Let the *madeleines* cool in the molds for 10 minutes. Unmold. (Note: If using metal molds, wash immediately with a stiff brush in hot water without detergent, so they retain their seasoning.) The *madeleines* may be stored in an airtight container at room temperature for several days.

Walnut Cake

This walnut cake reminds me of a traditional Italian breakfast cake, although I am happy to enjoy it with coffee at any time of day. The addition of toasted ground walnuts and a touch of lemon zest makes this cake positively addictive. Be warned, one piece might not be enough!

— 8 SERVINGS

EQUIPMENT: *A baking sheet; a food processor or electric spice mill; a fine-mesh sieve; an 8-inch (20 cm) round cake pan lined with baking parchment; a baking rack.*

1 cup (140 g) walnuts
3/4 cup (6 ounces/180 g) unsalted butter
3 tablespoons intensely flavored honey, such as chestnut, buckwheat, or mountain
1 cup plus 2 tablespoons (140 g) confectioners' sugar, plus more for dusting
1/2 cup plus 2 tablespoons (90 g) unbleached, all-purpose flour
1/2 teaspoon sea salt
6 large egg whites, free-range and organic
Grated zest of 1 organic lemon

1. Center a rack in the oven. Preheat the oven to 350°F (175°C).

2. Spread the walnuts in a single layer on the baking sheet. Bake, shaking the sheet from time to time, until the nuts are toasted and fragrant, 8 to 10 minutes. Transfer the nuts to a dish to cool.

3. When cool, place the walnuts in the food processor or spice mill and grind to a fine powder.

4. In a small, heavy-duty saucepan, melt the butter over medium heat, stirring as it melts. Turn the heat to low and simmer the butter until the milk solids

begin to brown and smell warm and nutty. Be careful, as the milk solids can burn quickly at this stage. The butter should not have any specks of dark brown or black. Remove from the heat and strain through the fine-mesh sieve into a bowl to stop the cooking process.

5. Whisk the honey into the brown butter. Set aside to cool.

6. In a large bowl, combine the ground walnuts, sugar, flour, and salt. Mix to blend. Add the egg whites and mix until thoroughly blended. Add the lemon zest and cooled brown butter mixture and mix until well incorporated. The mixture should be thin and pourable.

7. Pour the batter into the prepared cake pan. Bake until the cake springs back to the touch and a skewer inserted into the center comes out clean, 25 to 30 minutes. The cake should be a deep golden brown.

8. Let the cake cool in the pan for 10 minutes, then transfer it to the baking rack to cool completely. Cut into 8 even wedges. Dust with confectioners' sugar and serve.

Rosemary, Parmesan, and Sun-Dried Tomato Muffins

This master recipe converts surprisingly well into a savory version. Here the ground nut base is roasted hazelnuts, their earthy quality a natural pairing for rosemary and Parmesan. Toasting the hazelnuts dramatically intensifies their flavor, so don't miss this step.

— MAKES 12 MINI MUFFINS —————————————————————

EQUIPMENT: *A baking sheet; a food processor; a fine-mesh sieve; a pastry brush; a 12-cavity 2-1/2-inch (6 cm) mini-muffin pan.*

1 cup (140 g) hazelnuts
3/4 cup (6 ounces/180 g) unsalted butter
1/2 cup plus 2 tablespoons (90 g) unbleached, all-purpose flour
1/4 cup (30 g) packed grated Parmigiano-Reggiano
1 tablespoon minced fresh rosemary leaves
1/4 teaspoon sea salt
6 large egg whites, free-range and organic
1/4 cup (about 55 g) packed sun-dried tomatoes, finely chopped

1. Preheat the oven to 350°F (175°C).

2. Spread the hazelnuts in a single layer on the baking sheet. Bake, shaking the sheet from time to time, until the nuts are toasted and fragrant, 8 to 10 minutes. Place the nuts in a clean kitchen towel and rub them to remove their skins. Transfer the nuts to a dish to cool, discarding the skins.

3. When cool, place the hazelnuts in the food processor and grind to a fine powder.

4. In a small, heavy-duty saucepan, melt the butter over medium heat, stirring as it melts. Turn the heat down to low and simmer the butter until the milk solids begin to brown and smell warm and nutty. Be careful, as the milk solids can burn quickly at this stage. The butter should not have any specks of dark brown or black. Remove from the heat and strain through the fine-mesh sieve into a bowl to stop the cooking process. Set aside to cool to room temperature.

5. With the pastry brush, use the brown butter to thoroughly grease the muffin molds. Place the muffin tin on the baking sheet.

6. In a large bowl, combine the ground hazelnuts, flour, cheese, rosemary, and salt. Mix to blend. Add the egg whites and mix until thoroughly blended. Add the sun-dried tomatoes and cooled brown butter mixture and mix until thoroughly blended. The mixture should pourable.

7. Spoon the batter into the molds, filling them almost to the rim. Place the baking sheet in the center of the oven and bake until the muffins are golden brown and spring back when pressed with a finger, 15 to 20 minutes.

8. Let the muffins cool in the molds for 10 minutes. Unmold. The muffins may be stored in an airtight container at room temperature for up to 2 days.

Rustic Galettes: Sweet and Savory

One summer in Provence, my friend the singer Todd Murray prepared a rustic fruit *galette* for us with apricots and berries from our garden. Almost any filling can be used here: raspberries, blackberries, apples, pears, or figs. I have expanded the repertoire to include a savory version, filled with a classic ham-and-spinach combination. There are a few tricks to mastering the perfect *galette:* The egg white brushed onto the pastry and the crumbled cookies have vital roles in preventing the pastry from becoming soggy from liquid in the topping ingredients that is released during baking. A baking steel or a baking stone can be put to good use here, resulting in a very firm and well-cooked pastry.

Galette Dough

The tart dough is truly child's play: Any cook who has avoided pastry must try this one. It's easy, foolproof, and demands no futzing or prebaking. Whenever I prepare this, I think, *This is so simple, so honest, why would anyone make any other pastry?* Once you've mastered this dough, you can let your imagination run wild with the filling ingredients, creating your own personal *galette* specialty.

MAKES ENOUGH PASTRY FOR 2 *GALETTES*

EQUIPMENT: *A food processor; a rolling pin.*

2-1/2 cups (360 g) unbleached, all-purpose flour
1 tablespoon sugar
2 teaspoons fine sea salt
1 cup (8 ounces/250 g) unsalted butter, chilled and cubed
About 1/3 cup (80 ml) ice water

1. In the food processor, combine the flour, sugar, and salt and process to blend. Add the butter and process until the mixture resembles coarse cornmeal, about 10 seconds. With the machine running, slowly add the water through the feed tube and process just until the dough comes together (you may not need all the water), about 10 seconds more.

2. Divide the dough in two, flattening each half into a 5-inch (12.5 cm) disk. Wrap both disks securely in plastic wrap, reserving one disk for another use. Chill the disk you will be using first for at least 2 hours, or until the dough is firm. The second disk can be stored, well wrapped, in the refrigerator for 1 day or in the freezer for up to 1 week.

Three-Apple and Fresh Rosemary Galette

I have created endless variations on the theme of a rustic fruit *galette*, such as with all berries and all apricots, but a favorite winter version is prepared with three varieties of apples. Each variety offers its own texture, sweetness, and acidity, creating a symphony of colors and flavors. Options might include Gala, Jonagold, and Honeycrisp. (In France, I tend to use Gala, Reine de Reinettes, and Chantecler.) The addition of rosemary here surprises many, but its woodsy, piney, eucalyptus-like edge adds a bright flavor that marries beautifully with the apples. And note that this is not an overly sweet dessert; with just 2 tablespoons of added sugar, the fruit takes center stage.

─ 8 SERVINGS ──────────────────

EQUIPMENT: *A rolling pin; a pastry brush; a baking sheet lined with baking parchment, baking steel or baking stone (optional).*

1/2 recipe Galette Dough (page 319)
Flour, for dusting
1 large egg, free-range and organic, separated
1/2 cup (3-1/2 ounces/100 g) mixed berry jam
1/2 cup (45 g) crushed cookies, such as biscotti
3 apples, cored and cut into 8 wedges each (do not peel; see Note)
2 tablespoons Vanilla Sugar (page 440)
4 tablespoons minced fresh rosemary leaves
1 tablespoon heavy cream

1. About 30 minutes before baking the *galette*, center a rack in the oven with the baking steel or baking stone (if using). Preheat the oven to 425°F (220°C).

2. On a floured surface, roll the dough into a 12-inch (30 cm) disk. Fold the dough in half and transfer it to the parchment-lined baking sheet. Unfold

the dough. In a small bowl whisk the egg white with a fork. With the pastry brush, brush the dough with the egg white, leaving about a 1-1/2-inch (3 cm) edge of the disk untouched. Spread the jam in a thin layer over the top of the egg white, and sprinkle with the crushed cookies (the cookies add crunch and flavor but, most important, help absorb the cooked fruit juices and, as with the egg white, keep the pastry from becoming soggy.) Arrange the apples on top, in concentric circles alternating the variety each slice, continuing to leave a 1-1/2-inch (3 cm) space at the edge of the pastry. Sprinkle with the vanilla sugar.

3. Fold the outer edge of the pastry over the inner circle of fruit. Be very careful not to create any holes or thin areas that will let the juices escape. If the dough has gotten too soft, pick up the edge of the parchment and use it to fold the dough over.

4. In a small bowl, mix the egg yolk with the heavy cream until combined and with the pastry brush, paint the edges of the dough with it. (Any remaining egg wash can be drizzled over the top of the galette.) Sprinkle with 2 tablespoons of the minced rosemary.

5. Slide the baking parchment with the tart onto the baking steel or baking stone (if using), or place in the oven directly on the baking sheet and bake until the pastry is golden and the bottom is deep brown, 30 to 35 minutes. This is very important: Err on the well-done side. This is a rustic tart.

6. Let the *galette* cool, then carefully transfer it to a cake stand or round, flat serving dish. Garnish with the remaining 2 tablespoons minced rosemary. Serve at room temperature, cut into 8 even wedges.

NOTE: *Cutting the apples into 8 wedges will result in a galette with firm to soft cooked apples. For softer fruit, cut the apples into 12 to 16 wedges. Flavors and textures will vary, of course, according to the apple varieties used.*

Blackberry and Raspberry Galette

My eyes light up when berries come in season; they are so welcome in the kitchen, with their faint acidity, bright colors, and dense, sweet flavors, not to mention their versatility. We have a giant blackberry patch in Provence, and many mornings Walter sets a carton of just-picked berries on the kitchen windowsill, ready for a *galette* or sorbet. Make this with a single variety of berries, or a mix.

— 8 SERVINGS —

EQUIPMENT: *A rolling pin; a pastry brush; a baking sheet lined with baking parchment; a baking steel or baking stone (optional).*

1/2 recipe Galette Dough (page 319)
Flour, for dusting
1 large egg, free-range and organic, separated
1/2 cup (3-1/2 ounces/100 g) mixed berry jam
1/2 cup (1-1/2 ounces/45 g) crushed cookies, such as biscotti
1 pound (500 g) fresh blackberries and raspberries
2 tablespoons Vanilla Sugar (page 440)
1 tablespoon heavy cream
Grated zest of 1 organic lemon
Confectioners' sugar, for dusting

1. About 30 minutes before baking the *galette,* center a rack in the oven and set the baking steel or baking stone (if using) on top. Preheat the oven to 425°F (220°C).

2. On a floured surface, roll the dough into a 12-inch (30 cm) disk. Fold the dough in half and transfer it to the parchment-lined baking sheet. Unfold the dough.

3. In a small bowl whisk the egg white with a fork. With the pastry brush, brush the dough with the egg white, leaving about a 1-1/2-inch (3 cm) edge of the disk untouched. Spread the jam in a thin layer over the top of the egg white, and sprinkle with the crushed cookies (the cookies add crunch and flavor but, most important, help absorb the cooked fruit juices and, as with the egg white, keep the pastry from becoming soggy.) Scatter the berries within the inner circle. Sprinkle with the vanilla sugar.

4. Fold the outer edge of the pastry over the inner circle of fruit. Be very careful not to create any holes or thin areas that will let the juices escape. If the dough has gotten too soft, pick up the edge of the parchment and use it to fold the dough over.

5. In a small bowl, mix the egg yolk with the heavy cream until combined and, with the pastry brush, paint the edges of the dough with it.

6. Slide the baking parchment with the tart onto the baking steel or baking stone (if using), or place in the oven directly on the baking sheet and bake until the pastry is golden and the bottom is deep brown, 30 to 35 minutes. This is very important: Err on the well-done side. This is a rustic tart.

7. Let the *galette* cool, then scatter the top with the lemon zest and dust lightly with the confectioners' sugar. Carefully transfer the *galette* to a cake stand or round, flat serving dish. Serve at room temperature, cut into 8 even wedges.

Apricot and Lavender Honey Galette

One of France's biggest apricot-growing regions lies just north of our Provençal home, in the Drôme valley. We also grow our own, and come July, if we're lucky, our on-again/off-again apricot tree produces some gorgeous fruit. On the years that it pouts, we get our supply from a local organic market. Apricots are one of my favorite fruits, with their brilliant orange skins blushed with pink, their intense flavor, and their versatility. Beautiful as they are fresh, I love to roast them in the oven, where their flavor concentrates to become sweeter, more acidic, and a little sticky. Pair this *galette* with Fresh Rosemary Sorbet (page 91) to bring out its delicate fragrant notes.

— 8 SERVINGS —————————————————————

EQUIPMENT: *A rolling pin; pastry brush; a baking sheet lined with baking parchment; a baking steel or baking stone (optional).*

1/2 recipe Galette Dough (page 319)
Flour, for dusting
1 large egg, free-range and organic, separated,
1/2 cup (3-1/2 ounces/100 g) apricot jam
1/2 cup (1-1/2 ounces/45 g) crushed cookies, such as biscotti
1 pound (500 g) fresh apricots, cut in half, pits removed
2 tablespoons lavender honey
1 tablespoon heavy cream

I. About 30 minutes before baking the *galette,* center a rack in the oven, with the baking steel or baking stone (if using). Preheat the oven to 425°F (220°C).

2. On a floured surface, roll the dough into a 12-inch (30 cm) disk. Fold the dough in half and transfer it to the parchment-lined baking sheet. Unfold the dough.

3. In a small bowl, whisk the egg white with a fork. With the pastry brush, brush the dough with the egg white, leaving about a 1-1/2-inch (3 cm) edge of the disk untouched. Spread the preserves in a thin layer over the egg white and sprinkle with the crushed cookies (the cookies add crunch and flavor but, most important, help absorb the cooked fruit juices and, as with the egg whites, keep the pastry from becoming soggy). Arrange the apricots cut side up, continuing to keep a 1-1/2-inch (3 cm) space at the edge of the dough. Drizzle with the honey.

4. Fold the outer edge of the pastry over the inner circle of fruit. Be very careful not to create any holes or thin areas that will let the juices escape. If the dough has gotten too soft, pick up the edge of the parchment and use it to fold the dough over.

5. In a small bowl, mix the egg yolk with the heavy cream until combined and, with the pastry brush, paint the edges of the dough with it. (Any remaining egg wash can be drizzled over the top of the galette.)

6. Slide the baking parchment with the tart onto the baking steel or baking stone (if using), or place in the oven directly on the baking sheet and bake until the pastry is golden and the bottom is deep brown, 30 to 35 minutes. This is very important: Err on the well-done side. This is a rustic tart.

7. Let cool, then carefully transfer the *galette* to a cake stand or round, flat serving dish. Serve at room temperature, cut into 8 even wedges.

Savory Ham and Spinach Galette

Top-quality ham—such as Italian Parma ham—and fresh, vibrant green spinach star in this savory *galette*. A touch of pungent, grainy mustard—I prefer Edmond Fallot's from Beaune in Burgundy—adds an essential counterpoint.

— 8 SERVINGS ————————————————————————————————

EQUIPMENT: *A rolling pin; a large skillet with a lid; a baking sheet lined with baking parchment; a pastry brush; a baking steel or baking stone (optional).*

3 ounces (100 g) thinly sliced cured ham, cut into 1/2-inch (2.5 cm) squares
1-1/2 cups (about 10 ounces/300 g) tightly packed baby spinach
Flour, for dusting
1/2 recipe Galette Dough (page 319)
1 large egg, free-range and organic, separated
2 teaspoons whole-grain mustard
1/2 cup (45 g) crushed plain croutons
1/4 cup (65 ml) heavy cream, plus 1 tablespoon for the egg wash
1/4 cup (65 ml) plain Greek-style whole-milk yogurt
1/8 teaspoon freshly grated nutmeg
Coarse, freshly ground black pepper

1. About 30 minutes before baking the *galette*, center a rack in the oven and set the baking steel (if using) on top. Preheat the oven to 425°F (220°C).

2. Panfry the ham over medium heat in a dry pan until it begins to brown, 3 to 4 minutes. Transfer to a dish and set aside.

3. Place the spinach in the skillet over medium heat, cover, and cook until wilted. Remove from the heat and use the back of a wooden spoon to lightly press as much liquid as you can from the spinach. Set aside.

4. On a floured surface, roll the dough into a 12-inch (30 cm) disk. Fold the dough in half and transfer it to the parchment-lined baking sheet. Unfold the dough.

5. In a small bowl, whisk the egg white with a fork. With the pastry brush, brush the dough with the egg white, leaving about a 1-1/2-inch (3 cm) edge of the disk untouched. Brush the mustard evenly over the egg white and sprinkle with the crushed croutons (the croutons add crunch and flavor but, most important, help absorb any extra liquid from the ingredients and, as with the egg white, will keep the pastry from becoming soggy).

6. In a small bowl, mix 1/4 cup (60 ml) of the heavy cream, the yogurt, and half the ham. Cover the croutons with the yogurt mixture. Evenly distribute the wilted spinach over the yogurt mixture and scatter with the remaining ham. Season with the nutmeg and black pepper.

7. Fold the outer edge of the pastry over the filling, leaving the center of the filling exposed. Be very careful not to create any holes or thin areas that will let the juices escape. If the dough has gotten too soft, pick up the edge of the parchment and use it to fold the dough over.

8. In a small bowl, mix the egg yolk with the remaining 1 tablespoon heavy cream until combined. With the pastry brush, paint the edges of the dough with it.

9. Slide the baking parchment with the tart onto the baking steel or baking stone (if using), or place in the oven directly on the baking sheet and bake until the pastry is golden and the bottom is a deep golden, 30 to 35 minutes. This is very important: Err on the well-done side. This is a rustic tart.

10. Let cool, then carefully transfer the *galette* to a cake stand or round, flat serving dish. Serve warm or at room temperature, cut into 8 even wedges.

Clafoutis: Sweet and Savory

There are few more classic early summer French desserts than a *clafoutis*, fruit baked in a cream, almond, sugar, and egg mixture. This format works equally well for savory ingredients—such as in my trio of vegetable variations—making for an excellent lunch or light evening meal.

Cherry Clafoutis

This recipe is quick, easy, and always appealing. Here the cherries are cooked with their pits, allowing the fruit to give up an intense cherry flavor as the berries bake and, with the stems intact, making for a bit of drama in the presentation. Remember to tell your guests that the pits are still in the fruit, so they are not surprised!

4 SERVINGS

EQUIPMENT: *Four 6-inch (15 cm) individual porcelain gratin dishes; a baking sheet.*

1 plump, fresh vanilla bean
3/4 cup (185 ml) heavy cream
1/2 cup (45 g) almond meal (also called almond flour or almond powder)
1/2 cup (3-1/2 ounces/100 g) Vanilla Sugar (page 440), plus extra for dusting
2 large eggs, free-range and organic, lightly beaten
2 large egg yolks, free-range and organic, lightly beaten
1 tablespoon cherry eau-de-vie *(kirsch), or other fruit-flavored* eau-de-vie
1 teaspoon Homemade Vanilla Extract (page 439) or pure vanilla extract
1 pound (500 g) fresh cherries, with stems attached
Vanilla powder (page 441), for garnish

1. Center a rack in the oven. Preheat the oven to 375°F (190°C).

2. Flatten the vanilla bean and cut it lengthwise in half. With a small spoon, scrape out the seeds. (Reserve the pod to make Vanilla Sugar, page 440, and Vanilla Powder, page 441)

3. In a large bowl, whisk together the vanilla seeds, cream, almond meal, vanilla sugar, eggs, egg yolks, *eau-de-vie*, and vanilla extract.

4. Arrange the gratin dishes side by side on the baking sheet. Divide the batter among the dishes. Arrange the cherries—with their stems still intact and pointing in the air—in the dishes. Dust with vanilla sugar. Bake until the *clafoutis* are golden and the cherry juices are bubbling, 30 to 35 minutes. Serve warm, garnished with a touch of powder.

VARIATION: *Scatter with about 1/2 cup (65 g) fresh raspberries right after the* clafoutis *comes out of the oven.*

Summer Peach Clafoutis

A peach *clafoutis* is a culinary wonder, with its delicate fruity aroma, and sweet, fragrant juices that mingle so perfectly with vanilla, almond, cream, and *eau-de-vie*. Make sure your peaches are firm, as overripe fruit will turn to mush during baking.

---

4 SERVINGS

EQUIPMENT: *Four 6-inch (15 cm) individual porcelain gratin dishes; a baking sheet.*

1 pound (500 g) firm, ripe peaches, rinsed
1 cup (200 g) Vanilla Sugar (page 440)
1/2 teaspoon pure almond extract
1 plump, fresh vanilla bean
3/4 cup (185 ml) heavy cream
1/2 cup (45 g) almond meal (also called almond flour or almond powder)
2 large eggs, free-range and organic, lightly beaten
2 large egg yolks, free-range and organic, lightly beaten
1 tablespoon cherry eau-de-vie (kirsch) or other fruit-flavored eau-de-vie
1 teaspoon Homemade Vanilla Extract (page 439) or pure vanilla extract
Confectioners' sugar, for garnish

1. Center a rack in the oven. Preheat the oven to 375°F (190°C).

2. Halve the peaches, then cut each half lengthwise into two slices. Remove and discard the pit. With a small, sharp knife, carefully peel the peach quarters, then cut each quarter into two slices. Gently toss in a bowl with half the vanilla sugar and the almond extract.

3. Flatten the vanilla bean and cut it lengthwise in half. With a small spoon, scrape out the seeds. (Reserve the pod to make Vanilla Sugar, page 440, and Vanilla Powder, page 441.)

4. In a large bowl, whisk together the vanilla seeds, cream, almond meal, remaining sugar, eggs, egg yolks, *eau-de-vie,* and vanilla extract.

5. Arrange the gratin dishes side by side on the baking sheet. Arrange 8 peach slices like spokes of a wheel on the bottom of each gratin dish. Divide the batter among the gratin dishes. Bake until the *clafoutis* are golden, 30 to 35 minutes. While still warm, sprinkle with the confectioners' sugar. Serve immediately.

Clementine and Almond Clafoutis

I think of them as baby citrus, or miniature oranges; clementines, tangerines, and mandarins are all hybrids of our everyday orange. Each name tells of its history: The clementine, small and seedless, is said to have been created by a French missionary in North Africa, Marie-Clément Rodier. The tangerine is said to have arrived in France through the port of Tangiers in North Africa. The mandarin is, of course, native to China. Whichever sweet and juicy fruit is used here, make sure it has plenty of bright, fresh flavor. A touch of almond along the way is always welcome, here in slices for extra crunch.

— 4 SERVINGS

EQUIPMENT: *Four 6-inch (15 cm) individual porcelain gratin dishes; a baking sheet.*

1 plump, fresh vanilla bean
3/4 cup (185 ml) heavy cream
1/2 cup (45 g) almond meal (also called almond flour or almond powder)
1/2 cup (100 g) Vanilla Sugar (page 440)
2 large eggs, free-range and organic, lightly beaten
2 large egg yolks, free-range and organic, lightly beaten
1 teaspoon Homemade Vanilla Extract (page 439) or pure vanilla extract
6 clementines or other miniature orange varieties
1/4 cup (20 g) sliced almonds
Vanilla Powder (page 441), for garnish

1. Center a rack in the oven. Preheat the oven to 375°F (190°C).

2. Flatten the vanilla bean and cut it lengthwise in half. With a small spoon, scrape out the seeds. (Reserve the pod for Vanilla Sugar, page 440, and Vanilla Powder, page 441.)

3. In a large bowl, whisk together the vanilla seeds, cream, almond meal, Vanilla sugar, eggs, egg yolks, and vanilla extract.

4. Arrange the clementine slices like spokes on a wheel in the gratin dishes. Pour the batter over the fruit. Arrange the gratin dishes side by side on the baking sheet. Sprinkle with the sliced almonds. Bake until the *clafoutis* are golden, 30 to 35 minutes. Serve warm, garnished with a touch of vanilla powder.

Morel and Parmesan Clafoutis

Morels are pure pleasures from the earth. Fresh morels are a seasonal delicacy but dried morels can be found year-round. They are a pantry staple for me, making it easy to create an elegant dinner with minimal fuss, such as this savory *clafoutis* variation.

4 SERVINGS

EQUIPMENT: *A fine-mesh sieve lined with cheesecloth; four 6-inch (15 cm) individual porcelain gratin dishes; a baking sheet.*

1 cup (30 g) dried morel mushrooms
3/4 cup (185 ml) heavy cream
2 large eggs, free-range and organic, lightly beaten
2 large egg yolks, free-range and organic, lightly beaten
1/2 cup (30 g) freshly grated Parmigiano-Reggiano cheese
2 teaspoons fresh thyme leaves

1. Place the morels in a colander and rinse well under cold running water to get rid of any grit. Transfer the mushrooms to a 2-cup (500 ml) measuring cup. Add 1 cup (250 ml) hot water and set aside for 20 minutes to plump up the mushrooms. With your hands, carefully remove the mushrooms from the liquid and transfer them to a colander to rinse again under cold running water. (Filter the mushroom water, which may contain grit, through the cheesecloth-lined sieve and reserve it for use in soups or vegetable stock.)

2. If the mushrooms are large, cut them lengthwise into bite-size pieces.

3. Center a rack in the oven. Preheat the oven to 375°F (190°C).

4. In a large bowl, whisk together the cream, eggs, egg yolks, half the cheese, and half the thyme. Add the morels and toss to coat the mushrooms evenly.

5. Arrange the gratin dishes side by side on the baking sheet. Divide the batter and mushrooms evenly among the gratin dishes. Shower with the remaining cheese and thyme.

6. Bake until the batter has set and the *clafoutis* are golden and bubbling, 30 to 35 minutes. Serve warm with a colorful tossed salad.

Yellow Zucchini, Gruyère, and Lemon Thyme Clafoutis

In the summer months, yellow zucchini is a welcome partner in the kitchen, with its sunny disposition and pure sensation of lightness. A touch of Swiss Gruyère and a sprinkling of lemon thyme are wonderful additions to the team.

4 SERVINGS

EQUIPMENT: *Four 6-inch (15 cm) individual porcelain gratin dishes; a baking sheet.*

3/4 cup (185 ml) heavy cream
2 large eggs, free-range and organic, lightly beaten
2 large egg yolks, free-range and organic, lightly beaten
2 teaspoons fresh lemon thyme or regular thyme leaves
4 baby summer squash or zucchini (about 8 ounces/250 g total)
1/2 cup (50 g) freshly grated Swiss Gruyère cheese

1. Center a rack in the oven. Preheat the oven to 375°F (190°C).

2. In a large bowl, whisk together the cream, eggs, egg yolks, and 1 teaspoon of the thyme.

3. With a sharp knife or a mandoline, slice the zucchini into coins about 1/4 inch (5 mm) thick.

4. Arrange the gratin dishes side by side on the baking sheet. Evenly arrange the zucchini slices in the gratin dishes. Divide the batter evenly among the gratin dishes and shower them with the cheese.

5. Bake until the batter has set and the *clafoutis* are golden and bubbling, 30 to 35 minutes. Shower with the remaining thyme. Serve warm with an herb-filled green tossed salad.

Onion and Chorizo Clafoutis

This rich and fragrant Spanish variation, prepared with a fine *chorizo* sausage (a dramatic partner for the soft, sweet onions) is my go-to wintertime *clafoutis*. I like to enjoy it in front of the kitchen fireplace, with a few sips of red wine.

— 4 SERVINGS ————————————————————————————

EQUIPMENT: *A large nonstick skillet with a lid; four 6-inch (15 cm) individual porcelain gratin dishes; a baking sheet.*

3/4 cup (185 ml) heavy cream
2 large eggs, free-range and organic, lightly beaten
2 large egg yolks, free-range and organic, lightly beaten
3 tablespoons extra-virgin olive oil
1 pound (500 g) onions, peeled, halved lengthwise, and cut into thin half-moons
1/2 teaspoon fine sea salt
12 thick slices dried (Spanish) chorizo (2 ounces/60 g total), cut into 2 x 1/4-inch (5 cm x 5 mm) matchsticks

1. Center a rack in the oven. Preheat the oven to 375°F (190°C).

2. In a large bowl, whisk together the cream, eggs, and egg yolks.

3. In the skillet, combine the olive oil, onions, and salt and sweat—cook, covered, over low heat—until the onions are soft, about 5 minutes.

4. Arrange the gratin dishes side by side on the baking sheet. Evenly arrange the sweated onions in the gratin dishes. Divide the batter evenly among the gratin dishes and shower with the *chorizo* matchsticks.

5. Bake until the batter has set and the *clafoutis* are golden and bubbling, 30 to 35 minutes. Serve warm with a refreshing arugula salad.

Golden Baked Frittatas

Eggs are such an incredible gift of nature, and this Italian dish—think a crustless quiche without all the cream, or a more structured omelet—is one of the easiest ways I can think of to feed my friends and family a wholesome, light lunch at a moment's notice. The onions, sweated slowly with butter until soft and translucent, are for me an essential base to build upon for texture and flavor. Then it's merely a question of choosing the fresh herbs, cheese, vegetables, or citrus zest that inspires you that day—the number of variations is unlimited!

Feta, Onion, Mint, and Oregano Frittata

Onions and piquant Greek feta cheese form the background of this warming and homey *frittata*, brightened up with a festive, spritely touch of citrus zest. All you need to add is a vibrant green tossed salad.

—— 8 SERVINGS ————————————————————————————

EQUIPMENT: *A large nonstick skillet with a lid; a 10-inch (25 cm) round baking dish.*

Extra-virgin olive oil, for oiling the dish
6 large eggs, free-range and organic
3/4 teaspoon fine sea salt
1 tablespoon fresh oregano leaves, or 1 teaspoon dried
2 tablespoons (30 g) unsalted butter
3 medium onions, peeled, halved lengthwise, and cut into thin half-moons
1 tablespoon coarsely grated organic orange or lemon zest
6 ounces (180 g) Greek feta cheese, cubed
1/4 cup fresh mint leaves, cut into a chiffonade, for garnish

1. Center a rack in the oven. Preheat the oven to 400°F (200°C). Lightly brush the baking dish with oil.

2. Crack the eggs into a bowl. Add 1/2 teaspoon of the salt and the oregano. Whisk to blend.

3. In the skillet, combine the butter, onions, and the remaining 1/4 teaspoon salt and sweat—cook, covered, over low heat—until soft and translucent, about 5 minutes. Do not let the onions brown. Transfer the onions to the

baking dish and sprinkle with the citrus zest. Pour the eggs over all and dot with the feta cheese. (The dish can be prepared up to 1 hour before baking. Store at room temperature.)

4. Bake until the eggs are firm and the top is a deep golden brown, 20 to 30 minutes. Let cool slightly, then sprinkle with the mint chiffonade. Cut into 8 wedges and serve warm.

Zucchini Blossom, Goat Cheese, and Mint Frittata

Delicate, golden, nutrient-rich zucchini blossoms are the treasures of my garden. I use them as often as I can when they blossom, stuffing them with a zesty goat cheese filling and either steaming or frying them. But when the fiddly nature of such a recipe does not appeal, I turn to this simple frittata where I bake the blossoms whole, and it never disappoints. If zucchini blossoms are difficult to find, use ribbons of fresh baby zucchini, cut on a mandoline, instead. The goat's milk cheese adds a nice a gentle tang and elegant, creamy texture.

— 8 SERVINGS

EQUIPMENT: *A small nonstick skillet with a lid; a 10-inch (25 cm) round baking dish.*

Extra-virgin olive oil, for oiling the dish
6 large eggs, free-range and organic, lightly beaten
2 teaspoons fresh lemon thyme leaves
2 tablespoons extra-virgin olive oil
1 small onion, peeled, halved lengthwise, and cut into thin half-moons
1/2 teaspoon fine sea salt
12 zucchini blossoms, rinsed, or 2 baby zucchini, trimmed and cut into rounds
8 ounces (250 g) mild, soft goat's milk cheese, crumbled
1 tablespoon coarsely grated organic lemon or orange zest
2 tablespoons freshly grated Parmigiano-Reggiano cheese
2 tablespoons fresh mint leaves, cut into a chiffonade, for garnish

1. Center a rack in the oven. Preheat the oven to 400°F (200°C). Lightly brush the baking dish with oil.

2. Crack the eggs into a bowl. Add the thyme leaves. Whisk to blend.

3. In the skillet, combine the olive oil, onion, and salt and sweat—cook, covered, over low heat—until soft and translucent, about 5 minutes. Do not let the onions brown. Transfer the onions to the baking dish. Arrange the zucchini blossoms like the spokes of a wheel on top of the onions. Dot with the goat cheese and sprinkle with the citrus zest. Pour the eggs over all. Sprinkle with the Parmesan. (The dish can be prepared up to 1 hour before baking. Store at room temperature.)

4. Bake until the eggs are firm and the top is a deep golden brown, 20 to 30 minutes. Let cool slightly, then sprinkle with the mint chiffonade. Cut into 8 wedges and serve warm.

Ham and Mushroom Frittata

Ham and mushrooms are a perfect match, and welcome partners in almost any season. But I prepare this most often in the winter months, serving it as a lunchtime treat.

—— 8 SERVINGS ——

EQUIPMENT: *A large nonstick skillet with a lid; a 10-inch (25 cm) round baking dish.*

Extra-virgin olive oil, for oiling the dish
6 large eggs, free-range and organic
1 teaspoon fine sea salt
1 tablespoon fresh oregano leaves, or 1 teaspoon dried
4 tablespoons (60 g) unsalted butter
3 medium onions, peeled, halved lengthwise, and cut into thin half-moons
8 ounces (250 g) fresh mushrooms, trimmed and thinly sliced lengthwise
1 tablespoon coarsely grated organic lemon or orange zest
1/2 cup (2-1/2 ounces/75 g) cooked ham, cut into 2 x 1/4-inch (5 cm x 5 mm)
   matchsticks
1/4 cup (25 g) freshly grated Parmigiano-Reggiano cheese
3 tablespoons finely minced fresh chives, for garnish

1. Center a rack in the oven. Preheat the oven to 400°F (200°C). Lightly brush the baking dish with oil.

2. Crack the eggs into a bowl. Add 1/2 teaspoon of the salt and the oregano. Whisk to blend.

3. In the skillet, combine half the butter, onions, and 1/4 teaspoon salt and sweat—cook, covered, over low heat—until soft and translucent, about

5 minutes. Do not let the onions brown. Transfer the onions to the baking dish.

4. In the same skillet, combine the remaining butter, mushrooms, and the remaining 1/4 teaspoon salt and sweat—cook, covered, over low heat—until soft, about 5 minutes. Arrange the mushrooms on top of the onions and sprinkle with the citrus zest. Dot with the ham matchsticks. Pour the eggs over all. Sprinkle the Parmesan on top. (The dish can be prepared up to 1 hour before baking. Store at room temperature.)

5. Bake until the eggs are firm and the top is a deep golden brown, 20 to 30 minutes. Garnish with the chives. Cut into 8 wedges and serve warm.

Fennel Sausage and Parmesan Frittata

The options for using homemade pork sausage are seemingly endless: We use it on pizza, in pasta sauce, and in this warming lunch or dinner *frittata*. Can't get enough of it!

8 SERVINGS

EQUIPMENT: *A small nonstick skillet with a lid; a 10-inch (25 cm) round baking dish.*

Extra-virgin olive oil, for oiling the dish
1 teaspoon fennel seeds
6 large eggs, free-range and organic, lightly beaten
2 teaspoons fresh lemon thyme or regular thyme leaves
2 tablespoons extra-virgin olive oil
1 small onion, peeled, halved lengthwise, and cut into thin half-moons
1/2 teaspoon fine sea salt
8 ounces (250 g) Pork and Fennel Sausage (page 113), cooked
6 tablespoons freshly grated Parmigiano-Reggiano cheese
1 tablespoon coarsely grated organic lemon or orange zest

1. Center a rack in the oven. Preheat the oven to 400°F (200°C). Lightly brush the baking dish with oil.

2. In a small skillet, toast the fennel seeds over medium heat until they are fragrant, shaking the skillet to keep the seeds from burning, about 1 minute. Transfer to a plate to cool.

3. Crack the eggs into a bowl. Add the thyme leaves. Whisk to blend.

4. In the skillet, combine the olive oil, onion, and salt and sweat—cook, covered, over low heat—until soft and translucent, about 5 minutes.

Do not let the onions brown. Transfer the onions to the baking dish and arrange the sausage on top. Dot with half the cheese and sprinkle with the citrus zest. Pour the eggs over all. Sprinkle with the remaining cheese. (The dish can be prepared up to 1 hour before baking. Store at room temperature.)

5. Bake until the eggs are firm and the top is a deep golden brown, 20 to 30 minutes. Sprinkle with the fennel seeds. Cut into 8 wedges and serve warm.

FOLD

Folding is a simple yet artful and essential technique used for incorporating an ingredient that has had air bubbles whipped into it, such as whipped egg whites or whipped cream, into a heavier mixture like a batter, so that it retains its light and airy quality. It can be used to create a cloudlike quality for all manner of desserts.

When combining the two ingredients, you want to keep as much of the aeration from the light ingredient as possible. Whisking or beating the two together would knock the air and fluffiness straight out of the mixture. Folding, however—using the lightest hand possible—allows the mixture to remain well aerated. The best tools to do this with are a large rubber spatula or large metal spoon and a large bowl. The technique is simple and an essential for any cook.

METHOD FOR FOLDING

1. Place the heavier mixture in a large bowl.

2. When folding a light ingredient into a particularly heavy mixture, take about one-quarter of the light ingredient and gently stir it into the heavy mixture to lighten it up a bit.

3. Place the remaining light ingredient on top of the heavier mixture.

4. With a rubber spatula or large metal spoon (the large surface of a spoon is useful as it means you need fewer passes to fold the two mixtures

together), cut through the mixtures with the side edge of the spoon or spatula until you reach the bottom of the bowl, then draw the spoon along the bottom of the bowl. Turn your wrist to bring the spoon up the side of the bowl, lightly bringing the mixture from the bottom to the top, and as you do so, turn the bowl about 45 degrees and lightly overturn the spoon to gently fold the mixture on top of the light ingredient. Turning the bowl as you fold will incorporate the mixtures more efficiently. Continue cutting into the mixture and folding until just incorporated. I find that twenty turns are almost always the right number, so I count as I fold.

Always work slowly and gently. Do not be tempted to overmix and unnecessarily knock extra air out of the mixture. If necessary, err on the side of underfolding. When adding a light-colored mixture to a darker mixture (such as whipped egg whites to a chocolate mixture), be sure to fold until no streaks of white remain.

WHIPPING EGG WHITES

Egg whites can be beaten or whipped with a whisk, electric hand beater, or heavy-duty mixer using the whisk attachment. Beating raw egg whites vigorously makes the egg proteins uncurl, and as air bubbles are beaten in, the uncurled proteins link together, enclosing the bubbles and locking them in, resulting in a light and extremely airy opaque foam. Egg whites form undulating waves with soft peaks, when the tips of the peaks curl over on themselves, or stiff peaks, when they hold themselves straight upward, clinging tightly to the whisk when lifted up. The stiff peak stage (or just before) is required if you are folding egg whites into a heavier mixture and then baking in the oven.

Tips for Whipping Egg Whites

~ Eggs are easiest to separate when cold, but whites will beat to their fullest volume at room temperature. So plan ahead!

~ Use a large bowl, since egg whites can grow 10 to 12 times their volume when beaten.

~ If you have a copper bowl, use it; the copper reacts with the egg whites, helping to create a more stable protein structure. But you can whip egg whites very successfully in stainless steel or glass bowls. Avoid plastic bowls, as the surface can hold grease that keeps the whites from whipping properly.

~ Make sure your bowl is clean and dry before starting. If you notice any kind of greasy film on the surface of the bowl, use lemon juice or vinegar to clean the bowl before you begin.

~ Make sure your egg whites are free from contamination, especially a runaway drop of yolk, as the fats in the yolk can keep the whites from forming stiff peaks. Use a piece of eggshell to remove any unwanted egg yolk or pieces of shell from the egg white.

~ Egg whites can be overbeaten and become "dry," where the whites lose their silky appearance and begin to look clumpy and almost curdled. Stop whisking when the whites are stiff and fluffy.

~ Use whipped egg whites right away or they will begin to liquefy.

Meringues

Meringues are miraculous things. By simply combining whipped egg whites with a little cream of tartar (the acidity helps stabilize the egg white proteins) and sugar, and baking them slowly at a low temperature, you can easily (and very inexpensively!) create an elegant dessert that is wonderfully versatile. Baked long and slow, they become hard and dry, a sweet crispy counterpoint to acidic fruits and cloudlike whipped cream. With the addition of cornstarch and a few simple adjustments in the recipe, you can create irresistible pavlova desserts with sweet marshmallow centers.

Meringues are simple to make, but it's worth keeping these tips in mind for the best possible results:

~ Older eggs are best for meringues, as the protein structure in the whites begins to break down as the eggs age, making them easier to whip. But fresh eggs will make meringues just fine, too.

~ The meringue will begin to liquefy if left to stand, so be sure to prepare all the ingredients before whipping the egg whites. Bake as soon as the meringue is prepared.

~ When added to egg whites for whipping, cream of tartar stabilizes the egg proteins, helping to achieve stiff peaks and the fullest volume from the whites. If you don't have any to hand, a couple of drops of lemon juice or vinegar will do the trick.

~ Pay close attention when whipping egg whites, as over- or underbeating can result in the mixture weeping a sugary syrup during cooking.

Look for visual cues to know when the egg whites are at the right stage to incorporate the sugar: the stiff peak stage (or just before), where the whites stand tall on their own and cling firmly to the whisk. Overwhipping results in the egg whites becoming "dry," with a clumpy, curdled-looking texture.

~ Meringues are very sensitive to temperature, so use an oven thermometer to make sure the oven is not too hot. Too high a temperature will cause beading, coloring on the surface of the meringue, and cracking.

~ For dry, crisp meringues, wedge the oven door open with a wooden spoon for the last hour of baking to allow any moisture to escape and encourage the drying process. For pavlova recipes, however, a sudden drop in oven temperature can cause the mixture to fall, resulting in a less tall marshmallow-like interior, so avoid opening the oven door during baking and let the pavlovas cool in the oven with the door closed.

~ Avoid making meringues in very humid weather: The sugar in the egg white mixture absorbs moisture from the air, making it almost impossible to achieve thick, stiff peaks. Humidity may also cause meringues to weep or to soften once baked.

~ Superfine sugar is recommended when making meringues. It is more finely ground than granulated sugar, dissolves more quickly, and helps prevent weeping or sogginess in the meringues. When the sugar is undissolved in the meringue mixture, there is a tendency for the baked product to weep. Superfine sugar can be made at home by placing classic sugar in a food process and grinding it to a finer texture.

~ The classic ratio for most meringues is double the amount of sugar to egg whites. Since egg size can vary, you can use this formula to adjust any recipe. In general, 1 large egg white weighs about 1.25 to 1.4 ounces (35 to 38 g), so for 4 eggs whites, you will need 1 cup plus 6 tablespoons to 1-1/2 cups (280 to 300 g) of sugar.

Soft Individual Meringue Nests

It's amazing how versatile this classic three-ingredient French meringue can be. Baked long and slow at the lowest of temperatures, these sugary beauties come out of the oven dry, crisp, and perfectly white. Just firm enough on the outside and like billowy, welcome clouds on the inside, these are my preferred meringues. They are the ideal low-budget, make-ahead dessert, always in season, simply garnished with whipped yogurt cream and berries. It is important to have the oven at the proper temperature, so that the meringues remain lily-white, with barely a touch of color. These can be baked as elegant, professional, piped-layered meringue nests, or simple free-form meringues with a touch of whimsy.

MAKES 6 NESTS OR 12 FREE-FORM MERINGUES

EQUIPMENT: *A heavy-duty mixer fitted with a whisk; a large rubber spatula or large metal spoon; 1 or 2 baking sheets lined with baking parchment; a pastry bag fitted with a large nozzle (optional).*

4 large egg whites, free-range and organic, at room temperature
1 teaspoon cream of tartar
1 cup plus 6 tablespoons (280 g) superfine sugar (see page 355)
Whipped Yogurt Cream (page 416), for serving
Raspberries or a mix of berries, for serving

1. If preparing piped meringue nests, arrange a rack in the lower third of the oven. If preparing free-form meringues, arrange two racks in the lower half of the oven. Preheat the oven to 210°F (100°C).

2. In the bowl of the heavy-duty mixer, whisk the egg whites at low speed until frothy, about 20 seconds. Add the cream of tartar. Gradually increase the speed until just before the stiff peak stage, 1 to 2 minutes. Be careful not to overbeat or the whites may begin to break down and become lumpy. Slowly add about 3/4 cup (150 g) of the sugar to the whites, a tablespoon at a time, and whisk until the mixture becomes thick and satiny and stands in tall stiff peaks, about 1 minute more.

3. Remove the mixer bowl from its stand. Add the remaining sugar and gently fold it into the whites: With the rubber spatula or metal spoon, cut through the egg whites and sugar with the side edge of the spoon or spatula until you reach the bottom of the bowl, then draw the spoon along the bottom of the bowl. Turn your wrist to bring the spoon up the side of the bowl, lightly bringing the egg whites from the bottom to the top, and as you do so turn the bowl about 45 degrees and lightly overturn the spoon to gently fold the whites on top of the sugar. Turning the bowl as you fold will help the sugar to be incorporated more efficiently. Continue cutting into the mixture and folding until just incorporated. Always work slowly and gently. Do not be tempted to overmix and unnecessarily knock extra air out of the mixture. If necessary, err on the side of underfolding.

4. IF PREPARING PIPED MERINGUES: Using a few small dabs of the meringue as glue, stick the baking parchment to the baking sheet. Fold back the wide, open end of the pastry bag and fill the bag with the meringue. Unfold the open end of the bag, twist it closed, and pipe the meringue into 6 small 3-inch (7.5 cm) disks to form the bottom of the nests. Then, following the outside edge of the disk, pipe a ring of meringue to create the side of the nest. Repeat with two more layers on top.

IF PREPARING FREE-FORM MERINGUES: Use a soup spoon to form the meringues into wispy 3-inch (7. 5 cm) balls on the baking parchment, dividing 12 meringues evenly between the two baking sheets. I like my meringues to resemble a wild, undisciplined, spiked hairdo.

5. Bake until firm and dry, about 2 hours, switching the two baking sheets halfway through the baking time. Let cool completely. Serve on individual dessert plates, garnished with a dollop of whipped yogurt cream and berries.

MAKE-AHEAD NOTE: *Meringues can be made in advance and stored in an airtight container at room temperature for up to 1 week.*

Lemon Curd or Passion Fruit Curd Meringues

"Heavenly" is the only word to be used for these light and airy little meringues. The sweetness of the dry, crisp meringue is tempered by the tang and smoothness of a perfect lemon curd.

— MAKES ABOUT 60 MINI MERINGUES ————————————————

EQUIPMENT: *A heavy-duty mixer fitted with a whisk; a large rubber spatula or large metal spoon; two baking sheets lined with baking parchment; a pastry bag fitted with a large nozzle.*

4 large egg whites, free-range and organic, at room temperature
1 teaspoon cream of tartar
1 cup plus 6 tablespoons (280 g) superfine sugar (see page 355)
6 tablespoons Lemon Curd or Passion Fruit Curd (page 415)
Crème fraîche or sour cream, for serving

1. Arrange two racks in the lower half of the oven. Preheat the oven to 210°F (100°C).

2. In the bowl of the heavy-duty mixer, whisk the egg whites at low speed until frothy, about 20 seconds. Add the cream of tartar. Gradually increase the speed and whisk until just before the stiff peak stage, 1 to 2 minutes. Be careful not to overbeat or the whites may begin break down and become lumpy. Slowly add about 3/4 cup (150 g) of the sugar to the stiffened whites, a tablespoon at a time, and whisk until the mixture becomes thick and satiny.

3. Remove the mixer bowl from its stand. Add the remaining sugar and gently fold it into the whites: With the rubber spatula or metal spoon, cut through the egg whites and sugar with the side edge of the spoon or spatula until you reach the bottom of the bowl, then draw the spoon along the bottom

of the bowl. Turn your wrist to bring the spoon up the side of the bowl, lightly bringing the egg whites from the bottom to the top, and as you do so turn the bowl about 45 degrees and lightly overturn the spoon to gently fold the whites on top of the sugar. Turning the bowl as you fold will help the sugar to be incorporated more efficiently. Continue cutting into the mixture and folding until just incorporated. Always work slowly and gently. Do not be tempted to overmix and unnecessarily knock extra air out of the mixture. If necessary, err on the side of underfolding.

4. Using a few small dabs of the meringue as glue, stick the baking parchment to the baking sheet. Fold back the wide, open end of the pastry bag and fill the bag with the meringue. Unfold the open end of the bag, twist it closed, and pipe the meringue into about sixty 1-1/2-inch (4 cm) disks. With a demitasse spoon, place a small dollop of lemon curd in the center of each disk, so that it resembles a poached egg. Using the piping bag again, cover the curd with meringue, creating a circular cone that spirals upward to a peak.

5. Bake the meringues for 1-1/2 hours, switching the two baking sheets halfway through the cooking time. Remove from the oven immediately. Serve with a dollop of *crème fraîche* or sour cream. These are best eaten the day they are made.

VARIATION: *Use any fruit curd in place of the lemon curd, such as orange or lime.*

Individual Pavlovas with Orange Curd

Pavlova—that endlessly elegant dessert named after the Russian ballerina Anna Pavlova—is a meringue made with the addition of an acid to help achieve stiff peaks and the fullest volume from your egg whites (we use cream of tartar) and cornstarch to help stabilize the egg whites, resulting in a crisp meringue exterior and a soft, marshmallow interior. The best of both worlds! Classic versions call for summer berries but here we have tempered the pavlova's sweetness with a zesty orange curd. Of course any curd variation or tart fruit would work, paired with cream to cut through the sweetness of the sugar.

6 SERVINGS

EQUIPMENT: *A 3-inch (7.5 cm) pastry cutter or large glass; a heavy-duty mixer fitted with a whisk; a large rubber spatula or large metal serving spoon; a baking sheet lined with baking parchment.*

4 large egg whites, free-range and organic, at room temperature
1 teaspoon cream of tartar
1-1/2 teaspoons cornstarch
1 cup plus 6 tablespoons (280 g) superfine sugar (see page 355)
1-1/2 teaspoons Homemade Vanilla Extract (page 439) or pure vanilla extract
1 cup (250 ml) heavy cream
Orange Curd (page 415), for serving

I. Arrange a rack in the lower third of the oven. Preheat the oven to 340°F (170°C).

2. Using the pastry cutter or glass, trace six circles on the baking parchment, evenly spaced apart.

3. In the bowl of the heavy-duty mixer, whisk the egg whites at low speed until frothy, then gradually increase the speed to high until just before the stiff peak stage, 1 to 2 minutes. Be careful not to overbeat or the whites may begin break down and become lumpy. Add the cream of tartar and cornstarch and beat again to combine. Slowly add 3/4 cup (150 g) of the sugar to the stiffened whites, a tablespoon at a time, and whisk just until the sugar has dissolved and the mixture becomes thick and satiny.

4. Remove the mixer bowl from its stand. Add the vanilla to the whites and use the rubber spatula or large metal spoon to gently fold it in. Cut through the egg whites and vanilla with the side edge of the spoon or spatula until you reach the bottom, then draw the spoon along the bottom of the bowl. Turn your wrist to bring the spoon up the side of the bowl, lightly bringing the egg whites from the bottom to the top, and as you do so turn the bowl about 45 degrees and lightly overturn the spoon to gently fold the whites on top of the vanilla. Turning the bowl as you fold will help the vanilla to be incorporated more efficiently. Continue cutting into the mixture and folding until just incorporated. Always work slowly and gently. Do not be tempted to overmix and unnecessarily knock extra air out of the mixture. If necessary, err on the side of underfolding. Add the remaining sugar and, using the same technique, fold it gently into the whites.

5. Using some of the meringue as glue, stick the baking parchment to the baking sheet, making sure the drawn circles are on the underside of the paper so the markings do not transfer to the meringue during baking. Using the large spoon, scoop the meringue into large balls onto the baking parchment, dividing it evenly among the six circles.

6. Reduce the oven temperature to 230°F (110°C) and bake until the outside of the pavlovas are hard but not colored, 1 hour to 1 hour and 20 minutes; check the pavlovas without opening the door, since a rush of cold air while the pavlovas are still warm can cause them to collapse. Turn off the oven and leave the meringues in the oven to cool completely. The cooled baked pavlova can be stored in an airtight container at room temperature for up to 2 days.

7. When you are ready to serve the dessert, whip the cream into soft peaks in the bowl of the mixer. Spoon orange curd onto the pavlovas and top with the whipped cream.

Individual Rose and Raspberry Pavlovas

These fragrant, blush-pink individual pavlovas are an exotic twist on the classic recipe. The freeze-dried raspberries import a bright, fruity flavor without compromising the soft meringue texture. Don't overdo it on the rose water; just the subtlest hint of its floral notes is all that is needed.

--- 6 SERVINGS ---

EQUIPMENT: *A 3-inch (7.5 cm) pastry cutter or large glass; a heavy-duty mixer fitted with a whisk; a large rubber spatula or a large metal serving spoon; a baking sheet lined with baking parchment.*

4 large egg whites, free-range and organic, at room temperature
1 teaspoon cream of tartar
1-1/2 teaspoons cornstarch
1 cup plus 6 tablespoons (280 g) superfine sugar (see page 355)
1/2 teaspoon rose water
1-1/2 teaspoons Homemade Vanilla Extract (page 439) or pure vanilla extract
2 teaspoons freeze-dried raspberry powder (see Note)
1 cup (250 ml) heavy cream
1 plump, fresh vanilla bean, halved lengthwise
Fresh raspberries, for garnish

1. Arrange a rack in the lower third of the oven. Preheat the oven to 350°F (175°C).

2. Using the pastry cutter or glass, trace six circles on the baking parchment, evenly spaced apart.

3. In the bowl of the heavy-duty mixer, whisk the egg whites at low speed until frothy, then gradually increase the speed to high and whisk until just before the stiff peak stage. Be careful not to overbeat or the whites

may begin to break down and become lumpy. Add the cream of tartar and cornstarch and beat again to combine. Slowly add about 3/4 cup (150 g) of the sugar to the stiffened whites, a tablespoon at a time, and whisk just until the sugar dissolves and the mixture becomes thick and satiny. Add the rose water and whisk again briefly until combined.

4. Remove the mixer bowl from its stand. Add the vanilla extract to the whites, and, with the rubber spatula or metal spoon, cut through the egg whites and vanilla until you reach the bottom, then draw the spoon along the bottom of the bowl. Turn your wrist to bring the spoon up the side of the bowl, lightly bringing the egg whites from the bottom to the top, and as you do so turn the bowl about 45 degrees and lightly overturn the spoon to gently fold the whites on top of the vanilla. Turning the bowl as you fold will help the vanilla to be incorporated more efficiently. Continue cutting into the mixture and folding until just incorporated. Always work slowly and gently. Do not be tempted to overmix and unnecessarily knock extra air out of the mixture. If necessary, err on the side of underfolding. Add the remaining sugar and, using the same technique, fold it gently into the whites.

5. Add 1 teaspoon of the raspberry powder and fold it into the whites. You do not need to be thorough here—it's fine to leave the raspberry in streaks throughout mixture.

6. Using some of the meringue as glue, stick the baking parchment to the baking sheet, making sure the drawn circles are on the underside of the paper so the markings do not transfer to the meringue during baking. Using the large spoon, scoop the meringue into large balls onto the baking parchment, dividing it evenly among the six circles.

7. Reduce the oven temperature to 230°F (110°C) and bake until the outside of the pavlovas are firm but not colored, 1 hour to 1 hour and 20 minutes; check the pavlovas without opening the door, since a rush of cold air while

the pavlovas are still warm can cause them to collapse. Turn off the oven and leave the pavlovas in the oven to cool completely. The cooled baked pavlovas can be stored in an airtight container at room temperature for up to 2 days.

8. Put the cream in the bowl of the mixer. Scrape the seeds from the vanilla bean into the mixer bowl and whisk the cream into soft peaks. (Reserve the pod to make Vanilla Sugar, page 441, and Vanilla Powder, page 442.)

9. When you are ready to serve the dessert, spoon the cream on top of the pavlovas, sprinkle with the remaining 1 teaspoon raspberry powder, and top with fresh raspberries.

NOTE: *To make raspberry powder, blend freeze-dried raspberries into a fine powder in an electric spice mill.*

Frozen Desserts

There is something enduring about creamy frozen desserts. They can make for the most satisfying summer treat or a simple sweet end to a meal. But we don't all have ice cream makers or freezer space to fit the churning bowl. That's where *nougat glacé* and *semifreddo* desserts step in. They're easy make-ahead options when entertaining, and the mixture of flavors and textures is only as limited as your imagination.

The classic French *nougat glacé* is a miraculous semifrozen dessert that takes to a myriad of variations and can go through the seasons, garnished with all manner of seasonal fruits. Its Italian cousin, *semifreddo* (meaning "half cold"), is a richer version using egg yolks instead of egg whites, much like the custard base of Italian *gelato*.

Tips

~ A really cold freezer is essential here. In most modern freezers, this is no problem. If there is a thermometer in your freezer and/or you have an infrared thermometer, you can easily determine your freezer's temperature. The ideal temperature for freezing frozen desserts is 0°F (−18°C). Warmer than that, your dessert may not fully firm up.

~ Eggs are easiest to separate when cold, but whites will beat to their fullest volume at room temperature. So plan ahead!

~ To prevent freezer burn and protect the delicate consistency of frozen desserts, make sure your dessert is well wrapped. Once the dessert has firmed up in the freezer, take it out, remove the loaf pan or mold, and wrap it tightly in two layers of plastic wrap and then a layer of aluminum foil.

Honey Nougat Glacé with Candied Kumquats

The Provençal town of Montélimar is famous for its *nougat,* generally a semisoft confection of egg whites cooked with local honey. This chilled version, a honey-based *nougat glacé,* is a dessert that can be made in any season, folding in all manner of nuts and candied fruits, and garnished with any fruit of the season. In restaurants, all too often, I am served a *nougat glacé* that is hard as a rock. I have found in my tests that lightly cooking the sugar, honey, and invert sugar syrup and pouring the hot mixture into whipped egg whites softens the mixture, and the result is a feather-light, creamy-textured dessert. I make this often and find that a collapsible *pâté* mold works like a charm, simplifying the unmolding process.

---
12 SERVINGS

EQUIPMENT: *A 1-quart (1 l) rectangular loaf pan or a 1-quart (1 l) collapsible* pâté *mold l; a heavy-duty mixer fitted with a whisk; a large spatula or large spoon; 12 chilled dessert plates.*

3/4 cup (185 ml) heavy cream, chilled
1/4 cup (50 g) sugar
3 tablespoons mild honey, such as clover
3 tablespoons Invert Sugar Syrup (page 442) or light corn syrup
3 large egg whites, free-range and organic, at room temperature
Candied Kumquats (recipe follows) or mixed berries, for garnish

1. Line the loaf pan with baking parchment, leaving a generous overhang.

2. In the bowl of the heavy-duty mixer, whisk the cream at the highest speed until stiff peaks form, about 2 minutes. Transfer the whipped cream to a

large bowl. Wash the whisk and bowl of the mixer and reserve them to use to whisk the egg whites.

3. In a medium saucepan, combine the sugar, honey, and invert sugar syrup over medium heat. Whisking regularly, cook until the mixture is foamy and bubbling and has tripled in volume, 3 to 4 minutes.

4. In the clean bowl of the mixer, whisk the egg whites at the highest speed until stiff peaks form, about 2 minutes. Still whisking at the highest speed, slowly pour the hot sugar mixture into the egg whites and whisk until well blended. Remove the bowl from the mixer and spoon the whipped cream on top of the egg white mixture. Carefully fold in the cream by hand: Using the edge of the spatula or spoon, cut through the two mixtures until you reach the bottom, then draw the spoon along the bottom of the bowl. Turn your wrist to bring the spoon up the side of the bowl, lightly bringing the egg white mixture from the bottom to the top. As you do so, turn the bowl about 45 degrees, lightly overturning the spoon to fold the egg whites on top of the whipped cream. Turning the bowl as you fold will incorporate the mixtures more efficiently. Continue cutting into the mixture and folding until just incorporated.

5. Spoon the *nougat* mixture into the prepared pan or mold, using a spatula to smooth out the top. Carefully lift up on the edges of the overhanging baking parchment to loosen it and to ensure the mixture will not stick to the pan once frozen, then fold the baking parchment over the top. Cover lightly the *nougat* with aluminum foil and freeze until firm, at least 6 hours and up to 3 days.

6. To serve, carefully remove the frozen dessert from the pan, using the overhanging baking parchment as handles. (If the dessert is difficult to unmold, dip the bottom of the mold in hot water for a few seconds.) Remove the baking parchment. Cut the *nougat glacé* into 12 even slices. Serve on the chilled plates. Garnish with candied kumquats or mixed berries.

MAKE-AHEAD NOTE: *The* nougat glacé *can be made up to 3 days in advance and kept frozen.*

VARIATIONS

CANDIED CITRUS AND GINGER NOUGAT GLACÉ
Carefully fold in 1/4 cup (40 g) each of cubed candied lemon, orange, and ginger in step 3, or just use 3/4 cup (120 g) candied ginger.

YOGURT NOUGAT GLACÉ
For a tangier dessert: In step 1, combine 1/2 cup (125 ml) heavy cream with 1/2 cup (125 ml) thick Greek yogurt and whip as instructed.

Candied Kumquats

These shimmering orange candied fruits are great as a garnish on nougat glacé.

— MAKES 1 QUART (1 L) ———————————————————

EQUIPMENT: Eight 1/2-cup (125 ml) canning jars with lids, sterilized.

1-1/2 pounds (750 g) fresh kumquats
2 cups (500 ml) fresh blood orange, mandarin orange, or regular orange juice
1 cup (200 g) sugar

1. Stem the kumquats, halve them lengthwise, and remove and discard the seeds.

2. In a large saucepan, combine the kumquats, orange juice, and sugar. Simmer over medium heat, skimming the surface as needed, until the juice is thick and the kumquats are soft and translucent, about 1 hour. Skim off and discard any seeds that float to the surface. Let cool.

3. Transfer to the canning jars and secure the lids. Store in the refrigerator for up to 1 month.

Caramelized Pistachio Nougat Glacé

Pistachios play a starring role in this all-season dessert. Toasting the nuts brings out their sweet, rich, earthy flavors, and caramelizing them with sugar to make a sort of pistachio brittle only intensifies these qualities.

— 12 SERVINGS —————————————————————

EQUIPMENT: *A 1-quart (1 l) rectangular loaf pan or a 1-quart (1 l) collapsible pâté mold; a heavy-duty mixer fitted with a whisk; a large spatula or large spoon; 12 chilled dessert plates.*

3/4 cup (100 g) shelled pistachio nuts
3 tablespoons confectioners' sugar
3/4 cup (185 ml) heavy cream, chilled
1/4 cup (50 g) sugar
1/3 cup (80 ml) mild honey, such as clover
1/4 cup (60 ml) Invert Sugar Syrup (page 442) or light corn syrup
3 large egg whites, free-range and organic, at room temperature

1. Line the loaf pan with baking parchment, leaving a generous overhang.

2. In a large nonstick skillet, toast the pistachios over medium heat, shaking the pan regularly, cooking until the nuts begin to crackle, about 2 minutes. Watch carefully so they do not burn. Reduce the heat to low and sprinkle the nuts with the confectioners' sugar. The sugar will slowly melt and coat the nuts. Cook, stirring constantly, until the nuts are well coated with the melted sugar and nicely caramelized, about 2 minutes more. Immediately transfer the nuts to a large sheet of baking parchment to cool, spreading them out so they do not stick together.

3. In the bowl of the heavy-duty mixer, whisk the cream at the highest speed until stiff peaks form, about 2 minutes. Transfer the whipped cream to a

large bowl. Wash the whisk and bowl of the mixer and reserve them to use to whisk the egg whites.

4. In a medium saucepan, combine the sugar, honey, and invert sugar syrup over low heat. Cook, whisking regularly, until the mixture is foamy and bubbling, and has tripled in volume, 2 to 3 minutes. Let cool slightly in the pan.

5. In the clean bowl of the mixer, whisk the egg whites at the highest speed until stiff peaks form, about 2 minutes. Still whisking at the highest speed, slowly pour the sugar mixture into the egg whites.

6. Remove the bowl from the stand and spoon the whipped cream on top of the egg white mixture. Carefully fold in the cream by hand: Using the edge of the spatula or spoon, cut through the two mixtures until you reach the bottom, then draw the spoon along the bottom of the bowl. Turn your wrist to bring the spoon up the side of the bowl, lightly bringing the egg white mixture from the bottom to the top. As you do so, turn the bowl about 45 degrees, lightly overturning the spoon to fold the egg whites on top of the whipped cream. Turning the bowl as you fold will incorporate the mixtures more efficiently. Continue cutting into the mixture and folding until just incorporated.

7. Fold in about three-quarters of the caramelized nuts, reserving the rest for garnish. Spoon the nougat mixture into the prepared pan or mold and use a spatula to smooth out the top. Carefully lift up on the edges of the overhanding baking parchment to loosen it and to ensure the mixture will not stick to the pan once frozen, then fold the baking parchment over the top. Cover lightly with aluminum foil and freeze until firm, at least 6 hours and up to 3 days.

8. To serve, remove the dessert from the pan or mold, using the overhanging parchment as handles. Remove the baking parchment. Cut the *nougat glacé* into 12 even slices. Serve on the chilled plates, garnished with the reserved caramelized pistachios.

Lemon Semifreddo with Poached Strawberries

Guests have dubbed this dessert "lemifreddo," a simple, golden, egg-yolk-rich lemon version of the classic Italian frozen dessert. Here it is garnished with strawberries lightly cooked in their own juices, but use your imagination for the possibilities for variations and garnishes are endless. This is a great recipe to make after you've prepared meringues and *nougat glacé* and have lots of leftover egg yolks.

— 12 SERVINGS ————————————————

EQUIPMENT: *A 1-quart (1 l) rectangular loaf pan or a 1-quart (1 l) collapsible pâté mold; a double boiler; a heavy-duty mixer fitted with a whisk; a large rubber spatula or large spoon; 12 chilled dessert plates.*

1 cup (250 ml) heavy cream, chilled
4 large egg yolks, free-range and organic, at room temperature
3/4 cup (150 g) sugar
Finely grated zest of 1 organic lemon
1/4 cup (60 ml) freshly squeezed lemon juice
4 cups (about 350 g) strawberries, hulled and quartered, or mixed fresh berries, such as raspberries, blackberries, or blueberries, poached in their own juice until soft and cooled

1. Line the loaf pan with baking parchment, leaving a generous overhang.

2. In the bowl of the heavy-duty mixer, whisk the cream at highest speed until stiff peaks form, about 2 minutes. Transfer the cream to a large bowl. Wash the mixing bowl and whisk and reserve them to whisk the egg yolks.

3. In the top of the double boiler set over but not touching simmering water, whisk together the egg yolks, sugar, lemon zest, and lemon juice. Cook,

whisking regularly, until the yolk mixture begins to thicken slightly (but is not cooked or set), about 4 minutes.

4. Transfer the hot mixture to the clean bowl of the mixer and whisk at the highest speed until the yolk mixture has cooled and thickened, is a pale yellow, and has doubled in volume, about 4 minutes.

5. Remove the bowl from the mixer and spoon the whipped cream on top of the whipped yolk mixture. Carefully fold in the whipped cream by hand: Using the edge of the spatula or spoon, cut through the two mixtures until you reach the bottom, then draw the spoon along the bottom of the bowl. Turn your wrist to bring the spoon up the side of the bowl, lightly bringing the yolk mixture from the bottom to the top. As you do so, turn the bowl about 45 degrees, lightly overturning the spoon to fold the yolk mixture on top of the whipped cream. Turning the bowl as you fold will incorporate the mixtures more efficiently. Continue cutting into the mixture and folding until just incorporated.

6. Spoon the mixture into the prepared pan or mold and use a spatula to even out the top. Carefully lift up on the edges of the paper to loosen it and to ensure the mixture will not stick to the pan once frozen, then fold the baking parchment over the top. Cover lightly with aluminum foil and freeze until firm, at least 6 hours and up to 3 days.

7. To serve, carefully remove the frozen dessert from the pan or mold using the overhanging parchment as handles. (If the dessert is difficult to unmold, dip the bottom of the mold in hot water for a few seconds.) Remove the baking parchment. Cut the *semifreddo* into 12 even slices. Serve on the chilled plates, garnished with the berries.

MAKE-AHEAD NOTE: *The* semifreddo *can be made up to 3 days in advance and kept frozen.*

CITRUS SEMIFREDDO

Replace the lemon zest and juice with that of lime, blood orange, or yuzu, an Asian citrus fruit. Use your imagination for garnishes, varying the fruits, including sliced mangoes, crushed raspberries, a mixture of fresh berries, passion fruit pulp, or a puree of mango or papaya. Serve with Honey, Candied Lemon, and Almond Bars (page 304).

YOGURT SEMIFREDDO

For a tangier dessert: In step 1, combine 1/2 cup (125 ml) cream with 1/2 cup (125 ml) thick Greek yogurt and whip as instructed. Garnish with crushed raspberries.

SET

When the summer months roll around, as much as I can, I try to avoid turning on the oven. Set desserts are a great answer here, calling on the refrigerator rather than the heat of the oven to firm up the ingredients. It also means I can make them in advance, a necessity when I have a house full of guests or students. There are two classic ways to "set" a dish: with gelatin and with chocolate.

SETTING WITH GELATIN

Gelatin is a little like yeast in that it inspires fear in even the most confident of cooks. But with the right guidance and following a few simple rules, gelatin is very easy to use.

Gelatin comes in two forms: powder and sheet (or leaf) gelatin. Sheet gelatin is more common in Europe, while the powdered version is the easiest to come by in the United States. The right gelatin-to-liquid ratio is essential to making a dessert with a pleasing mouthfeel (not too sloppy and not overly set), and I have found that using 1 packet of powdered Knox brand gelatin in my master *panna cotta* recipe turns out perfectly set desserts every time. For conversion to sheet gelatin, see the note on page 386.

Tips for Setting with Gelatin

~ Make sure you get your quantities of gelatin right—many a *panna cotta* has been ruined by a cook's heavy hand in this department, resulting in a dense dessert that is far too firm.

~ Gelatin needs to be added to cold liquid to let it "bloom" and activate its gelling properties.

~ Add bloomed gelatin to warm liquids; if the mixture cools too quickly, it may create streaks of gelatin in the final product.

Panna Cotta

Some years ago I did a lot of experimenting with *panna cotta*, even preparing a truffled version for my black-truffle cooking class. I subsequently forgot about this miraculous (and make-ahead!) dessert until a few years ago, when an incoming student put in an advance special request to make it during class. Ever since then, this dessert has been on my menus, and what a blissful reunion it has been! I toyed around with a series of savory versions (with cheese and herbs and other concoctions), but they never seemed to sing quite like the sweet versions.

Lemon-Vanilla Panna Cotta
with Candied Lemon

Lemon, vanilla, cream, sugar: a culinary quartet that is right at home in this not-too-sweet silken dessert. The crowning glory is the accompanying homemade candied lemons with their sauce, which add a strong citrus tang, an essential counterpoint to the creaminess of the dessert.

— 6 SERVINGS

EQUIPMENT: *Six 1/2-cup (125 ml) ramekins; a rimmed baking sheet; a sifter; a fine-mesh sieve; a large measuring cup with a pouring spout; 6 chilled dessert plates.*

2 teaspoons (1 package/7 g) unflavored powdered gelatin (see Note)
2 cups (500 ml) whole milk, well chilled
1 plump, fresh vanilla bean
1 cup (120 g) confectioners' sugar, sifted
1 cup (250 ml) heavy cream
Grated zest from 1 organic lemon
1 recipe Candied Lemon and Syrup (page 414)

1. Place the ramekins side by side on the baking sheet. Set aside.

2. In a small bowl, sprinkle the gelatin over 1/4 cup (60 ml) of the milk and stir to blend. Set aside until the gelatin "blooms" or completely absorbs the milk, 2 to 3 minutes. The mixture should resemble light clouds.

3. Halve the vanilla bean lengthwise and use the tip of a small spoon to scrape out the seeds. Place the seeds and vanilla bean halves in a large

saucepan and combine with the remaining 1-3/4 cups (435 ml) milk, the sugar, cream, and lemon zest. Bring to a boil over medium heat, whisking to dissolve the sugar. Remove from the heat, cover, and let steep for 10 minutes to infuse with the vanilla flavor.

4. Bring the cream mixture back to a simmer and stir in the softened gelatin and milk mixture. Strain the mixture through the fine-mesh sieve set over the large measuring cup. (Remove, let dry, and reserve the vanilla bean halves to make Vanilla Sugar, page 440.)

5. Divide the strained mixture evenly among the ramekins. Cover with plastic wrap and refrigerate until set, about 8 hours.

6. To serve the *panna cotta*, quickly dip the bottom of each ramekin into a bowl of hot water for about 10 seconds, shaking to loosen the cream. Invert onto the chilled plates. Pour a spoonful of candied lemons and syrup over each serving of *panna cotta*. Serve.

NOTE: *To prepare* panna cotta *with sheet gelatin: Conversions of powdered gelatin to sheet gelatin are universally controversial. For best results, follow the package directions. I do not like a super-firm panna cotta, so would tend to err on the side of using less gelatin. Generally, three to five 3 x 5-inch (6.5 x 11 cm) sheets equal 2 teaspoons (1 package/7 g) gelatin, depending on how firm you want your* panna cotta. *To soften the sheet gelatin, soak in cold water for 5 to 10 minutes, drain, and add in step 5.*

MAKE-AHEAD NOTE: *The* panna cotta *can be prepared up to 2 days in advance and refrigerated until serving time.*

Crushed Raspberry Panna Cotta

This raspberry version takes on the ubiquitous vanilla *panna cotta* with berry *coulis* you find in so many Italian restaurants. Here, raspberries are crushed and incorporated into the cream mixture before setting, giving a much livelier burst of berry flavor and a twist on the classic *panna cotta* texture. Plus, one can generally find top-quality raspberries year-round, so there is really no excuse not to make this!

— 6 SERVINGS

EQUIPMENT: *Six 1/2-cup (125 ml) ramekins; a rimmed baking sheet; a potato masher or large fork; a fine-mesh sieve; 6 chilled dessert plates.*

2 teaspoons (1 package/7 g) unflavored powdered gelatin (see Note, page 386)
2 cups (500 ml) whole milk, well chilled
4 cups (500 g) fresh raspberries
1 plump, fresh vanilla bean
1 cup (120 g) confectioners' sugar, sifted
1 cup (250 ml) heavy cream
1/4 teaspoon fine sea salt

1. Place the ramekins side by side on the baking sheet.

2. In a small bowl, sprinkle the gelatin over 1/4 cup (60 ml) of the milk and stir to blend. Set aside until the gelatin "blooms," or completely absorbs the milk, 2 to 3 minutes. The mixture should resemble light clouds.

3. Place the raspberries in a large, shallow bowl and crush them lightly with the potato masher or fork.

4. Halve the vanilla bean lengthwise and use the tip of a small spoon to scrape out the seeds. Place the seeds and the vanilla bean halves in a large

saucepan and combine with the remaining 1-3/4 cups (435 ml) milk, sugar, and cream. Bring to a simmer over medium heat, whisking to dissolve the sugar. Remove from the heat, cover, and let steep for 10 minutes to infuse with the vanilla flavor.

5. Bring the cream mixture back to a simmer and stir in the softened gelatin and milk mixture. Strain the mixture through the fine-mesh sieve set over the large measuring cup. (Remove, let dry, and reserve the vanilla bean halves to make Vanilla Sugar, page 440.)

6. Stir in half the crushed raspberries, reserving the rest for garnish. Evenly divide the mixture among the ramekins. Cover with plastic wrap and refrigerate until set, about 8 hours.

7. To serve the *panna cotta*, quickly dip the bottom of each ramekin into a bowl of hot water for about 10 seconds, shaking to loosen the cream. Invert onto the chilled plates. Garnish with the remaining crushed raspberries. Serve.

MAKE-AHEAD NOTE: *The* panna cotta *can be prepared up to 2 days in advance and refrigerated until serving time.*

Saffron, Orange, and Rhubarb Panna Cotta

Make this in spring when ruby-red, garden-fresh rhubarb is readily available. The saffron threads and vanilla seeds make for a dramatic *tableau*, and the tart rhubarb sauce is a perfect companion for this creamy chilled Italian dessert.

If you have the time, make this dessert at least 24 hours in advance, since the orange-saffron flavor is even better the next day.

— 6 SERVINGS ————————————————————————

EQUIPMENT: *Six 1/2-cup (125 ml) ramekins; a rimmed baking sheet; a sifter; a fine-mesh sieve; a large measuring cup with a pouring spout; 6 chilled dessert plates.*

2 teaspoons (1 package/7 g) unflavored powdered gelatin (see Note, page 386)
2 cups (500 ml) whole milk, well chilled
1 plump, fresh vanilla bean
1 cup (120 g) confectioners' sugar, sifted
1 cup (250 ml) heavy cream
Grated zest from 1 organic orange
1/4 teaspoon saffron threads
Rhubarb-Orange Sauce (recipe follows)

1. Place the ramekins side by side on the baking sheet.

2. In a small bowl, sprinkle the gelatin over 1/4 cup (60 ml) of the milk and stir to blend. Set aside until the gelatin "blooms" or completely absorbs the milk, 2 to 3 minutes. The mixture should resemble light clouds.

3. Halve the vanilla bean lengthwise and use the tip of a small spoon to scrape out the seeds. Place the seeds and the vanilla bean halves in a large saucepan and add the remaining 1-3/4 cups (435 ml) milk, sugar, and the

cream. Bring just to a boil over medium heat. Remove from the heat. Place 1/4 cup (60 ml) of the cream mixture in a small bowl and add the orange zest and saffron threads. Cover and let steep for 10 minutes to infuse.

4. Bring the vanilla-cream mixture back to a simmer. Stir in the gelatin mixture. Strain the mixture through the fine-mesh sieve set over the large measuring cup. (Remove, rinse and reserve the vanilla bean halves to make the rhubarb-orange sauce.) Add the infused saffron–orange zest cream to the vanilla-cream mixture. Stir to incorporate.

5. Divide the mixture evenly among the ramekins. Cover with plastic wrap and refrigerate until set, about 8 hours.

6. To serve the *panna cotta,* quickly dip the bottom of each ramekin into a bowl of hot water for about 10 seconds, shaking to loosen the cream. Invert onto the chilled plates and pour a spoonful of chilled rhubarb-orange sauce over each serving. Serve.

MAKE-AHEAD NOTE: *The* panna cotta *can be prepared up to 2 days in advance and refrigerated until serving time.)*

Rhubarb-Orange Sauce

EQUIPMENT: A fine-mesh sieve.

1 pound (about 4 cups/500 g) fresh or frozen rhubarb, coarsely chopped into
    2-inch (5 cm) pieces
3 tablespoons confectioners' sugar
1 reserved scraped vanilla bean pod (from the *panna cotta* recipe)
1/2 cup (125 ml) freshly squeezed orange juice

1. In a medium saucepan, combine the rhubarb, sugar, vanilla bean pod, orange juice, and 2 cups (500 ml) water.

2. Bring to a boil over high heat, then reduce the heat to medium and simmer until the rhubarb is cooked through and has softened, about 10 minutes.

3. Strain the juices through the sieve into a measuring cup with a pouring sprout (reserve the strained rhubarb pulp for another use, such as a compote). Rinse the saucepan and return the sauce to the heat. Simmer over medium heat, uncovered, until the sauce has reduced by about half, 10 to 15 minutes. Set aside to cool, then place in the refrigerator to chill. Store in an airtight container in the refrigerator for up to 3 days.

Chocolate

Chocolate truffles are essentially chocolate *ganache* with the right ratio of chocolate to cream to allow the *ganache* to set into smooth decadent balls of soft chocolate. It is the cocoa butter in the chocolate that acts as the setting agent, so if the ratio of cream to chocolate is off, the truffles either won't set or will be too hard.

Chocolate Truffles

I know few people who can resist chocolate, and right up there on top of the all-time favorites list are chocolate truffles. The touch of honey here makes for fragrant, wholesome treasures.

Note that due to the setting times, you will need to start making these several hours or a day before you plan to serve them.

— MAKES 25 TO 30 TRUFFLES ——

EQUIPMENT: *A silicone spatula; a storage container with a lid, lined with baking parchment; a baking sheet lined with baking parchment; a miniature ice cream scoop or melon baller (about 1 inch/2.5 cm in diameter); a demitasse spoon; a miniature fine-mesh sieve.*

7 ounces (200 g) 70% bittersweet chocolate, coarsely grated (see Note)
2/3 cup (160 ml) heavy cream
1 tablespoon mild honey, such as clover
1 tablespoon (1/2 ounce/15 g) unsalted butter, at room temperature
3 tablespoons unsweetened cocoa powder

1. Place the chocolate in a large metal bowl.

2. In a small saucepan, combine the cream and honey and bring just to a boil over low heat.

3. Pour one-third of the cream mixture over the chocolate. Working rapidly with a silicone spatula, mix to obtain a smooth and glossy texture. Gradually add the remaining cream mixture, making sure to maintain

the emulsion, until the chocolate has completely melted and has reached a uniform texture. Stir in the butter and mix thoroughly one more time.

4. Let the *ganache* cool at room temperature. When cool, cover with plastic wrap and let set at room temperature for several hours, preferably overnight, to harden, until it is firm enough to scoop. (When the *ganache* has set, it can be refrigerated for up to 2 days.)

5. Place the cocoa powder in a small cup. Set the sieve in the cup, making sure it reaches into the cocoa powder.

6. To shape the truffles, use the ice cream scoop or melon baller to form 1-inch (2.5 cm) balls of *ganache*. Remove the chocolate balls from the ice cream scoop or melon baller with the demitasse spoon and roll the truffles between the palms of your hands into smooth balls.

7. Place one of the truffles in the sieve and shake gently to cover the truffle in cocoa powder. Lift the sieve and shake to dust off any excess powder. Transfer the truffle to the storage container. Repeat to coat the remaining truffles.

NOTE: *In our tests, we found best results with Lindt Excellence 70% chocolate, which is readily available in supermarkets.*

MAKE-AHEAD NOTE: *The truffles can be prepared up to 1 week in advance and stored in the refrigerator in a covered container. Bring to room temperature before serving.*

Chocolate Satin

I have to confess that I have been known to obsess over a recipe, and this one became a big-time obsession. I tinkered with it over an entire summer, working to find just the right proportion of whipped egg white and cream and the best kind of chocolate to use, to create a dessert that is at once creamy, fragrant, full-flavored, and, well, unforgettable. And of course it can also be made in the spring, fall, and winter! This dessert differs from a classic chocolate mousse, which would contain egg yolks as well as whites. The proof is in the pudding, as they say, and I have seen guests literally scraping the serving bowl clean. I consider this a success!

— 8 TO 12 SERVINGS —————————————————————————

EQUIPMENT: *A sifter; a heavy-duty mixer fitted with a whisk; a 6-quart (6 l) metal bowl; a 1-1/2-quart (1.5 l) saucepan; an attractive 2-quart (2 l) serving bowl.*

10 ounces (300 g) 70% bittersweet chocolate, finely chopped (see Notes)
1/2 teaspoon fine sea salt
1 teaspoon Homemade Vanilla Extract (page 439) or pure vanilla extract
2 cups (500 ml) heavy cream
3 large egg whites, free-range and organic, at room temperature (see Notes)
1 cup (120 g) confectioners' sugar, sifted

1. Place the chocolate in the metal bowl. Sprinkle with the salt and vanilla extract.

2. In the saucepan, bring the cream just to a simmer over medium heat. Pour the hot cream into the bowl with the chocolate and, working rapidly, mix with a wooden spoon to melt the chocolate until you have a smooth and glossy texture, about 2 minutes. Let cool.

3. In the bowl of the mixer, whisk the egg whites at the highest speed until frothy, about 10 seconds. Continue whisking until soft peaks form, about 1 minute more. Add the sugar 1 tablespoon at a time and whisk at the highest speed until satiny and stiff peaks form, about 2 minutes more. The mixture should be airy, glossy, and stiff like a meringue.

4. Add about one-quarter of the egg white mixture to the cooled chocolate mixture to lighten it. Whisk gently until no streaks of white remain. Spoon the rest of the whipped egg white on top of the mixture in the bowl. Fold in the whipped egg white by hand: Using the edge of the spatula or a large metal spoon, cut through the two mixtures until you reach the bottom, then draw the spoon along the bottom of the bowl. Turn your wrist to bring the spoon up the side of the bowl, lightly bringing the chocolate mixture from the bottom to the top. As you do so, turn the bowl about 45 degrees, lightly overturning the spoon to fold the chocolate on top of the egg whites. Turning the bowl as you fold will incorporate the mixtures more efficiently. Continue cutting into the mixture and folding until just incorporated.

5. Pour the mixture into the serving bowl and cover with plastic wrap. Refrigerate until firm, at least 6 hours or up to 1 week. The dessert will be firmer than a mousse but not as firm as a cake or brownie. Scoop into ice cream bowls with an ice cream scoop or large, rounded spoon. Serve chilled.

NOTES

~ In our tests, we found best results with Lindt Excellence 70% chocolate, which is readily available at supermarkets. Be cautious about using just any chocolate; in chocolate with less than 70% cacao, the final result will not always be firm enough.

~ Raw eggs are used in this preparation. Consuming raw eggs may increase the risk of foodborne illness. Raw eggs should be avoided by the very young and the very old, pregnant women, and anyone with a compromised immune system.

VARIATION: *Mix about 1/2 cup (60 g) cocoa nibs into the chocolate mixture before folding, and/or sprinkle the top of the satin with cocoa nibs at serving time.*

MAKE-AHEAD NOTE: *This dessert can be prepared up to 1 week in advance, covered with plastic wrap, and refrigerated.*

EXTRAS

Staple Stocks

Forget those dried powdered cubes full of additives and preservatives and manufactured flavors that try to pass themselves off as stock. Their harsh flavors can overpower a dish instead of giving fullness and depth of flavor, as a real stock or broth should do. Certainly it takes more time and some forward planning to make your own, but the rewards will be apparent in the end result. And in reality, it is the stove and the ingredients that do most of the work. It is merely a question of setting aside the time to save the ingredients you need, adding them to the stockpot, and planning to be somewhere in the vicinity of the stove while it bubbles away for the next few hours.

After making a roast chicken, keep the carcass for stock and your purchase will go even further in feeding your family. Keep a container for vegetable scraps in your fridge, and when you've collected enough, make a fresh and vibrant vegetable stock with it.

Stocks freeze well: Use ice cube trays if you plan to use the stock in small quantities for soups for one or sauces (when frozen, empty the stock cubes into a freezer storage bag and keep in the freezer for up to 3 months), or in larger containers for braising and soups in larger quantities.

Chicken Stock

For an omnivorous cook, having a freezer stocked with flavorful, top-quality chicken stock is essential. Soups are a part of any good cook's repertoire, and chicken stock forms the backbone of the best soups I know. Keep it on hand for such dishes as Asian Chicken and Cilantro Meatballs (page 121), Stracciatella (Roman "Egg Drop" Soup) with Spinach (page 33), or Magic Cèpe Mushroom Soup (page 69).

This recipe was inspired by chef Joël Robuchon, who taught me to sear onions over a live flame, giving the resulting stock a richer flavor and golden color. Likewise, he instructed me to add a touch of fresh ginger, lending an Asian accent to the final product.

Tips

~ Use a tall pot to limit evaporation. I always use a large pasta pot fitted with a colander, which makes it easy to remove the solid ingredients and begin to filter the stock.

~ For a clear stock, begin with cold water and bring it slowly to a simmer. Never allow a stock to boil or it will be cloudy, since the fat will emulsify. Cold water also aids in extracting greater flavor.

~ For the first 30 minutes of cooking, skim off the impurities that rise to the surface as the stock simmers.

MAKES 3 QUARTS (3 L)

EQUIPMENT: *A long-handled, 2-pronged fork; a 10-quart (10 l) pasta pot fitted with a colander; a fine-mesh skimmer; dampened cheesecloth.*

2 large onions, halved crosswise (do not peel)

4 whole cloves

About 4 pounds (2 kg) chicken backs, or 2 whole free-range chicken carcasses

2 teaspoons coarse sea salt

4 carrots, scrubbed and cut into thick rounds (do not peel)

1 plump, fresh garlic head, halved crosswise (do not peel)

4 celery ribs

1 leek, white and tender green parts only, halved lengthwise, rinsed, and cut into
    1-inch (2.5 cm) pieces

One 1-inch (2.5 cm) piece fresh ginger, peeled

12 black peppercorns

1 bouquet garni: *several bay leaves, fresh celery leaves, thyme sprigs, and parsley*
    sprigs encased in a wire-mesh tea infuser or bound in a piece of cheesecloth

1. One at a time, spear the onion halves with the long-handled fork and hold them directly over a gas flame (or directly on an electric burner) until scorched. Pierce a clove into each of the onion halves.

2. Place the chicken in the pasta pot and cover with 5 quarts (5 l) water. Add the onions, salt, carrots, garlic, celery, leek, ginger, peppercorns, and *bouquet garni*. Bring to a gentle simmer, uncovered, over medium heat. Use the skimmer to remove any impurities that rises to the surface, skimming until the broth is clear. Simmer gently until the broth is rich and golden and the chicken is cooked, about 2-1/2 hours.

3. Lift the colander insert out of the pot and discard the solids. Line a large colander with a double layer of the dampened cheesecloth and place the colander over a large bowl. Ladle—do not pour—the liquid into the colander to remove any impurities. Transfer the stock to airtight containers. Refrigerate, very lightly covered. When chilled, seal the covers and refrigerate; use within 3 days or freeze for up to 3 months.

Fish Stock

One usually comes across fish stocks that are rather neutral, without much personality. What makes this rich, multidimensional stock different? The flavorful fish bones are seared lightly before any liquids are added, creating an additional layer of flavor. Use any non-oily fish bones, such as monkfish or red snapper. For a pure, well-flavored stock with no bitterness, thoroughly rinse the bones, heads, and trimmings, removing the gills and any innards. Once cooked, extract the fish cheeks, if present, to enjoy as a special snack!

— MAKES 1-1/2 QUARTS (1.5 L) MILD STOCK OR 3 CUPS (750 ML) RICH STOCK —

EQUIPMENT: *A 6-quart (6 l) saucepan; a flat metal skimmer; a fine-mesh sieve; dampened cheesecloth.*

2 pounds (1 kg) non-oily fish bones, heads, and trimmings (gills removed), cut up
1/4 cup (60 ml) extra-virgin olive oil
1 shallot, peeled and minced
1 medium onion, peeled and minced
1/2 teaspoon fine sea salt
3 bay leaves, halved and crushed
Bouquet garni: *fresh celery leaves, thyme sprigs, and parsley sprigs encased in a wire-mesh tea infuser or bound in a piece of cheesecloth*

1. Thoroughly rinse the fish bones, heads, and trimmings under cold running water, so that no blood remains and the water runs clear, about 5 minutes. Drain and set aside.

2. In the saucepan, combine the oil, shallot, onion, salt, and bay leaves. Stir to coat the ingredients with the oil and sweat—cook, covered, over low heat—until soft, about 5 minutes. Add the fish bones, heads, and trimmings, increase the heat to high, and cook, uncovered, for 5 minutes more.

3. Add the *bouquet garni* and 2 quarts (2 l) cold water to cover. Bring to a simmer and leave to simmer gently, uncovered, for 20 minutes, skimming regularly to remove any foam or impurities that could add bitterness to the stock.

4. Remove the pan from the heat and set aside for 10 minutes to allow any additional impurities to settle to the bottom.

5. Line the sieve with the dampened cheesecloth. Set the sieve over a large bowl and ladle—do not pour—the stock into the prepared sieve. Rinse the saucepan and return the strained stock to the pan. Taste the stock for strength. For a mild stock, use as is. For a rich stock, boil the liquid until it has reduced to 3 cups (750 ml). Let cool to room temperature, then transfer the stock to an airtight container. The stock will keep in the refrigerator for up to 3 days or in the freezer for up to 1 month.

NOTE: *When straining stock, never pour the liquid from the vessel through the strainer, or you are likely to pour unwanted impurities into the stock. Rather, set the stock aside for at least 10 minutes, to allow the impurities to settle to the bottom, then ladle the liquid into a sieve lined with moistened cheesecloth.*

Shellfish Stock

Please don't discard those lobster or shrimp shells! They make the base of a rich and delicious stock, seasoned with fennel seeds, star anise, bay leaf, garlic, and a touch of tomato paste for color and a light hint of acidity.

— MAKES 2 QUARTS (2 L) BROTH ————————————————————

EQUIPMENT: *A 6-quart (6 l) heavy-duty stockpot; a fine-mesh sieve; dampened cheesecloth.*

2 tablespoons extra-virgin olive oil
2 pounds (1 kg) lobster or shrimp shells, well rinsed
1 tablespoon fennel seeds
2 whole star anise
4 bay leaves
1 plump, fresh garlic head, halved crosswise
2 teaspoons fine sea salt
1 tablespoon Italian tomato paste

1. In the stockpot, heat the oil over medium heat until shimmering. Add the shells and sear until they turn a bright pink and very fragrant, 2 to 3 minutes.

2. Add the fennel seeds, star anise, bay leaves, garlic, salt, tomato paste, and 3 quarts (3 l) cold water. Bring to a boil and let boil vigorously, uncovered, for 20 minutes. To extract maximum flavor from the shells, use a wooden mallet to gently crush and break up the softened, cooked shells (try not to splash the liquid all over). Taste occasionally for seasoning and strength.

3. Line the sieve with the dampened cheesecloth and place the sieve over a large bowl. Ladle the stock and solids—do not pour—into the sieve, pressing down hard on the solids to extract maximum juices and flavor.

4. Taste for seasoning. Serve warm in small cups as an appetizer or in warmed, shallow soup bowls as a first course. The stock will keep in an airtight container in the refrigerator for up to 1 day or freeze for up to 1 month.

Vegetable Stock

I always try to have minimal waste in my kitchen and vegetable stock is the perfect way to use up vegetable scraps. I like to keep a container in the refrigerator to collect the raw, well-scubbed vegetable peels, ends, and scraps from a day's cooking until I have enough to combine with fresh herbs and ginger to create a healthful, mild flavored stock. I favor celery and root vegetables such as carrots and onions over cruciferous vegetables such as cabbage and broccoli, which can overpower the stock.

MAKES 3 QUARTS (3 L)

EQUIPMENT: *A long-handled, 2-pronged fork; a 10-quart (10 l) pasta pot fitted with a colander; dampened cheesecloth.*

2 large onions, halved lengthwise (do not peel)
4 whole cloves
1 teaspoon coarse sea salt
4 carrots, scrubbed and cut crosswise into 1-inch (2.5 cm) pieces (do not peel)
1 plump, fresh garlic head, halved crosswise (do not peel)
4 celery ribs, with leaves
1 leek, white and tender green parts only, halved lengthwise, rinsed, and cut into 1-inch pieces
One 1-inch (2.5 cm) piece fresh ginger, peeled
6 black peppercorns
Bouquet garni: *several bay leaves, celery leaves, thyme sprigs, and parsley sprigs encased in a wire-mesh tea infuser or bound in a piece of cheesecloth*

1. One at a time, spear the onion halves with the long-handled fork and hold them directly over a gas flame (or directly on an electric burner) until scorched. (Scorching the onions will give the stock a richer flavor. The onion skins also give the stock a rich, golden color.) Stick a clove into each of the onion halves.

2. Place the onions in the pasta pot and add the salt, carrots, garlic, celery, leek, ginger, peppercorns, *bouquet garni*, and 5 quarts (5 l) quarts water. Bring to a boil. Lower the heat and simmer, uncovered, for about 45 minutes.

3. Lift the colander insert out of the pot and discard the solids. Line a large colander with a double layer of the dampened cheesecloth and place the colander over a large bowl. Ladle—do not pour—the liquid into the sieve to strain off any impurities. Measure the quantity of the stock. If the stock exceeds 3 quarts (3 l), return it to medium heat and cook until it has reduced to 3 quarts (3 l).

4. Transfer the stock to airtight containers and let it cool slightly, then cover and refrigerate the stock for up to 3 days or freeze for up to 3 months.

Pantry Staples, Sauces, Condiments

CLARIFIED BUTTER AND GHEE

Julia Child famously said, "With enough butter, anything is good." I wholeheartedly agree with Julia's sentiment and would perhaps add that with enough clarified butter, or *ghee*, the good can be elevated to the extraordinary.

Cooking with butter has the ability to radically enhance and transform the flavors of food, and cooking with butter that has been heated to bring out its nutty, caramelized flavors can add a remarkable depth of flavor to a dish.

On Butter

This most ancient of foods has over the past few decades been vilified as a "bad" fat, said to clog arteries and raise cholesterol. Recently, though, butter seems to be off the hook as a health hazard, if consumed in moderation. This is not an altogether surprising revelation; there is a reason that butter-making has endured for thousands of years.

If your budget allows, go for grass-fed butter, which has a far higher nutritional content than that made from the milk from corn-fed cows.

Clarified Butter and Ghee

Clarified butter is the result when butter is heated long enough to separate the milk solids from the butterfat. During this process some of the water is also cooked off, which means the butter can be preserved for longer. The resulting butter has a gentle nutty aroma, but its biggest advantage is that (like *ghee*) it can be heated to a high temperature (450 to 480°F/230 to 250°C, depending on how well it is clarified) without burning (it is the milk solids that burn when butter is heated). It is particularly useful when you want to panfry just about anything—toasted sandwiches, fruit, meat, or vegetables—with a clean, perfectly browned result.

Ghee, also known as butter oil or Indian clarified butter, is the extracted pure fat of butter. It is much like clarified butter, but is simmered for longer so that the milk solids separate from the fat entirely and all the water evaporates. What is left is a clear golden liquid (which quickly solidifies when refrigerated) with a deep nutty flavor. Like clarified butter, the removal of milk solids raises the smoke point from about 350°F (175°C) to 450 to 480°F (230 to 250°C).

— Makes about 1-3/4 cups cups (435 ml) —

EQUIPMENT: *A 3-quart (3 l) heavy-duty saucepan; a heat diffuser (see page 27); a fine-mesh sieve; dampened cheesecloth; a wide-mouth 2-cup (500 ml) glass jar with a lid.*

1 pound (500 g) unsalted butter, cubed

1. In the saucepan, melt the butter over low heat (using a heat diffuser as an insurance that the butter will not burn). Still over low heat, bring the butter to a gentle simmer, adjusting the heat if necessary. As the water evaporates, the butter will begin to sizzle and the milk proteins will separate from the butterfat into a layer of foam on the top (this is the whey protein) and solids

that clump together like curds (the casein). Let the butter simmer until it stops cracking, an indication that the butter is beginning to fry. This should take about 8 minutes. The liquid should be clear and golden. (You now have clarified butter.) Line the sieve with the dampened cheesecloth.

2. IF YOU ARE MAKING CLARIFIED BUTTER, at this point slowly strain the melted butter through the sieve into the glass jar, discarding the milky solids that remain in the cheesecloth. Cover securely and store in the refrigerator for up to 4 months.

3. IF YOU ARE MAKING GHEE, do not strain the melted butter at this point, but continue to gently simmer the liquid over low heat. The liquid will become translucent as the milk solids separate completely and fall to the bottom of the pan and the foam begins to subside, after a total of about 15 minutes. Continue to simmer gently until the milk solids at the bottom begin to brown, and the sizzling is barely audible (there will still be bubbles rising from the bottom, however), 5 to 10 minutes longer, but up to 20 (depending upon on how much water content there is in the butter, the pan used, and the heat). Watch carefully and keep the temperature low so as not to burn the milk solids. There is no need to remove the foam that rises to the top, as it will mostly subside naturally during the cooking process and the rest will be left behind in the cheesecloth during straining. This also prevents losing any butterfat in the skimming process.

4. Very slowly–to avoid splattering—strain the melted butter through the sieve into the jar. Cover securely and store in the refrigerator for up to 4 months.

Candied Lemon and Syrup

This recipe is my number one go-to condiment for desserts and baking, and the number of times it appears in this book will attest to that. While lemon is a favorite, oranges, blood oranges, clementines, and grapefruit can be easily be substituted. Avoid limes, however, as they turn a dingy gray when blanched.

— MAKES 1 CUP (250 ML)

3 organic lemons
3/4 cup (150 g) Vanilla Sugar (page 440)

1. Halve the lemons crosswise. Juice the lemons to measure 1/3 cup (80 ml) of juice. With a knife, trim off and discard the tips of both ends of the lemons so that they will stand up straight on a cutting board. With the knife, cut the peel and white pith lengthwise end to end into wide, 2-inch (5 cm) strips. Cut the strips lengthwise into 4 thin strips.

2. Fill a 3-quart (3 l) saucepan with 1 quart (1 l) water. Bring to a boil over high heat. Add the peel. Blanch for 5 minutes. Drain through a fine-mesh sieve. Repeat with fresh water two more times. (This helps soften the citrus and remove any bitterness in the peel or pith.)

3. In a small saucepan, combine the reserved lemon juice, the sugar, and 1/2 cup (125 ml) water. Bring to a simmer over medium heat and stir to dissolve the sugar, about 1 minute. Add the blanched peel, return to a simmer, and cook, uncovered, until the mixture has thickened slightly and reduced to about 3/4 cup (185 ml), about 10 minutes. Store in the refrigerator in an airtight container for up to 1 month.

Lemon Curd

Lemon is the quintessential curd, but this recipe works interchangeably using other citrus fruits or even passion fruit. Try substituting equal amounts of lime, tangerine, orange, or grapefruit juice and zest for the lemon.

— MAKES 1-2/3 CUPS (400 ML)

EQUIPMENT: *A fine-mesh sieve.*

1/2 cup (125 ml) freshly squeezed lemon juice
1/2 cup (100 g) sugar
3 large eggs, free-range and organic
1 large egg yolk, free-range and organic
1/8 teaspoon fine sea salt
1/2 cup (4 ounces/125 g) unsalted butter, cubed
2 teaspoons finely grated organic lemon zest

1. In a saucepan, whisk together the lemon juice, sugar, eggs, egg yolk, and salt. Add the butter and whisk over low heat until the butter has melted.

2. Raise the heat to medium and cook, whisking constantly, until the curd thickens and generously coats the back of a spoon, about 5 minutes.

3. Strain through a fine-mesh sieve into a bowl to remove any clumps of egg that may have cooked too fast. Add the lemon zest and stir to combine. Cover with plastic wrap and refrigerate until ready to use.

VARIATIONS

ORANGE OR PASSION FRUIT CURD

For Orange Curd, follow the recipe above, substituting 1/2 cup (125 ml) freshly squeezed orange juice and 2 tablespoons finely grated orange zest. For Passion Fruit Curd, follow the recipe above, substituting 1 cup (250 ml) passion fruit pulp (placed in a blender to pulse 8 to 10 times to break up seeds). Strain.

Whipped Yogurt Cream

The yogurt in this recipe adds a welcome touch of acidity to counter the richness of classic whipped cream. It is an ideal accompaniment for fruit-based desserts such as Blackberry and Raspberry Galette (page 323) and Roasted Plums with Vanilla, Star Anise, and Orange Zest (page 217), or as the filling for Soft Individual Meringue Nests (page 357).

— MAKES 1-3/4 CUPS (435 ML)

EQUIPMENT: *A heavy-duty mixer with a whisk attachment, or an electric whisk.*

1/2 cup (125 ml) heavy cream, well chilled
1 cup (250 ml) plain Greek-style whole-milk yogurt
4 teaspoons pourable honey

1. In the bowl of the mixer, whisk the cream at the highest speed until stiff, about 2 minutes.

2. Place the yogurt in a medium bowl. Add the honey and whisk to combine. Add 1 tablespoon of the whipped cream and whisk to lighten the mixture. Place the remaining whipped cream on top of the yogurt mixture, and with a spatula, gently fold the whipped cream into the yogurt until just incorporated (see page 351) for folding technique. Serve immediately.

Harissa

I love the spice and the earthy, pungent bite of this Middle Eastern condiment, which finds its way to our table often. This homemade version is so quick and simple, yet so superior to store-bought varieties, you'll never want or need to buy a pot again. I enjoy serving it with all cuts of lamb, but also use it to heighten the flavors of eggplant dishes, with sausages and meat patties, and even as a spread on toast. It's also great as a condiment for homemade French fries or "Cold-Fry" Frites (page 167).

— MAKES 1 CUP (250 ML) —

EQUIPMENT: *An electric spice mill; a mini food processor or a standard food processor fitted with a small bowl.*

1/4 cup (60 ml) cumin seeds
5 plump, fresh garlic cloves, halved lengthwise, green germ removed if present
3/4 cup (185 ml) vegetable oil, such as sunflower oil
2 tablespoons Italian tomato paste
3 tablespoons cayenne pepper
3 tablespoons Spanish sweet or hot paprika
1 tablespoon fine sea salt

1. Toast the cumin seeds in a small saucepan over medium heat until fragrant, 2 to 3 minutes. Transfer to a plate to cool, then grind to a fine powder in the spice mill.

2. In the food processor, mince the garlic. Add the remaining ingredients and process to a thick paste.

MAKE-AHEAD NOTE: *Store in an airtight container in the refrigerator for up to 2 months.*

Hummus (Chickpea and Sesame Dip)

I have this creamy Middle Eastern dip on hand at all times. It's great as a dip for raw vegetables, perfect for pairing with Falafel (page 162), and wonderful smeared on homemade sourdough bread as a snack. I always make this with home-cooked chickpeas, never those from a can or jar, which can often taste bland or overly salted.

— MAKES 2 CUPS (500 ML) ————————————

EQUIPMENT: *A food processor or blender.*

2 plump, fresh garlic cloves, peeled, halved, green germ removed if present
3 cups (500 g) home-cooked chickpeas (recipe follows), drained (reserve liquid)
1/4 cup (60 ml) freshly squeezed lemon juice, or to taste
3 tablespoons tahini (sesame paste)
1/2 teaspoon fine sea salt
2 tablespoons sesame oil or extra-virgin olive oil
1/4 cup (60 ml) fresh cilantro leaves
1/8 teaspoon Spanish sweet or smoked paprika

In the food processor or blender, mince the garlic. Set aside 1/2 cup (85 g) of the chickpeas for garnish. Add the remaining 2-1/2 cups (415 g) chickpeas, the lemon juice, tahini, salt, and 1 tablespoon of the oil. Blend until smooth, adding reserved chickpea cooking liquid if necessary to make a smooth puree. Taste for seasoning. Spoon the dip into a large, shallow bowl and garnish with the reserved chickpeas, the remaining 1 tablespoon oil, the cilantro, and the paprika. Serve. The dip can be stored, covered, in the refrigerator for up to 3 days.

HERBED HUMMUS
Blend in a handful of whatever fresh green herbs or leafy greens you have on hand: cilantro, basil, arugula, or baby spinach.

Home-Cooked Chickpeas

Scant 3 cups (500 g) dried chickpeas, rinsed and drained
2 tablespoons extra-virgin olive oil
1 medium onion, peeled, halved lengthwise, and sliced into thin half-moons
8 plump, fresh garlic cloves, halved, green germ removed if present, and crushed
Fine sea salt
Bouquet garni: several fresh parsley sprigs and bay leaves encased in a wire tea
infuser or bound in a piece of cheesecloth

1. Place the chickpeas in a large bowl and cover with cold water. Set aside at room temperature for 12 to 24 hours. This will help speed up the cooking time.

2. In a large saucepan, combine the oil, onion, garlic, and 1 teaspoon of salt and stir to coat with the oil. Sweat—cook, covered, over low heat—without coloring until soft and translucent, about 5 minutes. Drain and rinse the soaked chickpeas and add them to the saucepan. Stir to coat them with oil and cook for 1 minute more. Add 1 quart (1 l) cold water and the *bouquet garni.* Simmer, covered, until the chickpeas are tender, 30 minutes to 2 hours. The cooking time will vary depending upon the freshness of the beans; younger beans will cook more quickly and beans more than a year old will take longer. Taste for seasoning. The beans can be used immediately or frozen, with their cooking liquid, for up to 3 months.

Baba Ghanoush
(Smoky Eggplant Dip)

This recipe is an enduring summer classic—the eggplant's earthy notes are the perfect underlay for this smoky preparation. Like *hummus, baba ghanoush* is great as a dip to go with raw vegetables, but can also be used as an accompaniment for Grilled Leg of Lamb with Fresh Herbs (page 179), or as a part of a vegetable side dish such as Charred Green Bean and Almond Salad with Smoky Baba Ghanoush (page 139).

— MAKES 2 CUPS (500 ML) ——————————————————————————

EQUIPMENT: *A 2-pronged meat fork; a small, sharp knife or a serrated grapefruit spoon; a food processor or blender.*

2 small, fresh eggplants (about 1 pound/500 g total), rinsed and dried
2 plump, fresh garlic cloves, peeled, halved, and green germ removed if present
3 tablespoons tahini (sesame paste)
6 tablespoons freshly squeezed lemon juice, or to taste
1/2 teaspoon fine sea salt

1. With the meat fork, prick the eggplants all over. Place them directly over an open gas flame, hot coals, or an outdoor grill. Cook for 10 minutes, using tongs to constantly turn the eggplant, until the entire skin is blackened, blistered, and has collapsed in on itself, 25 to 30 minutes. Remove the eggplants from the heat and place in a paper bag or covered bowl. Let the eggplant cool for 10 minutes.

2. When the eggplants are cool, gently peel the skin away from the flesh with the knife or grapefruit spoon, being careful to remove all the charred skin. (Use paper towels to wipe away any recalcitrant bits.)

3. Mince the garlic in the food processor or blender. Add the tahini, lemon juice, and salt and process to blend. Add the eggplant pulp and process for just a few seconds to blend the ingredients. The mixture should remain rather chunky.

MAKE-AHEAD NOTE: *The baba ghanoush can be prepared up to 3 days in advance and stored in an airtight container in the refrigerator.*

Spicy Tomato Marmalade

Another refrigerated pantry item I have on hand at all times, this spicy, goes-with-everything marmalade can be served with cheese or anytime one might use ketchup (which is way too sweet for my palate!). This is a dependable and indispensable condiment if there ever was one. Serve it on toasted sourdough bread with an assortment of hard cheeses.

— MAKES 2 CUPS (500 ML) —

EQUIPMENT: *An electric spice mill; a 3-quart (3 l) saucepan.*

1 teaspoon cumin seeds
1-1/2 pounds (750 g) ripe red heirloom tomatoes, cored, peeled, and chopped
  (or two 14-ounce/400 g cans diced Italian tomatoes in juice)
2 tablespoons freshly squeezed lime juice
3 tablespoons peeled and grated fresh ginger, or 1 tablespoon ground ginger
1 teaspoon fine sea salt
1 teaspoon ground Espelette pepper or other mild ground chile pepper
1/8 teaspoon finely ground cloves
1/2 teaspoon ground cinnamon
1/2 cup (100 g) raw, unrefined sugar

1. Toast the cumin seeds in a small, dry skillet over medium heat, shaking the pan often to prevent burning, until fragrant, 2 to 3 minutes. Transfer to a plate to cool, then grind to a fine powder in the spice grinder.

2. In the 3-quart (3 l) saucepan, combine all the ingredients. Stir to combine and simmer, uncovered, over low heat, stirring frequently so it does not stick to the bottom of the pan, until the marmalade is thick and syrupy, about 45 minutes. Let cool. Transfer to an airtight container and store in the refrigerator for up to 1 month.

Mint Chimichurri Sauce

This wildly popular Argentinean green sauce for meat can be a mixture of
many herbs, always married to garlic, olive oil, and hot peppers. I like to
use it as a marinade for lamb or a quick sauce for Seared Beef Rib-Eye Steak
(page 125).

MAKES 1 CUP (250 ML)

EQUIPMENT: *A mini food processor or a standard food processor fitted with a
small bowl; a small airtight jar with a lid.*

2 plump, fresh garlic cloves, halved lengthwise, green germ removed if present
1/2 teaspoon fine sea salt
1 cup fresh mint leaves
1 cup fresh parsley leaves
3/4 cup (185 ml) extra-virgin olive oil
1/4 cup (60 ml) freshly squeezed lemon juice
2 teaspoons ground Espelette pepper or other mild ground chile pepper

In the food processor, mince the garlic. Add the salt, mint, and parsley and
pulse again to chop the herbs. Add the oil, lemon juice, and ground chile
and pulse once more. Taste for seasoning. Transfer to the jar, cover, and
refrigerate until ready to use. To heighten the flavors, refrigerate overnight.

MAKE-AHEAD NOTE: *Store in an airtight container in the refrigerator for up to
1 week.*

Tarragon Chimichurri Sauce

This sauce gives the tarragon hit of a béarnaise sauce without all the eggs and butter, making it great alongside Roasted Beef Rib-Eye Steak with Tarragon Chimichurri (page 212). Its spritely flavors also brighten up roasted winter vegetable dishes such as Honey-Roasted Squash with Mozzarella, Arugula Salad, and Tarragon Chimichurri (page 197).

— MAKES 1/2 CUP (125 ML) SAUCE ————————————————————

EQUIPMENT: *A blender, a mini food processor, or a standard food processor fitted with a small bowl; a small airtight jar with a lid.*

3 plump, fresh garlic cloves, peeled, halved, and green germ removed if present
1 small red bird's eye chile, trimmed, halved, and seeded
1/2 cup coarsely chopped fresh tarragon leaves
1/2 cup coarsely chopped fresh cilantro leaves and stems
1/2 cup coarsely chopped fresh chives
1/2 cup coarsely chopped fresh basil leaves
1/2 red onion, minced, soaked in a bowl of water for 15 minutes, then drained (optional)
1-1/2 tablespoons white balsamic vinegar or best-quality white wine vinegar
1/3 cup (80 ml) extra-virgin olive oil
1/4 teaspoon fine sea salt

In the blender or food processor, mince the garlic and chile. Add the tarragon, cilantro, chives, and basil and pulse again to chop the herbs. Add the onion (if using), vinegar, oil, salt, and 3 tablespoons of water and pulse until all the ingredients are well combined and form a unified sauce. Taste for seasoning. Transfer to the jar, cover, and refrigerate until ready to use. To heighten the flavors, refrigerate overnight.

Garlic-Yogurt Sauce

I have tripled my intake of Greek yogurt since I began making this intensely savory, refreshing sauce. I use it as the final touch on Chicken with Eggplant, Chickpeas, Pine Nuts, and Garlic Sauce (page 232), the garlicky garnish on my Yellow Tomato and Toasted Cumin Soup (page 110), and a cooling accompaniment to the spicy Roasted Eggplant with Harissa, Fennel Seeds, and Honey (page 195).

— MAKES 1 CUP (250 ML) ——————————————

1 cup (250 ml) plain Greek-style whole-milk yogurt
1 plump, fresh garlic clove, halved, green germ removed if present, and finely minced
1/2 teaspoon fine sea salt

In a small bowl, combine all the ingredients. Let sit for at least 15 minutes for the garlic to mellow.

VARIATION

HARISSA-YOGURT SAUCE
Add 1/4 teaspoon Harissa (page 417) and serve on salads or as the garnish on Merguez Lamb Sausages (page 115).

Asian Dipping Sauces

I always find it amazing that so many Asian sauces have such similar ingredients but can taste so different with just small tweaks in the quantities. The basic ingredients have long shelf lives and are worth the investment so that you can bring a splash of Asian flavor to your dishes with ease. Pay attention to the ingredients list of the bottles; many are full of preservatives and additives. See my list of recommended brands on page 449.

These sauces are so simple you can make all of them for a little variety, or simply serve your favorite one. Use for dipping Asian Chicken and Cilantro Meatballs (page 119) or splashing on Grilled Eggplant Slices with Asian Sauce and Scallions (page 184).

Clockwise from top: Quick Asian Dipping Sauce; Sweet and Spicy Dipping Sauce; Soy-Ginger Dipping Sauce

Quick Asian Dipping Sauce

This has to be the world's easiest dipping sauce: Just two ingredients can add volumes of flavor.

— MAKES 3/4 CUP (185 ML) ——————————————————————

EQUIPMENT: *A small jar with a lid.*

1/2 cup (125 ml) soy sauce
1/4 cup (60 ml) brown rice vinegar

Combine the ingredients in the jar, tighten the lid, and shake to blend.

VARIATION: *Add several tablespoons grated fresh ginger.*
MAKE-AHEAD NOTE: *Store in the covered jar in the refrigerator for up to 1 week.*

Soy-Ginger Dipping Sauce

This is a favorite dipping sauce for Mushroom, Seafood, and Shiso Tempura (page 153), but it can also be easily interchanged with other dipping sauces for Asian Chicken and Cilantro Meatballs (page 119) or grilled vegetables.

MAKES 1/2 CUP (125 ML)

EQUIPMENT: *A small jar with a lid.*

1/2 cup (125 ml) Chicken Stock (page 402)
2 teaspoons soy sauce
2 teaspoons mirin (see Note)
1 teaspoon minced shallot
1/2 teaspoon finely grated fresh ginger

Combine the ingredients in the jar, tighten the lid, and shake to combine.

NOTE: *Mirin is a sweet rice wine that is a staple ingredient in Japanese cooking. It can be found in the Japanese section of Asian supermarkets.*
MAKE-AHEAD NOTE: *Store in the covered jar in the refrigerator for up to 1 week.*

Sweet and Spicy Dipping Sauce

Five ingredients come together to create a magically complex sauce.

EQUIPMENT: *A small jar with a lid.*

2 tablespoons soy sauce

3 tablespoons brown rice vinegar

1 tablespoon sriracha or other spicy Asian chile sauce

2 teaspoons toasted sesame oil

2 tablespoons unrefined raw sugar

Combine the ingredients in the jar, tighten the lid, and shake to blend.

MAKE-AHEAD NOTE: *Store in the covered jar in the refrigerator for up to 2 weeks.*

Vietnamese Dipping Sauce

This classic sauce can be found in many variations, often served with Vietnamese spring rolls and *bò bún* (beef and noodle salad). The balance of spice, salt, and sugar lends itself to myriad uses.

MAKES ABOUT 3/4 CUP (185 ML)

EQUIPMENT: *A mini food processor or a standard food processor fitted with a small bowl; a small jar with a lid.*

2 plump, fresh garlic cloves, peeled, halved, green germ removed if present
1 fresh or dried red bird's eye chile
3 tablespoons Vietnamese fish sauce
3 tablespoons freshly squeezed lime or lemon juice
2 tablespoons sugar

In the food processor, mince the garlic and chile. Add the fish sauce, citrus juice, sugar, and 1/2 cup (125 ml) water. Pulse to blend and taste for seasoning. Transfer to the jar and tighten the lid.

MAKE-AHEAD NOTE: *Store in the covered jar in the refrigerator for up to 1 week.*

Mushroom Powders

Dried mushroom powder is a true secret weapon in the kitchen, and a small amount really packs a punch. Use it to flavor salts (page 84), butters (page 75), breads (page 288), and brioche rolls (page 273); as a base for infusions in soups (page 69) and pasta sauces (page 71); and with the addition of *nori* and sesame seeds, as a punchy dipping powder for Mushroom, Seafood, and Shiso Tempura (page 153). Store mushroom powders in a tightly sealed jar in a cool, dry place for up to 3 months.

Cèpe Mushroom Powder

— Makes 1/2 cup (8 tablespoons) ———————————————

EQUIPMENT: *An electric spice mill; a small jar with a lid.*

2 ounces (30 g) best-quality dried cèpe *(porcini) mushrooms (or substitute dried morels)*

Coarsely chop the dried mushrooms or cut them into pieces with scissors. Working in batches, grind them to a fine powder in the spice mill.

Cèpe-Nori Powder

— MAKES ABOUT 2-1/2 TABLESPOONS ————————————————

EQUIPMENT: *An electric spice mill.*

Large handful dried cèpe *(porcini) mushrooms (about 10 g)*
1/2 sheet dried nori seaweed, torn into small pieces
1/4 teaspoon sea salt
1 tablespoon plus 1 teaspoon dried bonito flakes

Grind the ingredients to a fine powder in the spice mill.

Cèpe-Sesame Powder

— MAKES ABOUT 1/4 CUP (4 TABLESPOONS) ————————————————

EQUIPMENT: *A electric spice mill.*

Small handful dried cèpes *(porcini) mushrooms (about 5 g)*
1/4 sheet dried nori, *torn into small pieces*
1/4 teaspoon fine sea salt
1 tablespoon plus 1 teaspoon dried bonito *flakes*
2 tablespoons sesame seeds

Place the dried *cèpes*, *nori*, salt, and *bonito* flakes in the spice mill and grind to a fine powder. Add the sesame seeds and pulse briefly to blend.

Side Dishes

Crunchy Jasmine Rice

My local organic shop in Provence introduced me to a version of this surprising rice mix. Ever since, this is about the only way I prepare rice, for I have a weakness for peanuts as well as that crunchy texture. Serve this as is or with a warming braise or stew such as Four-Hour Aromatic Braised Pork (page 223), Chicken with Morels (page 237), or Chicken with Eggplant, Chickpeas, Pine Nuts, and Garlic-Yogurt Sauce (page 232).

— 4 TO 6 SERVINGS —

EQUIPMENT: *An electric spice mill.*

1/2 cup (60 g) roasted and salted peanuts
1-1/2 cups (250 g) jasmine rice
1/2 cup (70 g) mixed sesame, flax, and sunflower seeds
1 tablespoon extra-virgin olive oil
1 bay leaf
1 teaspoon fine sea salt
2 cups (500 ml) Vegetable Stock (page 408) or Chicken Stock (page 402) or water

1. In the spice mill, coarsely chop the peanuts.

2. In a saucepan, combine all the ingredients. Bring to a boil over high heat. Reduce the heat to a simmer, cover, and cook until the rice is cooked through, about 10 minutes. Remove and discard the bay leaf before serving.

Herbed Couscous Salad

This light, refreshing couscous salad finds its way to the table in all seasons. Rich with herbal flavors, it pairs well with almost any cuisine, though I love it most when served with homemade Merguez Lamb Sausage with Harissa (page 115).

—— 2 LARGE SERVINGS OR 4 SMALL SIDE SERVINGS ——

1 cup (80 g) instant couscous
1/4 red onion (about 1/3 cup/45 g), finely chopped
1-1/2 tablespoons (20 g) unsalted butter
1/4 teaspoon fine sea salt
1 tablespoon fresh dill leaves
1/4 cup fresh cilantro leaves
1/4 cup fresh flat-leaf parsley leaves
Coarse, freshly ground black pepper

1. Bring 1 cup (250 ml) water to a boil in a covered medium saucepan (the cover prevents water evaporation). When the water comes to a boil, stir in the couscous. Turn off the heat, cover, and set aside for 10 minutes.

2. Meanwhile, soak the onions in a small bowl of cold water for 10 minutes, then drain. This helps to take the sharp bite out of the raw onion and make it more digestible.

3. When the couscous has absorbed all the water, bury the butter in the couscous, cover the saucepan, and leave it for 2 to 3 minutes to let the butter melt. Fluff the couscous with a fork until the grains separate with ease.

4. Add the onion, salt, and herbs and toss to mix. Season with pepper. Serve warm or at room temperature.

Socca (Chickpea Flour Crêpes)

Nothing more than chickpea flour, water, salt, and oil transform this classic crêpe from the Nice area of southern France into a crisp and golden rewarding pleasure. Seasoned with plenty of freshly ground black pepper, it's a regular at our table year-round.

—— 8 SERVINGS ——————————————————————————

EQUIPMENT: *A 14-inch (36 cm) round ovenproof* socca *pan or paella pan.*

1 cup (100 g) chickpea flour (garbanzo bean flour)
3/4 teaspoon fine sea salt
7 tablespoons fruity, extra-virgin olive oil
Coarse, freshly ground black pepper

1. Center a rack in the oven. Preheat the oven to 450°F (230°C).

2. In a bowl, whisk together the flour, salt, 3 tablespoons of the olive oil, and 1 cup (250 ml) water. The batter should be thin but a bit lumpy. (The batter can be prepared up to 24 hours in advance, covered, and stored at room temperature.)

3. Just before baking the *socca*, pour the remaining 4 tablespoons oil into the pan and brush to evenly distribute the oil. Place the oiled pan in the oven and heat for 5 minutes.

4. Pour the batter into the pan, swirling to evenly distribute the batter. Return the pan to the oven and bake until the *socca* is bubbling, colored a deep golden brown, and evenly dotted with little crater-like holes, 12 to 15 minutes. Sprinkle generously with pepper. Use a plastic scraper to scrape the *socca* into raggedy shards or cut into even wedges. Serve warm.

Powders, Extracts, and Sugars

Next time you open your pantry or are in a store that sells vanilla extract, please read the label! The laws regarding what can be called "vanilla extract" are pretty broad and very confusing. Although in our minds the idea of "pure vanilla extract" would ideally be fresh, fragrant vanilla beans marinated in a fabulous liquid, that is normally not the case. Many brands include all sorts of additives, including the vague "vanilla bean extract" (whatever that might be), glycerin, dextrose, sugar, artificial flavors, and corn syrup. So go for the real deal and make your own!

Here are recipes for making your own vanilla extract for use in baking; vanilla sugar for use in any sweet dish that might benefit from a scent of vanilla: and vanilla powder, which can be used in place of either homemade vanilla extract or vanilla sugar or as a garnish to add a vanilla essence to baked goods, fish, or shellfish.

Homemade Vanilla Extract

The U.S. Food and Drug Administration laws require that vanilla extract contain 35 percent alcohol and just under 3 ounces (100g) of vanilla beans per quart (liter). Double- and triple-strength vanilla extracts are also available. Here is my homemade version. You can begin either with untouched vanilla beans or with "leftover" vanilla bean pods from which you have scraped the seeds.

MAKES 1 CUP (250 ML)

EQUIPMENT: *A tall bottle (tall enough to hold the vanilla beans upright) with a lid.*

5 plump, fresh vanilla beans or 5 pods with seeds previously removed
1 cup (250 ml) vodka

Split the vanilla beans in half lengthwise, to expose the fragrant and flavorful seeds. Place the beans and seeds (or scraped bean pods from which you have previously extracted the seeds) in the bottle. Cover with the vodka to make sure the beans are completely submerged. Secure the lid on the bottle and give it a good shake. Store in a cool, dark place for at least 1 month. Taste the extract: If you want a stronger flavor, allow it to infuse a bit longer. As I use up the extract, I top it off with new vodka or periodically add fresh beans or leftover pods from which I have scraped out the seeds for baking.

Vanilla Sugar

Never discard vanilla beans, for once you have extracted the flavorful seeds from the pods, they can always be used to prepare this quick vanilla sugar, which you can use in any desserts that call for sugar.

— MAKES 4 CUPS (800 G) —

EQUIPMENT: *A small jar with a lid.*

4 plump, fresh vanilla beans, or 4 pods with seeds previously removed
4 cups (800 g) sugar

Flatten the beans and cut lengthwise in half. With a small spoon, scrape out the seeds and place them in a small bowl. Reserve the seeds for preparing any vanilla-flavored dessert. Combine the pods and sugar in a jar. Tighten the lid of the jar. Store at room temperature for 1 month for good vanilla flavor, topping off with sugar as needed.

Vanilla Powder

I keep vanilla powder on hand for sprinkling over desserts such as cherry *clafoutis* or for showering over just about any flavor of sorbet or ice cream.

When the seeds are removed, I let the vanilla pods dry on a windowsill until completely dried out, about 1 week.

MAKES 1/4 CUP (4 TABLESPOONS)

EQUIPMENT: *An electric spice mill; a small jar with a lid.*

4 vanilla bean pods with seeds previously removed, dried

With a large knife, coarsely chop the dried beans. Place in the spice mill and grind to a fine powder. Store in the jar with the lid securely tightened in a cool, dry place for several months.

Invert Sugar Syrup

This quick and easy, storable syrup (a perfect homemade substitute for corn syrup) is thick and clear and helps create a smoother mouthfeel in sorbets and ice creams. It also controls crystallization.

MAKES ABOUT 1-3/4 CUPS (435 ML)

EQUIPMENT: *A 2-quart (2 l) stainless steel saucepan.*

2-1/4 cups (450 g) sugar
2 teaspoons freshly squeezed lemon juice

In the saucepan, combine the sugar, lemon juice, and 1 cup (250 ml) water and bring to a boil over high heat. Reduce the heat to low and simmer until the mixture is slightly thick and viscous, like corn syrup or liquid honey, 8 to 10 minutes. The mixture should not darken or caramelize. Be aware that the liquid will thicken as it cools. I prefer to err on the runny side rather than risking a syrup that is too thick and nearly impossible to pour. Transfer to a heatproof container to cool, then cover.

MAKE-AHEAD NOTE: *When cool, store in an airtight container in the refrigerator for up to 6 months.*

Kaffir Lime Powder

I love having secret weapons in my kitchen, ingredients that with a mere sprinkle can elevate a dish or a snack from ordinary to fabulous. Kaffir lime powder is one of those. The deep-green, waxy leaf of the kaffir lime, with its distinctly fragrant citrus flavor common to Southeast Asian cooking, is traditionally tossed whole into curries and soups, but one of my favorite ways to use this zesty leaf is to grind it into a powder, imparting its balmy oils in a fine shower to infuse a sorbet (page 92) or as a final citrusy burst on seafood dish, such as Steamed Turbot with Lemongrass, Peas, and Baby Spinach (page 17).

MAKES 2 TABLESPOONS POWDER

EQUIPMENT: *An electric spice mill; a small jar with a lid.*

12 fresh, frozen, or dried kaffir lime leaves, coarsely chopped

In the spice mill, grind the leaves to a fine powder. Store in the jar with the lid securely tightened at room temperature for up to 1 month.

NOTES

~ The leaves, ground or whole, keep well in the freezer, so you can always have a stash to hand.
~ For sprinkling on desserts, you can add a touch of unrefined cane sugar to the grinder to make a sweeter powder.

Stocking the Pantry

Favorite Ingredients for a Well-Stocked Pantry, Refrigerator, and Freezer

The first and most important tenet of the kitchen is to begin with quality produce. Your cooking will only be as good as the ingredients you put into it, and having a well-stocked pantry and freezer means that you can pull together an impressive meal with virtually no advance planning. This is what my essential stocked kitchen looks like:

Pantry

Active dry yeast or instant yeast

Almond meal

Baking powder

Chickpea (garbanzo bean) flour

Chickpeas (dried)

Cornstarch

Durum wheat pasta

Épeautre (spelt) and *petit épeautre* (farro) grains

Extra-virgin olive oil

Fregola

Gelatin powder

Instant polenta

Intensely flavored honey, such as chestnut, mountain, or buckwheat

Jasmine and white rice

Mild, fragrant honey, such as lavender

Nut oils: pistachio, almond, walnut

Sesame oil

Soy sauce

Sunflower oil

Unbleached, all-purpose flour

Unrefined cane sugar

Vietnamese fish sauce

Vinegars: white wine, sherry, balsamic, brown rice

White beans (dried)

Seasonings and Spices

Bay leaves

Cèpe (porcini) mushrooms

70% cacao chocolate

Coarse sea salt (for salting pasta and blanching water)

Cumin seeds

Fennel seeds

Fine sea salt

Ground Espelette pepper (*piment d'Espelette*)

Hot red pepper flakes

Maldon salt (for garnish and making infused salts)

Spanish hot, sweet, and smoked paprika

Tellicherry black peppercorns

Turmeric

Vanilla beans

Canned Goods

Capers in vinegar

Diced Italian tomatoes in juice

Marinated artichokes

Oil-cured anchovies

Refrigerator (homemade or purchased)

Candied lemons

Clarified butter

French mustard

Harissa

Ghee

Parmigiano-Reggiano cheese

Spicy tomato marmalade

Various Asian sauces

Freezer

Artichoke bottoms

Brioche slices

Compound butters

Homemade pork and fennel sausage

Infused oils

Peas

Seaweed Quick Bread

Staple stocks: Chicken, fish or
shellfish, and vegetable

Truffle salt

White beans, shelled (*cocos blancs*)

Sources for the
Pantry and the Kitchen

In my cooking, I am very loyal to certain brands of ingredients that I have found to make a significant difference in the end result of a dish. All these ingredients can be found on my Amazon store, At Home with Patricia Wells, accessed via www.patriciawells.com. You'll find some favorite items that I use every day in my kitchen and recommend for their excellent quality, including:

Anchovy fillets: RUSTICHELLA D'ABRUZZO, from Italy

Chickpea (garbanzo bean) flour: BOB'S RED MILL

Chile pepper: dried *piment d'Espelette:* BIPERDUNA, *from France*

Cocoa powder and dark chocolate: VALRHONA or LINDT

Fish sauce: RED BOAT FISH SAUCE, from Vietnam

Honey, lavender honey: LE MAS DES ABEILLES, from Provence

Lemongrass: IMPORTFOOD.COM, U.S grown

Malt powder, for bread making: BARRY FARM

Mustard: EDMOND FALLOT, from France

Peppercorns, whole black Tellicherry peppercorns: THE PREPARED PANTRY

Nut and seed oils: LEBLANC roasted sesame, pistachio, and walnut oils, from France

Olive oils: CASTELAS, from France; CAPEZZANZA, from Italy; lemon-infused Gianfranco BECCHINA, from Sicily

Paprika, sweet and smoked Spanish paprika: HOT PAELLA, from Spain

Pastas: RUSTICHELLA D'ABRUZZO, from Italy

Salts: fleur de sel: LE PALUDIER; fine sea salt: CHEF SHOP, from Brittany

Seafood stock: MORE THAN GOURMET

Soy sauce: BLUEGRASS, from Kentucky

Tomatoes, canned chopped tomatoes and tomato concentrate: MUTTI

Wakame seaweed: CLEARSPRING

Yeast: SAF instant yeast

My store also features much of the equipment I suggest in my recipes and use every day in my kitchen, including bamboo steamers, cast-iron pizza pans, digital kitchen scales, electric spice mills, elevated plant gardens, enameled cast-iron pots, ice cream machines, instant-read thermometers, knife sharpeners, laser thermometers, linen-lined bread baskets, mandolines, pizza peels, and special salt and pepper mills. These are personal recommendations based on my own experience and there is no affiliation between myself and manufacturers.

In addition, here are some websites for ordering specialty items directly from select companies:

Magret Duck Breast

D'ARTAGNAN *(www.dartagnan.com)*, THE GOURMET FOOD STORE *(www.thegourmetfoodstore.com)*, *and* GRIMAUD *(www.grimaud.com): For making your own duck burgers, and more.*

Live Sea Scallops

FARM 2 MARKET *(farm-2-market.com): For fresh live, sea scallops in the shell, with roe attached, shipped, in season. They require cleaning and are quite expensive, but well worth it for a special occasion.*

PLANTIN *(www.plantin-truffle.com/en_US): My neighbors in Provence provide the world's top chefs and cooks with the finest.*

All Spices

THE SPICE HOUSE *(www.thespicehouse.com): An excellent source for spices, vanilla beans, and spice blends.*

Olive Oils

The world of olive oil can be totally confusing. Here are my choices for seriously good and dependable extra-virgin olive oils:

FRANCE: CASTELAS (www.castelas.com): Jean-Benoit and Catherine Hughes produce a clean, honest, variety of olive oils from their property in Les Baux de Provence.

ITALY: CAPEZZANA (www.capezzana.it): The Contini-Bonacossi family in Tuscany produce a wondrous oil. I especially love their rare *olio nuevo* or "new oil" come November.

Herb Plants

You don't need an extensive garden or a special green thumb to grow a few herbs yourself. I always say if you can only grow one plant in a pot, it should be rosemary, loved for its fragrance and versatility. For more unusual plants—bay leaf trees, lemon verbena, lemongrass, lovage—try The Growers Exchange (www.thegrowers-exchange.com).

There are a handful of trusted wine importers whom I recommend. Instead of going into a wine shop to look for a specific wine, ask the wine merchant if they have any wines imported by these companies:

ERIC SOLOMON/EUROPEAN CELLARS (704-358-1565, www.europeancellars .com, info@europeancellars.com: Specializing in wines from Spain and France, including our own Clos Chanteduc Côtes-du-Rhône, Domaine de la Janasse, and Domaine de Marcoux in Châteauneuf-du-Pape.

KERMIT LYNCH WINE MERCHANT (510-524-1524, www.kermitlynch.com, info@kermitlynch.com): Specializing in wines from Italy and France, including Auguste Clape in Cornas, Domaine Coche-Dury and Antoine Jobard in Burgundy, and Mas Champart in the Languedoc.

NORTH BERKELEY WINE (510-848-8910 or 800-266-6585, www .northberkeleyimports.com, retail@northberkeleywine.com): Specializing in wines from Chile, Italy, and France, including Le Clos du Caillou and Clos du Mont Olivet in Châteauneuf-du-Pape, Martinelle in Beaumes de Venise, and Domaine la Bouïssière in Gigondas.

DANIEL JOHNNES WINES (www.danieljohnneswines): Many great wines, including favorites from Domaine Saint Préfert in Châteauneuf-du-Pape.

Acknowledgments

If I could only acknowledge and thank one person, it would be Julia Child, my dear friend and the mentor to so, so many dedicated cooks. A friend once asked Julia what was the most important thing to know about cooking. Here was her response:

> *Read a recipe three times:*
> *The first time you read it*
> *The second time you absorb it*
> *The third time you understand it*

Need one say more? Oh, that all cooks would take her advice!

No book is the work of a single person, and I am seriously grateful to my assistant, Emily Buchanan, who cared about this project as much as I have, and put her talents, energy, passion, and brilliance into every bit of this book.

Thank you, editor Cassie Jones, first for your enthusiastic response to the "master" concept and also for your seriously attentive, hands-on, eagle-eyed editing throughout.

My agent, Amanda Urban, wholeheartedly responded to the manuscript, saying, "This book was written for me!" Thank you, Binky.

Throughout my life, day in and day out, professional chefs as well as home cooks inspire and motivate me with new ideas and remarkable flavor combinations, challenging me to march back into the kitchen and work harder. Thank you to chefs Joël Robuchon, Guy Savoy, Laurent Deconinck, William Ledeuil,

Frédéric Anton, Philip Zemour, Antoine Westerman, Eric Frechon, Aki-hiro Horikoshi, Eric Trochon, Pascal Barbot Nancy Silverton, and Dagobert Resneau for their special talents and inspiration. Various merchants have also shared their expertise and pride in their craft, including Paris butchers Antoine Guilhien and Johan Neveux and Provençal butchers Jean-Claude and Stéphane Raymond, as well as our dedicated Provençal fishmongers, the extended Laffont family, led by Christian and Guy. Cheese is a big part of my life, and I could not love it with the pleasure I do without the professionalism and enthusiasm of cheese merchants Marie Quatrehomme and her crew in Paris or Josiane Deal and her team in Provence. Bakers, including Eric Kayser and the late Lionel Poilâne, remain ever an inspiration. In the wine world, merchants Juan Sanchez and Mathieu Shillinger have greatly assisted in my ongoing wine education and pleasure.

Great cook and great friend Jeffrey Bergman gets special thanks, for all the shared ideas and pleasures. Thank you, Jeffrey and Katherine, for so many great moments in the kitchen, around the table, and around the world, with more yet to come. And thank you, Todd Murray, for your friendship, your beautiful voice, and your *galette*! I am always grateful to everyone at Plantin in Puymeras—especially Christopher Poron—for a never-ending supply of fresh summer and winter black truffles, as well as their incredible dried mushrooms.

At my Paris table, I most want to thank those who have shared moments there, including Johanne Killeen, Andrew Axilrod and Allyson deGroat, Ina and Jeffrey Garten, Eric Solomon and Daphne Glorian, Peter and Jeanne Fellowes, Jim Bitterman, Nancy Merritt, and Richard Asthalter.

At my Provence table, thanks go to Virginia Ward and Casey Gaines, Keith Love and Gina Cuff and their family, Vivian and Roger Cruise and their family, Brian Huggler and Ken Ross, Bill and Terry Whitaker, Suzanne Kay and Alain Vater, Mathieu and Miriam Schillinger, and Jean-Claude and Colette Viviani for sharing many a "test" meal!

Others who have inspired me include exceptional food scientist Nathan

Myhrvold in Seattle; the creators at the Moulin de la Vierge in Paris; and our ever-wonderful gardener, Cédric Ganichot—thank you especially for the summer bounty of tomatoes, herbs, and *legumes*.

And, of course, I want to thank each and every student from my more than twenty years of cooking classes, the teacher learns the most!

Also at William Morrow, I want to thank Cassie Jones's assistant, Kara Zauberman, as well as Liate Stehlik, Lynn Grady, Anna Brower, Mumtaz Mustafa, designer Suet Chong, Rachel Meyers, Tavia Kowalchuk, and Anwesha Basu. A special thank you to photographer David Japy and stylist Elodie Rambaud.

My friend Jonathan Burnham, also at HarperCollins, has believed in me from the beginning, and my only regret is that we do not share more meals together!

As ever, the single person I thank the most is that man in the kitchen with me, Walter Wells.

Patricia Wells

Universal Conversion Chart

Oven temperature equivalents

250°F = 120°C	350°F = 175°C	450°F = 230°C
275°F = 135°C	375°F = 190°C	475°F = 245°C
300°F = 150°C	400°F = 200°C	500°F = 260°C
325°F = 165°C	425°F = 220°C	

Measurement equivalents

Measurements should always be level unless directed otherwise.

1/8 teaspoon = 0.5 mL

1/4 teaspoon = 1 mL

1/2 teaspoon = 2 mL

1 teaspoon = 5 mL

1 tablespoon = 3 teaspoons = 1/2 fluid ounce = 15 mL

2 tablespoons = 1/8 cup = 1 fluid ounce = 30 mL

4 tablespoons = 1/4 cup = 2 fluid ounces = 60 mL

5-1/3 tablespoons = 1/3 cup = 3 fluid ounces = 80 mL

8 tablespoons = 1/2 cup = 4 fluid ounces = 125 mL

10-2/3 tablespoons = 2/3 cup = 5 fluid ounces = 160 mL

12 tablespoons = 3/4 cup = 6 fluid ounces = 185 mL

16 tablespoons = 1 cup = 8 fluid ounces = 250 mL

Index

Note: Page references in *italics* indicate photographs.